# CHALLENGES FOR GAME DESIGNERS

## BRENDA BRATHWAITE AND IAN SCHREIBER

**Charles River Media**

*A part of Course Technology, Cengage Learning*

COURSE TECHNOLOGY
CENGAGE Learning™

Australia, Brazil, Japan, Korea, Mexico, Singapore, Spain, United Kingdom, United States

**COURSE TECHNOLOGY**
CENGAGE Learning™

**Challenges for Game Designers**

Brenda Brathwaite and Ian Schreiber

Publisher and General Manager,
Course Technology PTR:
Stacy L. Hiquet

Associate Director of Marketing:
Sarah Panella

Content Project Manager:
Jessica McNavich

Marketing Manager: Jordan Casey

Acquisitions Editor: Heather Hurley

Project and Copy Editor: Marta Justak

CRM Editorial Services Coordinator:
Jen Blaney

Interior Layout: Jill Flores

Cover Designer: Tyler Creative Services

Indexer: Sharon Hilgenberg

Proofreader: Kate Shoup

For product information and technology assistance, contact us at
**Cengage Learning Customer & Sales Support, 1-800-354-9706**

For permission to use material from this text or product,
submit all requests online at **cengage.com/permissions**
Further permissions questions can be emailed to
**permissionrequest@cengage.com**

All trademarks are the property of their respective owners.

Library of Congress Control Number: 2008929225

ISBN-13: 978-1-58450-580-8

ISBN-10: 1-58450-580-X

**Course Technology**
25 Thomson Place
Boston, MA 02210
USA

Cengage Learning is a leading provider of customized learning solutions with office locations around the globe, including Singapore, the United Kingdom, Australia, Mexico, Brazil, and Japan. Locate your local office at: **international. cengage.com/region**

Cengage Learning products are represented in Canada by Nelson Education, Ltd.

For your lifelong learning solutions, visit **courseptr.com**

Visit our corporate website at **cengage.com**

Printed in the United States of America
9 10 11 12    17 16 15

# Acknowledgments

There were many people who contributed to the making of this book.

One of Brenda's MFA candidates at the Savannah College of Art and Design, game designer David McDonough, was offered the opportunity to assist in the development of the non-digital shorts that complete each chapter, and he jumped at the chance. Another of Brenda's MFA candidates, artist Blair Cooper, was asked to design the book's cover. Likewise, he was pleased to assist. For both their contributions, we are grateful.

Thanks are due also to members of the Design Army, and in particular SCAD graduates Michelle Menard (MFA, 2008) and Chris Schmidt (BFA, 2008), who read drafts of this book and made games from its challenges, a number of which are pictured within.

Professional game designers Jeb Havens, Ian Bogost, and Clint Hocking were kind enough to contribute material, and countless other designers, including Greg Costikyan, Sheri Graner Ray, Sam Lewis, Chris Crowell, and Linda Currie, listened to us talk about games obscure and new and added to the proverbial conversation.

Lastly, but most importantly, our spouses deserve much praise. Sharon Schreiber and Ian Brathwaite listened to keyboards click away for many a good evening while their game designer spouses got all excited about things that the average person would probably dismiss (or at the very least not find nearly as exciting). Fortunately, they also got to play a lot of good games.

# About the Authors

As a 26-year veteran of the video games industry, **Brenda Brathwaite** is a game designer and Chair of the Interactive Design and Game Development department at the Savannah College of Art and Design. She has worked on 22 internationally known titles, including the award-winning *Wizardry* series of role-playing games and the award-winning Jagged *Alliance* series of strategy role-playing games. Brenda serves on the board of the International Game Developers Association and is a passionate anti-censorship advocate. She is a regular speaker at universities and conferences, and according to a 2007 article in *Next Generation* magazine written by Ernest Adams, Brathwaite is the longest, continuously serving woman in video game development today. She is the author of *Sex in Video Games*.

**Ian Schreiber** has been in the industry for eight years, first as a programmer and then as a game designer. He has worked on five published game titles, including *Playboy: the Mansion* and the Nintendo DS version of *Marvel Trading Card Game*. He has also developed training/simulation games for two Fortune 500 companies. Ian has taught game design and development courses at Ohio University, Columbus State Community College, and Savannah College of Art and Design, and has mentored college students at those and several other universities.

# Contents

# Introduction and Welcome

This book is designed to challenge you, improve your brainstorming abilities, and allow you to have fun and sharpen your design skills whether you're a professional designer, an aspiring designer, a hobbyist, or a student of game design.

The chapters in this book cover a wide range of topics important to game designers. There are three key parts to each chapter:

- **Coverage:** A general overview of the topic is provided. All the material comes from actual industry experience of the authors.
- **Design Challenges:** Five challenges that allow you to apply the material, explore the topic, and expand your knowledge in the area. None of the challenges requires any computer programming or even a computer unless needed for research. Even then, good ol' books will do.
- **Non-Digital Shorts:** A range of topics that can be made into fully functional non-digital games. These are great for quick brainstorming sessions or homework assignments.

## PROFESSIONAL GAME DESIGNERS

If you already work as a game designer, the text in these chapters serves as a review or provides you with a frame of reference to conduct the challenges with others on your team, particularly junior designers. Feel free to jump around to whatever chapter is of interest or relevance to you. The material in this book comes from industry experience, and we welcome any feedback or contributions you may have for future editions.

If you work at a company where there is an entire design department (and not just you), take on a challenge every now and then with the other designers. If you have a large design department (eight people or more), you can divide into several teams and present your work at the end of each session. The authors regularly did these exercises with other designers when they worked together in the same office.

These exercises—particularly the Iron Designer exercises—also serve as excellent design tests for potential candidates.

You might also consider holding periodic "design exercises for non-designers" at your company, presenting some material and running a challenge for people who are interested in game design or who work closely with designers. As you surely know, lots of people are interested in becoming designers and would appreciate the effort and knowledge you convey.

## NOT A GAME DESIGNER... YET!

If you are interested in game design but don't have any industry credits as a designer, you may find the experience in each chapter enlightening. Start with Chapter 1, "The Basics," to get an idea of the kinds of skills and core knowledge you'll need. For every other chapter, after reading the text, we recommend playing a commercial or indie game of that type if you haven't already, and follow it up by doing some or all of the challenges at the end to practice your new skills. If you are doing this on your own (for example, not as assigned work for a class), you may be drawn to the challenges that look easy; resist this temptation. Find exactly those exercises that look daunting or just plain un-fun; those are the ones that will best build the skills you want to build.

If you are lucky enough to have some other colleagues who are as interested in game design as you, you will get better results by working in a group with them (think of it as a book club, except more fun). Many of the challenges in this book suggest working in a group for brainstorming; you will get very different results if you go it alone.

If you are looking to become a game designer some day, save the work that you create for these challenges. They can be used to fill out your design portfolio. There is no substitute for designing a video game that is fully implemented (such a piece should be the foundation of your portfolio), but additional work that shows your approach to common design problems in the field will give potential employers a better sense of what kind of designer you are, and a particularly innovative solution to a challenge in this book can be a talking point during an interview.

If you are a student and this textbook was required for one of your game design classes, this is not one of those books that you want to get rid of at the end of the course. There are far too many chapters and exercises here to cover in a single quarter or semester, but every chapter and every challenge is meant to be useful to a game designer. After the course is over, try reading some of the chapters that you didn't get to cover in class and even doing the challenges. You can use winter or summer break as an excuse to play around with this book. Even if you don't, you may become a game designer some day… and if you do, you will want to practice your skills so that you can be the best designer you can be.

## GAME DESIGN INSTRUCTORS

If you *teach* courses in game design, there are several ways you can use this book, depending on the class. It is currently being used in the following ways:

- As a primary text for an introductory class on the practice of game design
- As a supplemental exercise text for numerous classes
- As a primary text for a course on non-digital game design

If your students have already taken an introductory course in the theory of game design, this book can provide a series of challenges to form the basis for a course in *practical* game design. Give a quick refresher lecture (you can do this for most chapters in 30 minutes to an hour), and then leap right into the challenges at the end of a chapter. Assign research activities as homework and use class time primarily for group brainstorming and design activities.

The non-digital shorts also provide great opportunities for quick in-class projects or homework assignments.

For an advanced game development class, you can take most of the challenges in this book and enhance them into weeklong projects. If your students know how to program, any challenge that has a game concept as a deliverable can be extended by having the students implement a working rapid prototype. You could even extend this further, starting a course by giving students a choice of design challenges and having them extend that through the quarter or semester (or even an entire academic year) into a full working game.

## CONTINUING THE CONVERSATION

A painter gets better by making lots of paintings; sculptors hone their craft by making sculptures; and game designers improve their skills by designing lots of games. Unfortunately, designing a complete video game (and implementing it, and then seeing all the things you did right and wrong) can take years, and we'd all like to improve at a faster rate than that.

This book, at its heart, is a collection of challenges. Most are designed to take two hours or fewer, and each challenge focuses on a vital skill that is commonly used by practicing game designers. In other books, these might be referred to as inherently un-fun activities, such as *exercises* or *problems* or *homework*. The activities in this book are meant to be enjoyable, interesting, fun, and challenging; hence, *challenges*.

We welcome your questions and any suggestions you may have for future editions of *Challenges for Game Designers*. You may reach the authors via the book's site at designgames.wordpress.com.

## RANDOM TRIVIA: HOW THIS BOOK HAPPENED

Both authors have similar stories. They are game designers who recently left full-time game development to teach full-time and contract part-time. They both taught a class in practical game design, where the students were expected to regularly design games. They could be twins, if they didn't have such completely different personalities (and design skills, and looks, and…).

Brenda approached Ian, asking him to co-author a book proposal she was writing (not this one). Ian counter-offered with a book of game design exercises, based on the exercises they used to do when they worked together. Interest in "low-tech" game design exercises had already been shown on Game_Edu, an IGDA mailing list for game development educators, and no book like this existed. This book ended up taking precedence, because it was fun to write and born of experience. For more challenges or to submit your completed work, please visit the authors' site at http://designgames.wordpress.com.

# Part 1 Building Blocks

# 1 The Basics

Game design is an art form, and as designers, we grow by challenging ourselves often. Some are fortunate and good enough to do it professionally. Others design games as a part of their education or do it for personal pleasure (and the hope of reward).

This book was written by professional game designers. That means that certain terms will be flung about with an assumption that the reader actually knows what these terms mean. However, the authors realize that not all readers have experience working in the game industry. If we didn't define them or if we didn't give you an overview of the basics of game design, we would have failed to properly analyze our audience or meet its expectations. That's one of the cardinal sins of game design itself.

This chapter then serves as a tutorial or "intro level" to this entire book. If you're relatively new to the field of game design, this chapter is for you.

## What Is Game Design?

Game design is the process of creating the content and rules of a game. *Good* game design is the process of creating goals that a player feels motivated to reach and rules that a player must follow as he makes making meaningful decisions in pursuit of those goals.

### It's Also All About the Player

Good game design is player-centric. That means that above all else, the player and her desires are truly considered. Rather than demanding that she do something via the rules, the gameplay itself should inherently motivate the player in the direction the designer wants her to go. Telling players they must travel around the board or advance to the next level is one thing. If they don't have a reason and a desire to do it, then it becomes torture.

In creating a game, designers take a step back and think from the player's viewpoint:

- What's this game about?
- How do I play?
- How do I win?
- Why do I want to play?
- What things do I need to do?

### Meaningful Decisions

Distilled down to its essence, game design is about creating opportunities for players to make meaningful decisions that affect the outcome of the game. Consider a game like a boxing match. So many decisions lead up to the ultimate victory. How long will I train? Will I block or will I swing? What is my opponent going to do? Where is his weakness? Jab left or right? Even those few, brief questions don't come close to the myriad decisions a fighter must make as he progresses through a match.

Games invite players into similar mental spaces. Games like *Tetris* and *Chess* keep our minds busy by forcing us to consider which one of several possible moves we want to take next. In taking these paths, we know that we may be prolonging or completely screwing up our entire game. *The Sims* games and those in Sid Meier's *Civilization* series force dozens of decisions upon the player every minute. Few of these decisions are as direct as "Do you want to go east or west?" but each little decision affects the gameplay overall.

*Agribusiness* (see Figure 1.1) presents the player with numerous choices. Where will the player place the next crop tile? If it's a cheap crop, does he want to use his valuable land or place it on his opponent's? Does he want to uproot a cheap crop to place a more valuable crop instead? The decision by other players to place rocks around this player's water holes affects the player's ability to get more land and thus more crops.

**FIGURE 1.1**
*Agribusiness* (a.k.a. *Farmer*)—prototype 2.
© *Michelle Menard and reprinted with permission.*

Not sure if games are nothing more than a series of meaningful choices? Take a look back at the last game you played and lost. Odds are that you know precisely where things started to go wrong. Some decision or series of decisions ultimately led to your downfall. We remember these things in the rear-view mirror, and through repeated play, we become less likely to falter in our decision making the further we go. What if you don't remember where things went wrong, though? Odds are that you didn't entirely grasp the rules, and once those rules got in motion, it didn't get any better. When players don't grasp the rules, they don't grasp the cause and effect of those rules. Sometimes, they lose badly but don't understand why.

Each of these is an example of meaningful decision making in a game:

- Troop placement in a real-time strategy game (RTS) or a turn-based strategy game.
- Point allocation during character advancement in a role-playing game (RPG)
- Choosing which piece to move in *Chess*
- Aiming and firing your weapon in a first-person shooter (FPS)
- Pressing the right buttons at the right time in *Guitar Hero*

Whenever the player is allowed to exercise choice in a game and that choice affects the outcome of the game, then designers are creating *meaning*. In order to create choice, there has to be another option that has meaning as well.

Sometimes, however, the player has no choice at all. Consider a game like *Monopoly*. Once all the property is purchased, what choice is there beyond "roll the dice and pay"?

Mind you, "roll the dice and pay" isn't even a choice, since there are no other options. Unless house rules are invented to take it beyond this limited scope, there's nothing more to do, and there are no more decisions to make. The player fully understands everything he needs to know about *Monopoly*, and the outcome of any given game becomes predictable. That's why *Monopoly* can become boring for people after just a few trips around the board.

## WHAT GAME DESIGN IS NOT

Game design is one of the most misused terms in use today. Some seek to learn game design, but learn game art instead. Still others learn pure programming. While programming and art are important fields and indeed incredibly important to digital games, game design is its own art form and has been around long before computers, polygons, and even the discovery of electricity.

It is these basic principles of game design that we cover in this book—design distilled down to its basic essence. Not surprisingly, many of today's greatest game designers got their start playing and designing non-digital games, and some still use paper prototyping in their present-day designs.

When thinking of game design, think in terms of the board game *Go*, a Chinese game thousands of years old (see Figure 1.2). It requires no computer programming or polygon models to play. Yet its rules, simple as they are, allow for a depth of strategy so great that it is still played heavily today. While many of the games enjoyed today may not be as popular as *Go* a thousand years from now, there is no reason why such a game could not be created.

**FIGURE 1.2**
*Go* board.
*Image from the Wikipedia Commons*

## TYPES OF DESIGN

Just as there are many types of games, there are many types of game design, too.

- **World design** is the creation of the overall backstory, setting, and theme of the game. While it's generally performed by the lead or sole designer, it often determines the scope of the other design tasks listed below.
- **System design** is the creation of rules and underlying mathematical patterns in a game. This is the only game design task that is common to all games, because all games have rules. Therefore, most of the challenges in this book involve system design. In particular, Chapters 2, 5, 6, 7 and 8 give a starting point for system designers.
- **Content design** is the creation of characters, items, puzzles, and missions. While it's much more common in video games, role playing and collectible card games also feature a significant amount of content. Chapter 3 gives plenty of practice creating puzzles, while Chapters 9, 10, 19, and 20 involve incorporating special kinds of content within a game.
- **Game writing** is the writing of dialogue, text, and story within the game world. Chapter 9 deals with stories in games.
- **Level design** is the crafting of levels in a game, including the layout of maps and placement of objects and challenges within those maps. Though level design is a shared discipline—dungeon masters have been mapping levels in tabletop paper games since the 1970s—when one refers to a "level designer," it is a video-game level designer that they are referring to.
- **User interface** (UI) design consists of two things: how the player interacts with the game, and how the player receives information and feedback from the game. Chapters 17 and 18 include many challenges of UI design. All types of games have UI, even non-digital ones. Boards are designed to fit on an average table and cards are designed to be held in an average-sized hand. The game components must present information that is easily understood, used, and interpreted by the players.[1]

In addition to these specific types of design, all designers need to have the aptitude to produce a game or their assigned portion of a game on the medium they've selected, whether it's a board game, a console game, or even a television game show.

## WHAT IS A GAME?

There are many definitions of the word "game," none of which has been universally accepted for the purposes of defining the limits of game design. One of the authors of this book put forth the following tentative definition: "An activity with rules. It is a form of play often but not always involving conflict, either with other players, with the game system itself, or with randomness/fate/luck. Most games have goals, but not all (for example, *The Sims* and *SimCity*). Most games have defined start and end points, but not all (for example, *World of Warcraft* and *Dungeons & Dragons*). Most games involve decision making on the part of the players, but not all (for example, *Candy Land* and *Chutes and Ladders*). A video game is a game (as defined above) that uses a digital video screen of some kind, in some way."[2]

In this book, and in our own careers, when we speak of a game, we are referring to games in general—from the ancient *Go* to the latest *Madden*. Digital or non-digital, the underlying fundamentals of a game and therefore of game design are all the same. Though technology may advance, modern video game designers use the same core skills today that were used when designing games on paper.

## THE CORE OF A GAME

The "core" or "core dynamic" of a game is the single thing gameplay is about—the single play experience the designer is trying to convey. For instance, games in the *Ratchet & Clank* series are about blowing stuff up in fun and creative ways. *Risk, Carcassonne*, and *Go* are about acquiring territory. A core is usually tied to a specific "core mechanic," be it blowing your enemies away, flipping over tiles on your turn, or selling units to another person. These core mechanics can, in turn, lead to "core dynamics," which is a particular pattern of play. In the industry, when someone says "core," the dynamic is typically what they are referring to. "Core statements" (sometimes called the game's "vision") are usually written by the development team to reflect the core mechanic or the core dynamic and sum up what the game is about, often in a single sentence.

- "This game is about…"
- "This game is the experience of being…"
- "This game teaches…"
- "This game simulates the experience of…"

As is well known by those who have tried to pitch their game to a publisher, if you can't sum up your game in two sentences, you don't have a game.

In games, the following core dynamics tend to show up again and again:

- **Territorial Acquisition:** With this core, things are usually "zero sum," meaning there's only so much to go around, and when it's gone, it's gone. Other times, it's a question of controlling a piece of territory, as it is in some first-person shooters. Games like *Risk, Carcassonne*, and many turn-based strategy games feature this core dynamic.
- **Prediction:** Some games are about doing the right thing or being in the right place at the right time. In many cases, these are children's games, although numerous carnival or party games also feature this core dynamic. All the individual mechanics in the game work toward allowing the players to guess what will happen, and they are rewarded for predicting the possible outcome of a game before it continues to the next round. Most times, the player's prediction involves luck or consideration of odds. Games like *Roulette* or *Rock-Paper-Scissors* fit this core dynamic.
- **Spatial Reasoning:** Puzzle games often incorporate spatial-reasoning skills into video games. Games like *Tetris* make the player think not only of the piece that they're putting in, but also the piece they may put in, or the piece that they desperately need to put in before the whole pile goes to pot. Many board games also make use of spatial skills, such as *Tic-Tac-Toe, Connect Four*, and *Pente*. The prototype for *All Systems Down!* (see Figure 1.3) shows the use of spatial reasoning within a game.

**FIGURE 1.3**
*All Systems Down!*–prototype 2.
*© 2008 by Christopher Schmidt*
*Reprinted with permission of the author.*

- **Survival:** Human beings are naturally wired to survive and thrive, and it's no different in the game world. We will protect ourselves out of sheer instinct before we're even told the point of the game. Survival is a core within many games. However, it's important not to confuse a core with a lose condition in a game. In many video games, you can die, and if you do it's game over. Still, some of these games do not involve constant life-or-death struggles as the primary activity of the game. If the player is concentrating on gaining power, killing enemies, or reaching the exit, then survival is a secondary activity that supports another core (such as building or destroying).

- **Destruction:** The flip side of the survival dynamic, or the companion side if it's a player versus player (PvP) game, is the wreck-everything-in-sight dynamic. Every FPS ever made features this core dynamic, but it is also common in board and card games with a warfare theme, like *Nuclear War*, *Plague and Pestilence*, and *Car Wars*.

- **Building:** In addition to their drive to survive, human beings are also naturally wired to build, even though they're not told that it's the point. It's not surprising then that building is a prime core mechanic featured in many games. In most RPGs, the core dynamic is character development—building up the power level of a character. Video games in the so-called "city builder" genre, such as the *SimCity* and *Caesar* series, feature building as their core. In some board games, like *Settlers of Catan*, players spend most of their time developing their own resources.

- **Collection:** As humans, we're also natural pattern matchers. As humans, we're also natural pattern matchers. You just noticed those two sentences were identical and put them together without even consciously thinking about it. As a human, you can't help it. We match similar objects together instinctively. Collection features prominently in collectible card games (obviously), casual games (match three things together), platformers (collect rings, bolts, or gold coins), or games where getting the most of a resource determines the winner.

- **Chasing or Evading:** Ancient humans had to run a lot, either to capture prey or escape predators. So it should not be a surprise to see this dynamic in many games. It is prominent in most contact sports, as well as video games like *Pac-Man* and board games like *Scotland Yard*.

- **Trading:** Not all play is necessarily competitive. In many games, players cooperate with each other (even if they are opponents). With games that have multiple kinds of resources that belong to each player, it is common to see players trading and negotiating with one another. Trading is a core dynamic of many non-digital games, such as *Pit* and *Settlers of Catan*. It happens outside of the game with collectible card games. Even video games like *Animal Crossing* and *Pokemon* feature the ability to trade with other players.

- **Race to the End:** Being the first to cross the street, the first to cross the finish line, or the first to learn a particular technology are each common uses of the "race to the end" core dynamic of gameplay (see Figure 1.4). Like survival, building, and collection, humans will also intuitively try to do things more quickly, in large part because the brain signals us that faster is better and is a sign of mastery over a given skill. Games featuring this mechanic are typically easy to create and play. The mechanic is often used in children's games.

**FIGURE 1.4**
A "race to the end" prototype.
*Robo Rumble prototype by Blake Harris, Nate Berna, Erika Scipione, AJ Rebecchi, and Keli Washington*

In considering a feature list for a given core, designers tie every feature in the game back into that single core mechanic (or set of mechanics) in some way that ultimately makes the game stronger.

However, developing and implementing a feature set from that core mechanic is another matter entirely, and it represents the real craft of the game designer. Feature sets list all the individual features of the product. Within a feature set, designers generally try for part innovation, part improvement, and part convention. For a game's feature set, game designers use the standard conventions that define the genre and that players expect, but they try to find some way to innovate on previous games in the genre or with a similar theme, if there are any.

Digital games actually greatly expanded the core possibility that we as game designers can choose from since they are capable of so many things that non-digital games cannot do. Taking into account the whole variety of games—from big-budget titles to serious games— the range of game cores is tremendous.

## WHERE DO IDEAS COME FROM?

Anything—anything at all—can be turned into a game. From bean farming, to sheep herding, to knitting, everything is fair game when it comes to game design. Nonetheless, for working game designers, the question "Where do you get your ideas?" is a common one.

There are multiple answers:

- **Playing lots of games.** Through playing games, you develop a vocabulary of mechanics and dynamics that are the necessary building blocks of successful game design. It is important to play many different kinds of games, not just those you are familiar with. Imagine if you were an architect and spent your entire life in a townhouse community, and then you tried to design a new house. That house would probably be similar to the ones you already know. Likewise, think of the level designer raised (for some odd reason) in an auditorium. All of his levels would reflect, in some way, the world that he grew up in. With exposure to lots of different games, however, your designs or the designs of your group are likely to reflect multiple influences (see Figure 1.5). Expose yourself to many new kinds of games to develop your range of knowledge and skills. Watch documentaries. If something interests you, look for the game inside.
- **Networking with other designers.** Two designers talking about the possibility inherent in a topic is a sure-fire way to produce a game. Mind you, it might be a bad game, so it's important to have a qualified pool of people to give you objective feedback as well. Still, designers share methods and always spur each other on to deeper thinking.
- **Everywhere.** Look for game ideas in everything you do and challenge yourself to make a game or think about making a game about a topic at least once a day. Right now around you, there are sounds you are completely tuning out: the flip of the page, the sound of your own breathing, and perhaps music or a television in the background. Game design can be tuned out or tuned in the same way. If you actively listen for the possibility and go with it, you will find game ideas everywhere.

**FIGURE 1.5**
A group of game-design students working on their own table-top RPG, complete with combat system and game master (GM). Their final design was influenced by a wide variety of games.
You Are Dead *prototype by Michelle Menard, Chris Schmidt, Darren Malley, and Jeff McNab*

## LEARNING GAME DESIGN

Game design is a field you must apply to learn. Truly, there is no substitute for making games. In that process, you learn so much more than you would by merely reading about making games. Fortunately, throughout the course of this book, you'll be doing a whole lot of that.

Game design has been likened to cooking in this respect. Imagine a chef who only reads cookbooks or books on various techniques but never actually sets foot in a kitchen or tries to cook a meal. Odds are his first dishes will be terribly unappetizing. Or imagine a painter who has never picked up a brush. Beyond some initial study of basic concepts, the best way to get better at painting is to paint and then paint some more.

Likewise, by creating and playing your own designs, you learn how particular mechanics work and don't work under a variety of circumstances. It is also only through the process of play that dynamics arise, and some of these may surprise you.

In the prototype pictured in Figure 1.6, one of this book's authors was attempting to simulate displacement for an installation that would appear as a part of an art exhibit. As play progressed, the gameplay developed two dynamics that the game designer didn't see coming.

**FIGURE 1.6**
*Where My People Come From*—prototype 1.
© *2008 by Brenda Brathwaite*

The first surprising dynamic was the change in the pace of play as one group of tokens crowded the others into a smaller and smaller piece of territory. Interesting strategies for "survival" developed where players would allow their tokens to get displaced more than once to ensure an optimum distance from the oncoming forces.

The second surprising dynamic was the distinct phases that were present in the game play. Phases are to be expected in a game—*Risk* has very clear phases—but the designer was surprised by the clear delineation of phases in this game, too.

By reading a rulebook or writing a design document, these dynamics would never have been evident. In order to design, you must practice design, and you must play what you practice. It doesn't work any other way.

## COMMON TERMS IN GAME DESIGN

Like any other industry, the game industry has terms it uses to define specific events or milestones in a project or things related to games in general. None of these definitions are set in stone, however. For every term used in the industry, there are probably five different definitions depending on the company, the person, or the discipline you're talking about. The following terms are used liberally throughout this book:

- **Feature List:** A list that details key features or selling points of the game. In published games, these are typically found on the back of the box.
- **Brainstorming:** A process to generate ideas, usually done in a group. Generally, participants in a brainstorming session are instructed to call out any idea that occurs to them, no matter how strange, silly, or crazy it seems. One participant writes all of these ideas down on a space where everyone can see them. Participants may elaborate on or play off of others' ideas, but criticism or elimination of ideas is not allowed until after the session is over.
- **Prototype:** A prototype is a playable early version of the game or part of the game constructed by the designer to assist in understanding and enhancing the player experience. It may be done with software ("digital prototype") or with physical materials as a tabletop game ("physical prototype" or "paper prototype")
- **Balance:** A term used to describe the state of a game's systems as either "balanced" or "unbalanced." When the play is unbalanced, it is too easy, too difficult, or optimal for only certain groups of players. When play is balanced, it provides a consistent challenge for its target audience. For competitive multiplayer games, it also includes the idea that no single strategy should be inherently better than any other, and that no exploits exist that let a player bypass the challenge of the game. We also sometimes call individual game elements "balanced" with each other, meaning that the cost of obtaining it is proportional to its effect, as with cards in a CCG or weapons in an FPS or RPG.
- **Mechanics:** The rules of a game. Common non-digital mechanics include trick taking, turn taking, rolling a die, and moving. Examples of mechanics from video games are running, jumping, and shooting. Mechanics are covered extensively in Chapter 2.
- **Dynamics:** As popularized in Robin Hunicke, Marc LeBlanc, and Robert Zubek's MDA (mechanics-dynamics-aesthetics) model,[3] dynamics result when rules are put in motion. The rules that allow players to attack each other might be a mechanic, but players actually using these rules to team up against the player in the lead is a dynamic. In some first-person shooter games, players always begin in certain locations ("spawn points"), which is a mechanic; standing next to a spawn point and killing players that come out of it ("spawn camping") is a dynamic. In *Chess*, the moves of the pieces are mechanics, but "book openings" (well-known sequences of moves at the start of the game) are dynamics.
- **System:** A collection of game mechanics that is responsible for producing a given outcome within a larger game such as character creation, combat, or casting spells (see Figure 1.7).
- **Avatar:** The direct representation of a player in a game. In *Monopoly*, the pieces moved around the board (shoe, dog, and so on) are avatars. In *Tomb Raider*, the main character Lara Croft is the avatar. In non-digital games, these are often called "tokens."
- **Playtesting:** The systematic testing of gameplay, systems, balance, and interface to find all the errors, inconsistencies, or issues and report them to the design team.

**FIGURE 1.7**
Paper prototype of several systems comprising
a role-playing game.
Totemic *prototype by Clay Kisko, Ben Rodgers,*
*Szymon Marciniak, and Jarrod Morrison*

The following terms are usually reserved for digital game design:

- **Platform:** The console, device, or system upon which the game will be played.
- **Concept Doc:** A one- to three-page document that provides a high-level overview of a proposed game. It usually contains the following sections: an introductory paragraph explaining the theme of the game; demographic breakdown, including target audience, genre, and intended platform(s); and a bullet-point feature-list and a feature list breakout that explains each of the features in more detail. An outline for a sample concept doc is also provided on the book's Web site at http://designgames.wordpress.com.
- **Proposal:** A five- to 20-page document that provides a more in-depth view of the potential game than a concept document. Like a concept document, it typically contains an introductory paragraph, a demographic breakdown, a gameplay summary, a feature list, and a feature-list breakout. It also contains budget and time estimations, competitive analysis (how it stacks up against the competition), and expansion plans (for example, sequels) beyond the initial product release. Typically, it contains screen mockups or concept art. An outline for a proposal doc is also provided on the book's Web site at http://designgames.wordpress.com.

- **Pitch:** A brief "elevator speech" given to a game publisher or VC (venture capitalist) to solicit funding for the project. An elevator speech gets its name from the length of time that people have to present their ideas—the amount of time you'd spend riding with someone in an elevator before one of you had to get out.
- **Design Document:** A "living" document that is continuously undergoing revision, it contains the entire design vision for the game. It may be in a document file or in a wiki. Some teams use Agile development, which requires no design document at all. More information on Agile can be found at AgileManifesto.org. Game design documents (GDDs) are usually separate from the technical design document (TDD) for programmers and the art style guide for the art team.
- **Bugs:** Errors in the game's design, code, art, sound, or writing.
- **Engine:** The core program that runs the game. Unreal and Gamebryo are popular engines used in the game industry. Developers will layer additional technology on top of the engine to achieve the exact design specifications of the product.
- **Alpha:** The milestone at which all systems have been implemented and all code is theoretically complete. It is usually full of bugs, however, and not terribly balanced. Some companies also require that all content—art, sound, and narrative—be implemented for alpha, too. Therefore, alpha is content- and code-complete.
- **Beta:** The milestone at which all systems and content are in the game. It is significantly more stable than the alpha version, and many of the big bug and balancing issues have been addressed.
- **Gold:** The final version of the game that is then released.
- **Game Jam:** A timed period during which a group of individuals attempts to create a complete game while working around the clock. These events are usually 1–3 days in duration.
- **Milestone:** A point at which the developer is expected to deliver some type of predetermined content. It may be a document, numerous art assets, or a complete game.

Non-digital games also have some common terms:

- **Game Bits:** The informal name given to the pieces and parts that ship with a game, including the game tiles, board, and cards (see Figure 1.8). These are more formally called "components" or "game objects."
- **Card Game:** A game that uses playing cards. They may be a standard deck of cards, *Pokemon* cards, *Magic: The Gathering* cards, or other cards.
- **Board Game:** A game whose board serves as the playing field for the game.
- **Tile Game:** A type of game where the game "board" is made out of tiles, usually square or hexagonal (see Figure 1.9). The tiles may start in a predetermined configuration (as in *Settlers of Catan* or *Hey, That's My Fish!*) or built during play (like *Carcassonne*).
- **Dice Game:** A game that uses dice as the main bits, typically lacking a board, cards or tiles.

**FIGURE 1.8**

Examples of game bits. These are unpainted, solid wood player tokens posed with dice and a business card to show width and height. (The business card is not *normally* considered a game bit, but it could be in the right game.)

**FIGURE 1.9**

A typical tile-based board-game layout. The board is formed of loose tiles that come together to form a playspace.

Age of Discovery *prototype by Tom Whitener, Josh Markham, Sam Paley, and Kevin Pollard*

## APPROACHES TO GAME DESIGN

Different designers have different approaches to game design, depending on the situation and the medium in which they're designing. In creating the list that follows, certain liberties have been taken with the names. In other words, we've made them up to describe processes that we both experience and regularly hear about.

- **Blue-sky:** Pure blue-sky design allows designers to consider lots of possibilities and ideas with a few exceptions imposed by time, money, interest, or all of the above. In some respects, game design is like treasure hunting without a map. Designers are always looking for new ideas, because the experience of creating a game right from the inception is inherently pleasurable to the designer. For most designers, in fact, the game lies in *creating* the game. Most of the time, a professional designer is working under a particular constraint—an externally imposed restriction on the design. Blue-sky design, however, assumes no constraints other than the designer's imagination.

- **Slow boil:** When given a theme and a setting—say, the Irish in 1880s Boston—game designers begin what can only be described as a massive research mission, but one that often has little direction as long as it encompasses the theme. As one designer noted, "I stuff my head full of everything I can get on the topic, and then I wait. A design will emerge." Fortunately for most designers, they are expert generalists with a love for learning and a natural curiosity that leads them in this direction. Sometimes, that design takes days, but other times, it may be weeks, months, or even years. Game designer Reiner Knizia regularly has 30 different designs on the go and has noted that he prefers to mull games over in his mind, playing them repeatedly, before moving to a prototype stage (see Figure 1.10). One common mistake new designers make is forcing a game out too early or not giving it enough time to develop. Periodically writing down the ideas in one's head can help spur still more ideas, particularly if the ideas take the form of a potential design document or rule set.

- **Mechanic:** Mechanic-driven design is more common than one might think. Consider the classic *Super Mario Bros.* game. Mario jumps onto things, over things, and into things. The strength of the game is based on the sheer strength of this mechanic, and nearly all games in the platformer genre have followed that game's lead from long, long ago. Other more recent games, like those in the *Katamari Damacy* series, feature a mechanic in which a sticky ball rolls over something and picks it up. Again, that same mechanic is used over and over to great effect. Perhaps the largest mechanic-driven games feature the mechanic right in the genre's title: first-person shooters. The mechanic of firing a gun, a wand, or a something evidently never gets old. Even Mario could shoot fireballs.

**FIGURE 1.10**
Reiner Knizia, a prolific non-digital game
designer. Over 200 of his games have been
published as of the writing of this book.

- **MDA:** Using the mechanics-dynamics-aesthetics model of game development, designers create aesthetic models for various types of gameplay. Aesthetics don't refer to the
looks of the game but rather the emotional response the designer and development
team hope to evoke in the players through the game dynamics. If mechanics are the
rules and dynamics are the play of the game, then aesthetics are typically the fun (or
lack thereof) experienced by playing. Designers ask themselves which aesthetic they
hope to achieve, define the dynamics that would lead to this feeling, and then create the
mechanics to produce the desired dynamics. More information on MDA can be found
at Marc's homepage at http://mahk.8kindsoffun.com/.

- **IP:** Standing for "intellectual property," games based on IP are very common in the
game industry, and most designers find themselves developing a game for a pre-existing
IP at some point in their career. The term "IP" is used to refer to pretty much anything
or *anyone* upon whose likeness a game is built. Examples of IPs include *Spiderman*,
*Halo*, *The Sims*, and individuals like John Madden. Even non-digital games are covered
in IP. Most popular television shows release board-game versions, and popular video
games are often made into card and board games. *Pokemon* and *World of Warcraft* are
just two examples of game IP that have gone "off the grid." Game publishers like to use
IP because it mitigates risk. The more people who already know about it and like it, the
larger the potential market based on the strength of the license alone, which means the

publisher has less risk of the game falling short of sales goals. As an example of the power of an IP, consider NFL football. Now, think of another professional football league. Though some have been tried in the real world and in video games, none ever came close to the strength of the true NFL.

▪ **Story:** Developing a game based on a story is also a common design approach, but more common in video games than non-digital games. This is often done hand-in-hand with IP when the license holder wants the developer to stick closely to the story of the book, television show, or movie in question. The story can also represent the chronological timeline of a person or a company. Author Tom Clancy has licensed many of his books for games, and the epic *The Lord of the Rings* was turned into an acclaimed board game by Reiner Knizia. More often than not, however, in non-digital games, the designer takes a thematic approach as Knizia did.

▪ **Research:** Increasingly, games are being used to research a variety of topics or as the topic of research itself. For her MFA thesis, Savannah College of Art and Design student Michelle Menard created a production-grade board game, a documentary, and completed a research paper which explored the idea of using emotion to create game mechanics (see Figures 1.11 and 1.12). Likewise, USC's Jenova Chen created *flOw* to explore the concept of flow and dynamic difficulty adjustment in games.

**FIGURE 1.11**
*Mesuline.* Michelle Menard's MFA graduate thesis from the Savannah College of Art and Design (www.artemic.com).

**FIGURE 1.12**

*Mesuline.* A playtest session in which Michelle Menard gathers information about player's responses to gameplay.

## ITERATIVE DESIGN

Game design, like most forms of design, is an iterative process. That means that the game is quickly prototyped, played, and refined again and again before it is finalized. It requires the understanding that no one gets it right on the first try, not even the most skilled designer, and that the greatest, most successful games are only achieved through a series of repeated failures on the way. Any moderately complex game or system within a game usually requires many iterations before it is considered finished.

A typical iteration includes the following components:

1. **Rapid Prototype:** Designers focus on play over graphics. Think for a moment about how one would prototype the video game Mario Kart in a board-game format. A "race to the end" core dynamic would be used, tokens would represent cars, and players would have a variety of actions they could perform, depending on their location on the board. From there, other mechanics could be made to improve the play of the non-digital counterpart. The key point of prototyping is that it has to be rapid. The more iterations a game can undergo, the higher quality it will be, so spending three months discussing a rough prototype's issues ends up just being a waste of time. Sometimes, designers are hoping to answer a specific question with a prototype ("Would including a blue shell weapon be too powerful?"), and other times they're hoping to gauge the overall feel of the game. There is a great tendency among designers to debate the outcome of something that could be shown in half the time if only it were prototyped.

2. **Playtest:** This is a full or partial play session to identify strengths and weaknesses in the design.
3. **Revision:** Changes are made in the design to fortify weaknesses and build upon strengths. Sometimes, changes are small incremental changes incorporated one at a time. Other times, designers happen upon unexpected play dynamics that cause the game to go in a completely different direction.
4. **Repeat:** Go back to the prototype and start the next iteration.

In prototyping games, there are also a couple general rules that the authors of this book follow:

- Don't write your rules down until you have to write your rules down. If you as the designers can't keep them straight in your head, how do you expect your players to? If, on the other hand, your players have things like monster lists in front of them while playing, so should you. If writing is a part of your brainstorming process, though, or if you're likely to forget parts of your game due to the length of time between design sessions, jettison this rule.
- In identifying problems in games, be wary of putting a Band-Aid on top of a problem, but leaving the problem in the game. In some cases, designers end up with Band-Aid upon Band-Aid when the initial bad mechanic should have been removed. When you repeatedly try to fix something that's just not worth it, it might be better to remove it entirely. If nothing else, your time away from it may improve your perspective and give you new insight into a solution.

## CONSTRAINTS ON GAME DESIGN

Constraints are the confines in which designers build games. Think of constraints as a box that you usually cannot alter. For instance, consider the type of game you would build if you had $20 versus $200,000.

### VIDEO-GAME CONSTRAINTS

In mainstream video games, designers often start their design process with constraints like the following:

- What is the approximate budget for this game?
- What is the desired time frame for completion?
- What is the desired platform for the game (for example, console, multiple consoles, cell phones, PCs, ARGs)?

These three questions influence the whole course of the design. In fact, these various constraints may conflict with one another. It's not uncommon for people new to games (a corporation hoping to get a training game made, for instance) to completely underestimate the cost of an average game's development. In pitching a game, it's possible that the publisher is open to negotiation and will ask you to suggest various possibilities.

With the key questions out of the way, there are other questions that designers ask:

- What is the target audience for the game?
- What is the desired rating for the game? (Although the game won't be rated by the ESRB (Entertainment Software Rating Board) until it's nearly finished production, if at all, publishers have an ideal rating in mind and strive to develop a game to fit that rating.)
- Do you have any particular genre or category of game in mind?
- Are there any features that you'd like to see in the game?

Some developers also ask potential clients for some adjectives that describe the game that they want to make. It tells the developer a lot about the game's overall style. If someone says "edgy and realistic," it steers the pitch in a completely different direction than "light and cartoon-like."

While this is a very simplified view of the process that takes place regularly behind the doors of game developers, with this information in hand, a developer can craft a competent pitch (provided he is a competent developer).

For nonlicensed games in which the developer is working from scratch in hopes of creating her own IP, the same questions generally apply. However, she has a bit more latitude in answering those questions since she is, technically, the IP holder.

*NOTE*

### *Publishing Your Game*

*In today's market, it is not possible to sell an idea for a great video game to a publisher, unless you are an already established game designer with multiple best-selling titles under your belt. Even then, it might be challenging. If you are just starting out and have a great idea, your best bet is to make it and sell it on the indie market, or get a job inside a game company and work your butt off for years until you reach a position where you can have that kind of effect.*

### NON-DIGITAL CONSTRAINTS

In non-digital game design, designers often *end* with constraints. The design of the game comes first—the mechanics, the theme, the play experience—and then, based on publisher response, changes are made. Some common constraints include the following:

- **Cost to manufacture per unit.** Is it worth using wooden tiles, or could cheaper plastic cards work just as well? Can lighter components be used to reduce shipping costs? For certain types of games, there is a target price point. Heavy strategy games can cost more than light, casual family games.
- **Physical dimensions.** In practical use, the people playing the game have a limited amount of tabletop or floor space on which to play, so the board (if there is one) and other components have to fit in a relatively small area. For games that are playable by small children, cards and other pieces should be such that they can be manipulated by small hands. Tactile considerations are particularly important to board-game players.

- **Publisher.** Not all publishers are identical in the board-game industry. Many of them specialize in certain genres. A company that is known for family games is unlikely to publish your historical war game, no matter how brilliant it is. Some publishers do not take outside submissions at all. Non-digital designers' choice of publishers will be limited by the nature of the game they have designed.
- **Timing.** If a similar game was just released, publishers may prefer to wait until the following year before manufacturing another game of the same type. Some non-digital designs may be functionally complete for years before they see the light of day.

In cases where a non-digital publisher approaches a particular designer for a specific game, the constraints can be similar to those of a video game. The publisher may want a game designed around a specific IP, to be released at a certain time, with a certain cost, targeted at a certain age group, and have a total playtime within a given range.

Unlike digital game design, the physical constraints of the game (making it tile-based, on a board, or using cards, for instance) usually come about as the result of the design, rather than as an initial constraint. For instance, after exploring an idea and doing a few prototypes, the designer may decide that it's best to make the game tile-based. Once the design is complete, the cost of materials can be a constraint that forces the designer to reconsider. However, in the initial design, the non-digital designer has many components and mediums from which to choose. This is in contrast to digital game design, where the designer almost always starts with medium constraints (such as platform and genre).

## OVERCOMING DESIGNER'S BLOCK

Even the best game designers end up with complete duds from time to time. The following tricks are sometimes employed to force a massive dynamic change upon existing game designs when you feel stuck and aren't sure how else to proceed (much like writers have ways to overcome "writer's block"). While the designs these tricks may produce might not lead to immediate shippable results, they will force you to play with a radically different dynamic and address a new set of problems and perhaps give your brain the ideas it needs to solidify a particular design.

### MAKE A RESOURCE LIMITED (OR UNLIMITED)

When a resource—money, land, med packs—are limited and finite, designers say that these resources are "limited." There is only a certain number of them to go around, and when one player gets one, it means that the other player will therefore lose the opportunity to get the same one. For instance, if there are 20 med packs in a level, and one player gets 12 of them, the other player will get eight at most. These med packs would be considered a limited resource.

In *Monopoly*, the property, houses, and hotels are limited, while the money is not. You can get as much cash as chance will allow.

In order to effectively use this trick, make a list of all the resources in your game and note whether they are limited or unlimited. Next, and one at a time, change the resources from unlimited to limited (or vice versa), and play a session of the game. Consider for a moment how you would play a FPS if you knew that the bullets on a level were limited versus unlimited. Think of how *Monopoly* would play if you could get all the property you wanted to.

When resources are limited, they tend to force a resource-gathering and management strategy on players. When they are unlimited, this strategy is less important, but as you can likely tell by the *Monopoly* example, interesting new play dynamics can be revealed.

### INTERACTING WITH YOUR FRIENDS

While it's always fun to win a game, it's occasionally as fun to stop someone else from doing the same or otherwise affect their play. Look at the various actions your players are performing in a game. Next, ask yourself, "How could someone else stop that from happening or make it happen even faster?" You can even take it one step further and ask how players could then protect themselves from aggressive moves or solicit help more directly from their opponents.

Allowing players to affect the play of other players is an effective means of introducing a bit of uncertainty even in the most mundane games. It also forces a minor amount of strategy on players who must consider preparing a counter to that attack or a means to ally with another player. Collectible card games are the best places to see examples of these principles in action.

### MESS WITH THE PLAY ORDER

Many games have a set play order—take turns going counterclockwise, for example. Consider allowing players to mess with the sequence of events in your game. For instance, instants in *Magic: the Gathering* allow players to initiate a move even when it is not their turn. Mechanics such as "go again" and "skip a turn" in board games are also common.

Games like *Fluxx* are excellent at messing with the player order, the rules, and everything else in the game.

### KILL A RULE

While this sometimes strikes the game's designer as sacrilege, killing a rule is usually a good thing to do in the prototype stage. At this point, it's common for people to have too many rules to make up for their lack of player trust and trust in the game as a whole. "What if the player doesn't do X?" one designer says. Another answers, "Let's add a rule to make them do it." Before long, the rules of the game are unwieldy. Identify the core of the game and start by killing every rule that doesn't directly affect the core of the game. (Simply saying "it doesn't work" doesn't mean anything.)

### Use the "Rule of Two"

If something seems off but you're not sure what, take one of the game's values and either multiply or divide it by two. Making such a drastic change gives you insight into how the game's values interact with each other and what effects they have on play, and you'll often realize things you never would have seen if you made smaller, incremental changes.

## Resources

[1] "Types of Game Designers," Applied Game Design, Brenda Brathwaite, November 20, 2007. Available online at http://bbrathwaite.wordpress.com/2007/11/20/types-of-game-designers/. Accessed May 18, 2008.

[2] IGDA Curriculum Framework. Available online at http://www.igda.org/wiki/images/e/ee/Igda2008cf.pdf. Accessed May 18, 2008.

[3] MDA Framework, by LeBlanc et al. Available online at http://www.cs.north-western.edu/~hunicke/MDA.pdf. Accessed May 20, 2008.

# 2 Game Design Atoms

Chemists and physicists have spent centuries trying to identify the smallest identifiable pieces of matter and how they interact with one another. Game design is a much younger field, but designers have likewise attempted to identify the smallest identifiable parts of a game. Each part can be designed individually, and understanding what the parts are and how they interact is necessary to design or analyze a complete game. These parts of a game, these "atoms" of game design, are what this chapter is all about.

When designing a game, many novice designers have no idea where to start. A complete game like *World of Warcraft* is so huge and expansive that designing the entire thing from scratch seems like an impossible task. Even for a relatively simple game like *Monopoly*, it's not clear where the design begins: Does it start with the playing pieces, the Chance and Community Chest cards, the board, the rules, or something else? By looking at a game as a collection of atoms, the process of design itself becomes clearer.

A word of warning—among developers and academics, there are dozens of definitions of the word "game" and still more ideas on how a game is put together. What follows is *one* way to categorize games, not *the* way. Designers who find these discussions interesting are encouraged to expand these definitions.

## THE GAME STATE AND GAME VIEWS

To understand games, it's useful to first take a look at the big picture. For a moment, imagine a game that you've recently played. Consider everything that's going on in a game or may change if someone takes a turn or leaves the Pause menu. We call this picture the *game state*—a collection of *all* relevant virtual information that may change during play.

In *Chess* (see Figure 2.1), the game state consists of a list of pieces, their positions on the board, and certain information based on previous moves (for example, which players are eligible to make a castling move, which pawns are vulnerable to *en passant* capture, and whose turn it is right now).

In *Poker*, the game state consists of each player's hand and chips, the size of the pot, whose turn it is to bet, who has folded on the current hand, which cards are in the deck and in what order, and so on. In video games, the game state can be extremely complicated; in the latest *Madden* game, for example, the game state contains information about every player, every possible move, and every previous move in the entire game.

**FIGURE 2.1**
*Chess* board.
*Image from the Wikipedia Commons.*

From the previous examples, it's clear that players are not always aware of the entire game state. The portions of the game state that a player can see, we will refer to here as the *game view*. In *Chess*, the game state *is* the game view, as there is no hidden information. In a real-time strategy game (RTS), the fog of war gives each player his own incomplete game view revealing only the land or terrain he has uncovered. In a massively multiplayer online game (MMO), the player can't possibly know what's going on half a virtual world away.

This leads finally to the *game space*, the entire area of the game. It may be the board on which the game is played, an enormous MMO, or a single level in a first-person shooter (FPS) campaign. In an alternate or augmented reality game (ARG), it may be the player's city, the Internet, the player's normal living space, or the entire world.

## PLAYERS, AVATARS, AND GAME BITS

A game space can be as small or as large as it likes, but it wouldn't be a game without players. By definition, all games have players since it's the players who set the rules in motion.

In digital worlds, the player is frequently represented in the game by an avatar. In non-digital games, the player is also represented, though the terminology is not consistent and varies from game to game ("token" and "pawn" are commonly used names that appear in game rules). For the sake of this book, we will refer to that thing which represents the player in the game world as an avatar. It's how players mark their location in the game view. In *Monopoly*, the avatars include the thimble, the car, and the little dog. In *Trivial Pursuit*, it's the pie. In *Chess*, it's the king (the other pieces are there to protect the king). In the typical FPS, it's a soldier or the portion of the gun on the screen. In many 3D video games, you watch the back of your avatar as he explores the world (see Figure 2.2).

**FIGURE 2.2**
*Mesuline* avatar. *Mesuline* uses hand-painted avatars.
© 2008 Michelle Menard. Reprinted with permission

In some games, there is no avatar in the game space. Instead, the player represents him- or herself. This is true of *Poker, Risk,* and the video game *Civilization Revolution*. In the latter, the little soldiers and artillery pieces are defending the player—the leader. Similarly, most RTS video games have no avatar. An avatar differs from what board-game designers informally call "game bits," which are the physical items required to play the game. Bits include things like property cards, dice, the plastic army pieces in *Risk,* action and mana cards, or jewelry pieces as in *Pretty Pretty Princess*. In video games, we frequently refer to these game bits as "art assets" when discussing the icons, sprites, and models, and as "objects" when talking about their representation in the programming code. Individually, they are referred to by names you're likely familiar with, such as NPCs, items, monsters, enemies, and so on. The *Steampunk* gunslinger in Figure 2.3 is one such character created by game artist and designer Benjamin Rodgers.

The current condition of all avatars and bits (and players, in the case of physical-dexterity games like *Twister*) is part of the game state in the overall game space.

**FIGURE 2.3**
*Steampunk gunslinger.* This character could be an avatar,
an NPC, or a fierce enemy.
© *2008 Benjamin Rodgers. Reprinted with permission.*

## MECHANICS

What really makes the game space a very interesting place to be are game mechanics. "Game mechanic" is another term for what others might commonly call a "rule." Among those in the industry, though, the term "mechanic" is commonplace. Mechanics are how something works. If you do X, then Y happens. If X is true, then you can do Y. In *Monopoly*, if you land on a property, you can buy it. If you roll the higher number, you get to go first. Each is a simple mechanic.

For game designers, gameplay mechanics are amazingly fun things. Think of a chef with a spice or a carpenter with a piece of wood. A mechanic makes every game designer ask, "What can I make with this?" A mechanic is all about possibility. For many designers, this process of creation is even a game unto itself.

Put another way, mechanics are the rules that act upon the players, avatars and game bits, game state and game views, and describe all of the ways to change the game state.

Mechanics are the ingredients of game design. Having an understanding of these is critical for all game designers. In fact, you can even search board games by mechanics on BoardGameGeek.com (http://www.boardgamegeek.com/browser.php?itemtype=game&sort-by=mechanic).

Here are some common classes of mechanics that are usually found in games:

- **Setup.** There must always be at least one rule that describes how the game begins.
- **Victory conditions.** There must always be at least one rule that describes how the game is won. Some games, like open-ended role-playing games (RPGs), have no victory condition. As a result, some designers do not consider them games. Others consider the achievement of a specific goal a victory as they race off to the next goal.
- **Progression of play.** Who goes first, and how (see Figure 2.4)? Is the game turn based or real time? For turn-based games, does the game start with one player and then proceed clockwise, or do players bid resources in an auction for the right to go first each round, or is there some other method? For real-time games, when two players try to do something at the same time, how is that resolved?

**FIGURE 2.4**
Two players enjoying a game of *Carcassonne.* Play begins with an initial tile and proceeds clockwise. Each player takes a turn placing a tile and claiming ownership of a farm, road, castle, or cloister on that tile.

- **Player actions.** Sometimes referred to as "verbs," some of the most important mechanics describe what players can do and what effect those actions have on the game state.
- **Definition of game view(s).** Mechanics define exactly what information each player knows at any given time. Note that some mechanics may change the view, such as partially lifting fog of war in an RTS under certain conditions.

Some mechanic combinations are also easier for people to grasp than others. For instance, in the board game *Scotland Yard*, Mr. X roams around London trying to evade capture. He only surfaces every three turns, but otherwise remains hidden. The game is based purely on strategy. As such, it's not as easy for people to play as, say, *Sorry!*. In Chapters 5–8, the concept of strategy and luck in mechanics is examined fully.

## DYNAMICS

A "game dynamic" is the pattern of play that comes from the mechanics once they're set in motion by players. For instance, throughout this book, some very common dynamics are referenced, such as "race to the end" and "territorial acquisition." Territorial acquisition is itself just a form of a larger dynamic collection (and, by default, retention).

The following games involve territorial acquisition, among other dynamics:

- *Civilization*
- *Starcraft*
- *Risk*
- *Axis & Allies*
- *Diplomacy*
- *Go*

All of these games are based on race to the end:

- *Mario Kart*
- *Candyland*
- *The Game of Life*
- *Chutes & Ladders*

Though these games share the same dynamic, the mechanics used to achieve that dynamic are different from game to game.

Notice that the dynamics are part of the play experience, but not all are explicitly defined or enforced by the mechanics—for example, interactions that take place between players outside of the game state (commonly referred to as the "metagame"). Some examples of metagame dynamics are player negotiations, discussion, alliances, online chat, and trash talking (see Figure 2.5).

**FIGURE 2.5**
A play session of *Melusine* in which the slumped player lost with much trash talking.

## GOALS

Layered on top of all things are game goals. The ultimate game goal is, of course, the victory condition. Sometimes, goals in games are called "missions" or "quests."

Goals typically provide rewards that motivate players to defeat creatures, search for treasure, equip themselves with better and better armor, and compete against their friends. In FPSs, the goal is often to defeat the enemy, capture the flag, or rescue the hostage. In *The Age of Discovery* (see Figure 2.6), one of the player's goals is to discover new lands at sea.

**FIGURE 2.6**
*The Age of Discovery.*
*© 2008 Thomas Whitener, Sam Paley, Kevin Proulx,*
*Kevin Powell, and John Markham. Conner Scott is*
*pictured.*

## THEME

*Bohnanza* is a game about bean farming. *Super Mario Bros.* is a game about a plumber searching through the Mushroom Kingdom to save a princess. *Katamari Damacy* is a game about a prince who must create the stars in the sky that were accidentally destroyed by the King of All Cosmos. This does not apply to all games; *Tetris* isn't about anything.

None of this information is strictly necessary to the gameplay. *Clue* could just as easily be about finding a lost mitten or your soul mate with exactly the same mechanics. At the same time, something about hunting down a murderer makes the game more appealing.

This concept of what the game is "about" goes by many names. It can be referred to as theme, color, story or narrative, among other terms. Throughout this book, we will use the term "theme" to describe this aspect of games that lies outside of the mechanics and yet somehow, when chosen well, can make the mechanics feel more natural.

## WHAT COMES FIRST?

Game state, avatars, mechanics, dynamics, theme… where does a designer begin?

For game developers, it can go in just about any order. Let's say you want to make a game based on resource collection. If the dynamics are decided, the question now becomes one of mechanics. How exactly does one go about collecting resources? There's also the question of theme. What is being collected, and what is the player's motivation for collecting them?

A designer might start with a theme. The board game *Redneck Life* (see Figure 2.7) is so heavily themed that it's likely the designer created the theme first, and then found a game to fit.

**FIGURE 2.7**
*Redneck Life* is an example of a game whose theme factored heavily into its design.

An individual mechanic can also be used as the basis for a game. In the case of *Katamari Damacy*, the mechanic of rolling over objects and picking them up forms the basis for the entire rest of the game, and it was probably designed first. Likewise, countless FPSs start with the mechanic of shooting and layer from there.

## PUTTING IT ALL TOGETHER

As an example, let's say you're designing a physical card game and the theme is automobile production (see Figure 2.8). The desired dynamic is race to the end and requires the player to finish building a car first. The mechanics that might let us do this are:

- Draw a card
- Play a card (either place it or discard it)

The game bits would be:

- Cards (each one has a piece of a car on it, and it takes 10 pieces to build a complete car)

The player represents himself, so an avatar won't be necessary.

**FIGURE 2.8**
Prototype of car game. In the first iteration of this game, it takes
10 pieces to build a full car, but the game isn't terribly fun.

By itself, it's not much of a game at this point. In fact, at this point, *most* games aren't. The point is to get a basic game, and then make it more interesting to the player through the addition of elements of strategy or chance, or by adding or removing mechanics to strengthen the game. While this is covered fully in Chapter 14, "Adding and Subtracting Mechanics," for the sake of illustration, we could add mechanics and game bits, if necessary, for each of the following:

- A production pipeline
- Production pricing that would force players to allocate workers, parts, and the like, to determine optimum output
- Sabotage, so that one player could affect another's production pipeline
- Random cards that introduce luck into the equation by causing production breakdowns, price drops, favorable publicity, and so on

Depending on the cards and on the strategy required, this game could evolve into something fun. For many designers, creating games not only keeps them sharp, but allows them to have a whole lot of fun in the process.

Learn to experiment and take joy in your designs and in the process of design. Remember that you can make a game about anything. It's normal to feel intimidated by the process at first. Ironically, some game players are more comfortable making FPS levels in a digital editor than they are making board games. However, the two mediums possess the exact same building blocks.

Design a game and be hooked.

## CHALLENGES

The challenges in this chapter grow progressively more difficult and are designed to get you comfortable with the process of game design in a non-digital format. In the remaining chapters, we build upon the foundation started here. Variants offer you a chance to take each suggested design further.

### CHALLENGE 1—THE PATH

For this game, you are going to explore the race to the end gameplay dynamic discussed earlier. The game should allow two to four players, be about progressing on a path, and make them go from point A to point B. The first player to point B wins.

As the game's designer, it's up to you to figure out the theme, the game bits, and the mechanics.

#### Components Required

- Materials to create prototype

#### Deliverable

- Board-game prototype or
- Card-game prototype or
- Tile-based–game prototype or
- One-page write-up of detailing a potential game design

#### Suggested Process

1. **Determine a theme and a goal.**
   Where are the players going, and why are they going there? Choose a theme that involves some interaction between the participants, to make things interesting.
2. **Identify mechanics.**

Start simple. Visualize a track that goes from beginning to end that's broken up into a bunch of different sections. It may be 100 spaces or tiles or cards that ultimately build the track on which your players are going to "race." Now think of the mechanic that will get your players moving on that track. The simplest one is rolling a die. Next consider things you could do to make play more interesting. For instance, you could have an action that speeds you up or slows your opponent down. Does the narrative suggest any obvious mechanics? For example, if your game is about a relay foot race, you'll need a way to pass the baton (perhaps suggesting a tradeoff where maintaining a higher running speed gives a higher chance of accidentally dropping the baton). To add some player interaction in a foot race, perhaps you'd change the theme so that the racers are robots with lasers that can shoot at one another, which suggests mechanics for shooting and dodging.

3. **Identify the conflict between players.**

   How can you screw up someone else's progress or accelerate yours? What's the tradeoff?

4. **Playtest.**

   Every time you add a mechanic to the game, test it. Does it make the game more fun or less fun? Does it support the core of the game? Does it work the way you originally thought it would?

5. **Create deliverable.**

### Variants

Try going through the process again and design a different game. This time, start with the mechanics (step 2 above) and then figure out a fitting theme (step 1 above). Notice that both ways can let you design a perfectly good game, but the thought process involved is quite different.

### CHALLENGE 2—IT'S MINE!

For this challenge, you'll be exploring the dynamic of territorial acquisition. If you haven't noticed already, this dynamic is present in the great majority of board games made today.

As in the previous example, this game should allow two to four players. The game must obviously have some kind of territory which will be acquired. You may select from one of two win conditions:

- The first player to get all the territory wins.
- The player with the most territory after X turns wins.

As the game's designer, it's up to you to figure out the theme, the necessary game bits and the mechanics.

### Components Required

▪ Materials to create prototype

### Deliverable

▪ Board-game prototype or
▪ Card-game prototype or
▪ Tile-based–game prototype

### Suggested Process

1. **Determine a theme, if you desire.**
   Precisely what are the players trying to conquer here? A swamp? A piece of turf? Maybe it's a wild band of monkeys who are determined to take over the zoo at night. Remember that you don't need a theme, but having one often helps game designers new to the process identify potential mechanics.
2. **Continue using the same process as in Challenge 1.**

## CHALLENGE 3—WHEN I FIND YOU...

We've talked about two common gameplay dynamics in this chapter: territorial acquisition and race to the end. These are just two of a whole collection of dynamics, however. Other common dynamics include building, exploration, and stomping everything in sight.

For this exercise, you will focus on the exploration dynamic. First, consider how it is used in MMOs, adventure games, and RPGs. In some adventure games, the "explore every location" dynamic is the whole of play. Consider how it is used in board games such as *Clue*.

You are tasked with creating a game that two to four individuals can play. Since the game involves exploration, it needs some kind of space to explore, even if that space isn't a physical one. You may use this dynamic in conjunction with another.

It will be up to you to determine the theme, mechanics, components, and additional dynamics, if any, for this exercise.

### Components Required

▪ Materials to create prototype

### Deliverable

▪ Board-game prototype or
▪ Card-game prototype or
▪ Tile-based–game prototype

**Suggested Process**

1. **Determine a theme, if you desire.**
   What are the players exploring? Anything from a parking garage to a treetop village to downtown Chicago to a fantastical world in the sky are up for grabs. Think of things your player might do while exploring, too. These dynamics will give rise to the mechanics you need.
2. **Continue using the same process as in Challenge 1.**

## CHALLENGE 4—PICK IT UP

Walking over an object to pick it up is a phenomenally common mechanic in video games, and leads to the collection dynamic. There are, of course, other ways to collect something. Consider how collecting comes into play in the *Mario* games, *Poker*, or *Bejeweled*.

For this exercise, you're going to take this mechanic and make a game out of it. This is slightly more challenging than starting with a dynamic, which, by itself, suggests both a beginning and an ending.

You must create a game for two to four players in which players "walk" over objects and pick them up. What players need to collect (three of a kind, similar color, and so on) and how much they need to collect is up to you. Mechanics that modify the primary mechanic are acceptable. For instance, you could have players pick something up when they land on it, or have a wheelbarrow that they first must acquire in order to pick up the objects.

You must choose the theme, components, and tokens, if applicable. You may also add additional mechanics, as needed. In particular, play attention to the narrative. It will help as you brainstorm. Think of this as a gardening game, then a gangster game, and then a car-racing game. Each theme brings different possibilities into play.

**Components Required**

■   Materials to create prototype

**Deliverable**

■   Board-game prototype or
■   Card-game prototype or
■   Tile-based–game prototype

**Suggested Process**

1. **The object of the game is…**

   If you can't think of how to begin, one way is to start by naming the goal or objective that ends the game. This will suggest additional mechanics and dynamics for you.

   For example, if the object of the game is to have the most points when time runs out, it immediately gives you two more questions: how do players receive points, and how is time handled in the game?

   The object may be connected to a theme, so you may find it easier to develop a narrative and objective concurrently, or start with the theme first and then find the objective. For example, if you are gangsters returning from a bank heist, maybe the object is to keep as much money for yourself and get out before the cops show up.

2. **Identify mechanics and dynamics.**

   From the theme and goal, you probably already have all kinds of ideas for mechanics and dynamics in the game to support the core pick-up action. If nothing occurs to you, come up with a new theme and goal and try again.

3. **Identify the conflict between players.**

4. **Playtest.**

5. **Create deliverable.**

**Variants:**

Think of another common mechanic in video games, such as shooting targets, avoiding collision with enemies, or leveling up a character. Repeat this challenge using this mechanic instead of picking up.

## Iron Designer Challenge 5—War Without Frontiers

In games featuring the territorial acquisition dynamic, and especially in war-themed games, territories are rarely acquired through a comical foot race. They're usually acquired through the death, regardless of how abstracted, of another player's bits. As a result of that death, the player gets the other player's territory. Whoever has the territory wins the war. Another common dynamic, "destroy the opposing side," is used for games that don't have territory.

For this exercise, however, you'll be pushing yourself beyond those traditional borders. Simulate and resolve a Civil War battle *without* using territorial acquisition or destruction of all units on the enemy side as the primary gameplay dynamic.

Split into teams of two to four players. Each team should do its best to come up with a game that fits the above constraints. For a greater challenge, have each team choose an additional mechanic or dynamic that the other team is not allowed to use.

### Components Required

- Materials to create prototype

### Deliverable

- Board-game prototype or
- Card-game prototype or
- Tile-based–game prototype

### Suggested Process

1. **Determine a theme.**
   Which battle does your game simulate?
2. **Identify mechanics.**
   Without territorial acquisition, does it make sense to even have territory? It might, or it might not. Consider how a player can win a battle other than claiming territory. What is the goal, if not territory? What kinds of mechanics can players perform to achieve that goal?
3. **Identify the conflict between players.**
4. **Playtest.**
   Every time you add a mechanic to the game, test it.
5. **Create deliverable.**

### Variants

Instead of the Civil War, choose a different conflict. World Wars I and II are obvious choices. You could also use other conflicts like corporate acquisition, feuding neighbors, or competing chain stores.

## RESOURCES

*I Have No Words, and I Must Design*, Greg Costikyan, www.costik.com/nowords.html

*Formal Abstract Design Tools*, Doug Church, http://www.gamasutra.com/features/19990716/design_tools_01.htm

# 3 | Puzzle Design

Exactly what is a puzzle?

The word is often overused, particularly in games. The so-called "puzzle game" genre, as exemplified by *Tetris* and *Bejeweled*, does not involve much in the way of puzzle solving, particularly when compared to games with an actual and game-ending solution like a crossword puzzle (see Figure 3.1) or Sudoku puzzle. Meanwhile, challenges referred to as "puzzles" seem to find their way into digital games as varied as the *Zork*, *Zelda*, *MYST*, *Final Fantasy*, and *Monkey Island* series. Consider the common video-game pattern in this "puzzle": "find object X and put it in location Y."

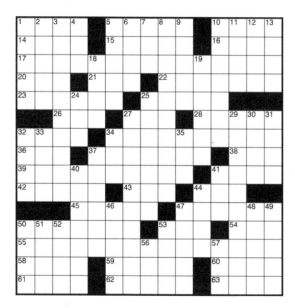

**FIGURE 3.1**
Crossword puzzle template.[1]

Also common are the puzzles referred to as "mini-games." These games offer brief interludes or challenges to be solved within the context of the larger game. Many video games use mini-games to open locks that allow the player to access the next section of the level.

Dictionary.com provides no fewer than 12 different definitions for the word "puzzle," only one of which seems relevant to games: "1.a toy, problem, or other contrivance designed to amuse by presenting difficulties to be solved by ingenuity or patient effort."[2]

For the purposes of this book and mirroring the use of the word in the video-game industry, a *puzzle* is very broadly defined as a noncombat event or series of events that requires the player to complete a task or an action or some series of tasks or actions in order to progress play. Completing these puzzles may be optional or required.

Unfortunately, as far as a player is concerned, there is sometimes no difference between a puzzle and a stop sign. In this chapter, we'll explore how and when to design puzzles and incorporate them as part of a larger game.

## Basic Puzzle Characteristics

Designing a new *kind* of puzzle is similar to designing a game. There's the "state" of the puzzle (similar to a game state), mechanics for changing the state, and a goal state that is the victory condition. Once the mechanics are decided, the designer tweaks them to come up with different dynamics. There is also usually a theme. In the game *BioShock*, for instance, there is a "hacking" mini-game that the player can solve to unlock doors and take control of electronic objects. The theme here is computer hacking, and the mechanics involve rotating pipes to form a path between the input and output of a board. A screenshot and in-depth description of the inner workings of the hacking mini-game can be found at http://guides.gamepressure.com/bioshock/guide.asp?ID=3348.

When designing the rules for a puzzle or mini-game, the following traits are necessary:

- **Affordances:** It should be easy to figure out the rules and controls.
- **Identifiable patterns:** Patterns within the puzzle should be clear so that players are able to identify a series of possibilities required for the game to be solved. Colors and shapes are commonly used, as are other forms of pre-existing knowledge like the spelling of words or the function of common objects.
- **Ease of use:** Good user interface (UI).
- **Reward player skill:** If a player is encountering the puzzle many times, the player should be able to improve his or her skill.

When designing the rules for a puzzle or mini-game that fits in a larger game, the following additional traits generally cause the puzzle to be more interesting to the players:

■ **Immersion:** Smooth transition between the main game and mini-game (this mostly falls to the artists making sure that the mini-game interface is done in the same visual style as the rest of the game, but the designer must consider the fit with the story and world).

■ **Meaningful consequences in the game, outside of the mini-game:** Not just "you unlock a door" but "you get cool items."

## WHAT MAKES PUZZLES FUN?

If the game designer's goal is to make a game fun, then the inclusion of puzzles in a game should only be done to make the game *more* fun—that is, to support the core of the game. In some games, puzzles are not appropriate at all. In other games, the designer is limited to certain kinds of puzzles. For example, most kinds of puzzles (especially logic puzzles and riddles) would likely feel out of place in a fast-paced action shooting game. Even in a "puzzle game," the designer is limited primarily to spatial puzzles. Pausing a game of *Tetris* to require the player to answer a riddle or explore a map to find an item would take away from the core of the game.

In general, puzzles are a direct obstacle to players, preventing them from reaching a goal until they solve the puzzle. The fun in a puzzle generally comes from the thrill of victory, the sense of achievement of solving a difficult puzzle, and the gradual sense of mastery that precedes those moments. At best, a good puzzle makes players feel great about themselves for what they can accomplish.

Done poorly, puzzles can reduce or eliminate the fun in the rest of the game just like a traffic jam can ruin a decent drive. A puzzle that players can't solve prevents them from experiencing the game further and causes them even greater frustration, and a puzzle that players see as arbitrary or unfair causes them to hate the game (and its designer).

## PUZZLE TYPES

There are many different puzzles. Luckily, they can be classified into general categories, where each category of puzzles shares certain design practices.

### RIDDLES

"My tines be long / My tines be short / My tines end ere my first report. / What am I?" (Riddle from *Beyond Zork*)

Riddles are questions that have one right answer, but that answer is not obvious. Typically, a riddle involves a play on words that requires the player to interpret it in a nonstandard way in order to solve it.

Riddles are far less common in games today than they were 20 years ago. This is partly for practical reasons. A riddle takes a fair amount of time and effort to create, yet is only encountered by a player once. Riddles also have no replay value, as a player who solves it the first time can recall the solution on future play-throughs. This property of riddles makes them costly compared to other kinds of content.

Riddles also aren't particularly fun to *try* to solve for the majority of players. Once the solution is known, there's a sense of reward. However, players either immediately know the answer to the riddle or they don't, and if they don't, then they're stuck for good or are off on an Internet search mission (unless the solution eventually occurs to them on their own). Not exactly the stuff of fun gameplay.

That said, there are a few tricks to making riddles less frustrating if a designer insists on including them:

- **Make the riddles purely optional.** In the classic RPG *Betrayal at Krondor*, riddles were used as locks on treasure chests. Opening a chest would give the player useful but nonessential items.
- **Offer clues.** *Betrayal at Krondor* did not simply ask the player to type in the answer to a riddle. Instead, the player was shown exactly how many letters were in the answer, and each letter only had a few choices. A determined player could write down each possibility and search for valid words, turning a riddle into a *Boggle*-like word search instead. Players could also find hints to some riddles by talking to NPCs in the game.
- **Allow alternate solutions.** Perhaps the player could solve a riddle *or* complete a different challenge. In *Dungeons & Dragons*, a Sphinx will allow the heroes to pass if they answer a riddle, but they can also attack the Sphinx and defeat it in combat.

To create a riddle, designers usually start with the answer and create the puzzle afterward. So, starting with an answer of "car," a valid riddle could be, "It sits on four and those on two sit within."

For the curious, the answer to the riddle posed at the beginning of this section is "lightning."

## LATERAL THINKING

Like riddles, lateral-thinking puzzles are trick questions that have a single correct answer. These puzzles are constructed in such a way that players make assumptions that are not true, and solving the puzzle requires the player to question his or her assumptions. Here is a classic example:

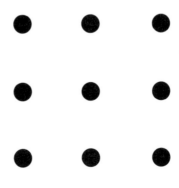

Place a pencil on this sheet of paper. Without removing the pencil from the page, draw four straight lines in such a way that all nine dots are connected. (If you'd like to try solving it, do not read further until you're done.)

By approaching this puzzle the obvious way, it takes at least five lines to connect all the dots. Most people, however, work on the unstated assumption that the lines we draw must remain within the square formed by the dots. By removing this assumption and allowing ourselves to draw lines that extend farther, the puzzle can be solved:

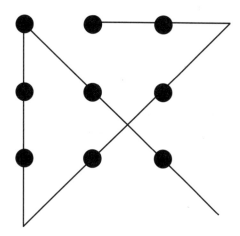

The analysis from riddles applies here as well. Lateral-thinking puzzles are expensive to create, they are only experienced once, and they can be frustrating if they block a player's path and the player can't think of the solution. Like other forms of puzzles, make these optional, offer alternate ways to solve them, and give players additional clues to point them in the right direction if they are taking a long time to solve them.

## Spatial Reasoning

Spatial puzzles involve the manipulation of objects, either in the mind or on the playing surface (see Figure 3.2). *Tetris* is essentially a continuous, fast-moving spatial puzzle. The *Adventures of Lolo* series and *Sokoban* are examples of a series of spatial puzzles made into a complete game. Other games (notably RPGs and adventure games) often use spatial puzzles as smaller quests in a larger game. Consider the myriad sliding crate puzzles in console RPGs and action games.

**FIGURE 3.2**
*Shift* prototype. *Shift* used squares with different connecting lines.
Players could turn the squares and shift entire rows depending on
their orientation.
*Shift prototype by William Miller, Raymond Champagne,
Clemmie Murdock, John Yoshikawa, and Spivey Lipsey.
Reprinted with permission.*

Spatial reasoning is also often used in boss battles where the players must use the level or the structure of the creature itself to succeed in battle. *Shadow of the Colossus* mastered this in each of its battles, effectively turning the creatures into their own playable levels.

## PATTERN RECOGNITION

Pattern-recognition puzzles require the player to look for and identify a pattern when presented with information. Code breaking is the height of this form of puzzle solving, of course. In electronic games, patterns can come at the player faster and faster, making recognition more difficult, or have mild differences in them, such as a missing component every fifth time the pattern is presented. In sports, people regularly study the patterns of competing teams in order to establish both a superior offense and defense.

Boss battles often involve players recognizing the pattern in the boss and identifying the weak point at which the boss is vulnerable to attack.

## LOGIC

"You have four orbs, colored black, blue, red and yellow. You must place them on four pedestals in the correct order. Black is on the left. Red is next to blue. Yellow is to the right of red."

Logic puzzles require the player to take a set of given information and derive additional information to find the solution. These puzzles are most frequently seen in puzzle magazines and adventure games, but they can also be used as challenges in other types of games.

As with riddles and lateral thinking puzzles, there is a single solution that the player must solve to progress, so logic puzzles should be used with caution. On the other hand, logic puzzles can be forgiving. In the case of the preceding example, if there is only a minor penalty or no penalty for guessing wrong, players could try all combinations of orbs until they get it right. The game could also be designed to give hints, showing player how close they are to the correct solution. In either case, the player should either get a penalty for a wrong guess or a bonus for getting the answer right away; otherwise, the puzzle seems like an arbitrary, pointless barrier to the rest of the game that just wastes the player's time.

## EXPLORATION

Mazes, dungeons, world maps… exploring the environment is found in a wide variety of games. Examples of exploration activities might be locating a specific person in a large town, finding a path through a maze-like series of corridors, or finding all of the treasure chests on the current level. In FPS games, exploration and knowledge of a level is second only to player skill when it comes to survival. Adventure games like *The Legend of Zelda* are well known for exploration-based puzzles, as are RPGs. *Katamari Damacy* elevated level design by forcing players to consider levels in a new way—as subsets of even greater levels that would be revisited again and again at different sizes. In 2D and 3D platformers, exploration of a level is often *the* puzzle. How do you get from A to B to Z to finish the level? In this case, you're not fighting against the enemy so much as you are trying to complete the level.

For many players, exploration *is* fun in and of itself. The thought of going down into a dungeon and mapping its corridors is the digital equivalent of spelunking (caving). In the early days of video games, in fact, the *Wizardry* series even shipped with graph paper and later included an auto-map as a feature—after the player found the automap kit in the game! Nowadays, automaps are commonplace and many identify "stuck points" that require players to find some kind of item, solve a puzzle, or complete a specific quest to pass.

While exploration is a great reward for many and, in fact, an aesthetic many games elevate to an art form, it can also become an obstacle when players encounter an area they cannot enter or cross (perhaps an open pit or a locked door). When players become stuck in levels and have no alternate way forward, the effect is similar to that of a bad riddle or a puzzle. It functions as a stop sign and frustrates the player.

## ITEM USE

Some games, notably graphic adventure games like *Myst* and action RPGs, use puzzles that involve the use of objects. The player must figure out which item(s) to use, in what order, to solve a particular challenge. A simple example is using a lighter to light the wick on a candle, and then using the candle as a light source to see around a dark room.

Item-based puzzles are more challenging if items can be combined or used on each other, or if they are used in non-obvious ways. A particularly difficult puzzle in *Maniac Mansion* required the player to moisten some postage stamps in order to stick them on an envelope, but the game did not have a "lick stamps" command. The solution: fill an empty bottle with water and place the bottle and the stamps in a microwave.

To reduce player frustration, the designer can give clues about non-obvious item use, for example, by showing an NPC early in the game who is using the item in question.

## LEVEL DESIGN AND PUZZLE DESIGN

There is a parallel between level design and puzzle design, and it is a strong one. In level design, you're using existing mechanics (monsters, walls, weapons, switches, doors, etc.) and putting them together to create unique and interesting play experiences. Mechanically, there's no difference between shooting an alien in a long narrow corridor and shooting an alien in a small enclosed room. However, the dynamics are totally different. It's the level designer's job to use the different building blocks of a level to change the dynamics.

Similarly, in puzzle design, the designer uses existing mechanics, like the rules of sliding crate puzzles, for instance, and attempts to put them together in new ways. In this case, it's the placement of crates. In crossword puzzles, it's the placement of words. In Sudoku, it's the placement of numbers.

## ALL FOR ONE AND ONE FOR ALL

Puzzles are one of the most difficult things to do well when designing a game. What's too hard for one player might be too easy for another. How do you find something that's appealing to all?

In order to be meaningful to the player, puzzles must be challenging enough to get the player to work hard and find the solution, without being so frustrating that the player turns away in disgust or to the Internet for a spoiler. It is a careful balancing act to begin with, made even more difficult by the fact that different players have different levels of puzzle-solving ability and different tolerances for challenge in puzzles. To make things even harder for a puzzle designer, it's extremely difficult to gauge the difficulty of your own puzzles, since you already know the solution. Your own puzzles are usually much harder than they initially seem to you. The only way to get a true picture of a puzzle's difficulty level is to watch testers try to solve it.

Many game puzzles become "stuck points," where the player cannot proceed without solving the puzzle (and if they cannot solve it, they are stuck). When stuck, players have five choices: try again, buy a strategy guide, contact a friend, go online for a FAQ, or give up. None of these scream "fun."

At the other extreme, puzzles can be so easy that they present no challenge to a player at all. When a player immediately sees a solution and has to spend five minutes fiddling with the interface to implement it, it feels like busywork.

Once it's determined that a puzzle is too easy or too difficult to solve, there are a few things the designer can do to balance things accordingly:

- **Add or remove additional clues.** As mentioned earlier, giving the player successive hints makes puzzles easier to solve.
- **Move the clues around.** If the clues are located right next to the puzzle that they help to solve, players can see the connection easily. If they are found halfway across the map, the player may not immediately make the connection, which increases the difficulty.
- **Allow multiple solutions.** This is especially useful if you notice many of your testers trying a particular invalid solution. You can either change the puzzle to make that solution correct, or provide additional clues to make it clear that the invalid solution will not work.
- **Offer dynamic, play-sensitive help.** Games like the *Ratchet & Clank* series and *Portal* offer the player additional help after he has failed at a task the first time. This serves to get the player going without robbing him of his initial shot at the puzzle (and subsequent reward).
- **Make use of dynamic difficulty adjustment (DDA).** With DDA, the game makes itself easier or harder based on how the player is doing in order to preserve a proper level of challenge. This was practiced in tabletop RPGs for years; few are the dungeon masters or game masters who haven't fudged a few die rolls to keep a character alive, or made a monster easier or harder to defeat than it was originally supposed to be. DDA first crossed over into digital games in 1985 with Dani Berry's *Heart of Africa;* the game would move key locations if the player was having trouble finding them.
- **Remove linearity.** If players are prevented from going in a particular direction for one reason or another, they should have another direction to go or other options. Players always need something to do—a goal to progress actively toward. Multiple goals in a multilinear design facilitate this.
- **Add a time limit.** A relatively simple puzzle becomes more challenging when the player is under time pressure.
- **Add or remove feedback.** Some early text-adventure and graphic-adventure games gave very little direction to the player when an incorrect solution was tried, other than "you can't do that" or "that didn't work." With no feedback, the player must continue trying with no additional information. But if players are given some indication of *why* their solution did not work, they can adjust their approach. For example, if a player is prevented from entering a dark room without a light source, the game could say "it's really dark in there, and you're scared of the dark" instead of simply saying "you can't go that way right now."
- **Test the game on a variety of players.** The most skilled players of a video game are often the ones who have tested it from the beginning. Some game designers make the mistake of using these testers as their only gauge of difficulty, and as a result their games end up a bit too challenging for the average Joe or Jane. Nothing reveals potential stuck points like a fresh battery of testers introduced to the game on a regular basis.

There is also a method that a designer should *not* use to balance difficult puzzles: Do not put the solution in the game's official strategy guide and require players to purchase it.

## JEB HAVENS ON PUZZLE DESIGN

*Jeb Havens is a game designer with Maxis and has worked on multiple digital and non-digital games including* Spore *and* Mother Sheep.

One of the most important elements of what makes a puzzle fun is the "aha moments." These are the moments when something locks into place, adding a layer of sense and understanding to something that was previously chaotic or meaningless. The human mind is designed to find order and apply meaning and structure to the huge amount of sensory data it constantly takes in. Without this ability and instinct to classify, compartmentalize, and chunk, we would be overwhelmed. So, when confronted with the disorder of a puzzle, the human mind naturally desires to figure it out so that it can be processed more easily. For example, if I told you that you had to memorize the sequence—ANEBARPRAYUNULUGEPCTOVEC—you might have a bit of trouble.

Try it. Close your eyes and try reciting it. No really, try it and then keep reading. How many did you get? Perhaps you saw the words "bar" and "pray" within the sequence, which you used to help you remember? See? Your brain is already trying to break it down into more meaningful parts. Now, what if I told you that the sequence is nothing more than the second and third letters of the 12 months of the year (jAN, fEB, mAR, aPR, etc.)? Doesn't seem like so much information to remember anymore, does it? Close your eyes and try reciting it again. Solving a puzzle almost always means bringing elements together in a way that gives all the parts a more cohesive meaning. It's like being able to zoom out from a scene, and now things make more sense. And when things make more sense, they are easier for the brain to handle. And if something makes the brain's job easier, chances are that evolution made it feel good to do. Hence the nice warm feeling you get when you get that "aha moment," when things click into place. When the world around you becomes more manageable and understandable, you become more powerful, since it's easier to control things you understand at a more fundamental level. So, I guess puzzles are just nerdy power trips.

So, the brain loves to solve things, bring things together that were previously unrelated. However, seeing the connection between unrelated things is hard. That's why they're unrelated. So, as a puzzle designer, your job is to gently guide your solver toward the relationships. One way to do this is by understanding and manipulating the player's previous experiences in the game. If your puzzle involves finding a novel way to use an existing item, the player should have already used the item several times to get a solid understanding of what it does in various other contexts, and the player should be allowed and encouraged to freely experiment with the item. It is important that general object classes in the game behave consistently, so that the player can start to build up a lexicon of object classes and interactions (all enemies of this type run away from loud noises, all crates disintegrate when smashed, all control panels malfunction when they get wet, etc.).

Continued

Another important way to guide a puzzle solver toward the solution is by having the puzzle unfold gradually, with a series of "aha moments." At each step, the solver is encouraged that they are on the right track or have grasped a key component of the full solution. This can be as simple as a dinging sound, or as complex as a change in the animation state for an NPC, but it must be something that is unmistakably a re-action to the player's actions, and not some random background event. As long as something changes in a way that signals that the steps the player just took are head-ing in the right direction, even the most difficult puzzles and leaps in logic are solv-able. Along with feeling good at each small step along the way, the player gets that extra jolt of triumph at the end, looking back upon their full solution, feeling owner-ship of it, even if they were somewhat handheld along the way.

## CHALLENGES

In spite of their difficulty—and creating a good puzzle is difficult—designers are continually called upon to create them. Fortunately, creating a good puzzle is sometimes a puzzle in itself.

### CHALLENGE 1—IT'S DA BOMB!

As with games, sometimes when designing a puzzle you're given a theme and you must cre-ate the mechanics to fit the theme.

In this case, you're designing a game based on the old TV show *MacGyver*, and part of the storyline in the game involves the main character defusing a bomb. Rather than making it a non-interactive cutscene, you've chosen to make it into a timed puzzle, where taking too long to solve the puzzle or solving it incorrectly results in the game being over. If *that* doesn't provide some tension to the player, *nothing* will.

Consider the different kinds of puzzles mentioned in this chapter and choose at least three puzzle types that would be appropriate to the theme. Then choose your favorite type and create a working prototype of the puzzle.

#### Components Required

- Materials to create prototype
- Kitchen timer to count down the time remaining for the player

#### Deliverable

- Three paragraphs and accompanying sketch, one per puzzle type, describing the basic mechanics of the puzzle
- Playable prototype of one of the three puzzles

**Suggested Process**

1. **Brainstorm.**
   Think about the different ways a character could defuse a bomb. You could have the bomb attached to a sliding-tile puzzle, but this would seem arbitrary. Think of puzzle mechanics that fit the given theme. What kinds of puzzles (riddles, lateral thinking, spatial, logic, exploration, item use) lend themselves well to your mechanics? Keep thinking until you identify at least three different core mechanics for a bomb-defusal puzzle.

2. **Choose one puzzle.**
   Take one of your core mechanics and flesh it out. Create the rest of the mechanics. Identify the general goal. Then choose the details for this specific puzzle: the beginning state, the goal state, and the correct and incorrect solutions.

3. **Playtest and iterate.**
   Try your puzzle on some friends. Did they solve it correctly? How long did it take them? Did they approach the puzzle in the way that you expected them to? Go back and modify your puzzle if some aspects of it weren't clear, or if it was too hard (or too easy, although it's rare for a puzzle designer to actually create something too easy).

4. **Create deliverable.**

5. **Add difficulty levels (optional).**
   After you show off your prototype, the publisher of your game insists that there be multiple difficulty levels, and that the difficulty of the puzzle should be affected. Find at least three ways to modify the difficulty of your bomb puzzle—other than changing the amount of time given to the player. Be specific.

### CHALLENGE 2—MORE THAN A MAZE

Consider the maze to be a type of exploration puzzle. A basic maze with arbitrary paths is not particularly compelling to a player who has seen many mazes before. Many older RPGs required players to make a map of a series of mazes as they played. Today, most gamers would consider this "busywork" and prefer that the game provided an automatic mapping function. For this challenge, though, let's give the player a reason to make his own map.

Brainstorm as many mechanics as you can think of that can be added to a simple maze, which makes the process of mapping a puzzle in and of itself. Come up with at least three ideas.

One example (which you're not allowed to use as one of your own ideas for this challenge) is the maze from the classic Atari 2600 game *Adventure*. In this game, the maze "wraps around" so that moving to the left may cause you to reappear on the right side of the maze. You may pass near the same point several times when you're actually in a completely different section of the maze. In this way, mapping and navigating are made more difficult, and become quite a puzzle, even though the maze itself is not very large.

**Components Required**

■ Graph paper

**Deliverable**

■ A short sentence up to a paragraph describing each mechanic that you can think of
■ A sample hand-drawn maze illustrating the mechanics described

**Suggested Process**

1. **Brainstorm.**
   It's tempting to start by thinking of any games you played that had nonstandard mapping or navigation mechanics. However, this runs the risk of constraining your creativity, because you may have trouble coming up with your own ideas if you're constantly thinking of other people's. Try to be original first, and then think of existing games only when your own ideas are spent.
2. **Create deliverable.**

### CHALLENGE 3—WHAT'S THE PASSWORD?

A person walks into his home and punches four or five numbers handily into the security pad. At work, at home, and at bank machines, these codes are a part of our lives. They are frequently used in video games, too, as a means to let one group in and keep another out.

For this challenge, your goal is to design three different password puzzles. There are three parts to this:

■ Determine the code (it need not be numbers)
■ Determine how the player enters the code
■ Determine how the player gets the code in the first place

There's an easy way out here: make the code four numbers, and kill four creatures, each with one part of the number. Then the player needs only to figure out the order. While this route would work, it's almost too obvious. Consider things that players don't expect, like physical interaction within a level to manipulate some object into entering a code or finding particular items that match a necessary pattern. Research the many unique "keys" that were used to keep people out (and to keep people in) in the medieval period.

**Components Required**

■ None

**Deliverable**

■ Mockups of the individual puzzles
■ Description of how the puzzle works
■ Level design on graph paper, if applicable

**Suggested Process**

1. **Research.**
   In modern day and in the past, what methods were used to keep valuable objects safe from those who were not supposed to have access to them? What methods were used to *allow* access? Your puzzles should be plausible. Sure, you could say that a high-security area has a passcode that's written down on the walls of several offices, in the form of a math problem that could be solved by anyone with a rudimentary knowledge of algebra, but would anyone in the real world actually *do* that? If not, the puzzle will seem contrived and arbitrary.
2. **Brainstorm.**
   Of the password methods you've seen, which ones seem the most game-like? Think of ways to adapt them to a puzzle found in a larger game.
3. **Work out the details.**
   Try creating a few puzzles from your own ideas. You don't have to design a complete game, just a set of rules for puzzles.
4. **Create deliverable.**

### CHALLENGE 4—A SHOCKING PUZZLE

Electricity makes for great puzzles in video games, since passing its current from one side to another can logically result in some action being performed, provided it is, in fact, passed correctly. For this challenge, your goal is to create a paper prototype of a puzzle in which electrical current is passed from one side of the screen to the other. You may use any interface you like, provided that it requires spatial reasoning on the part of the player.

**Components Required**

■ Materials to create prototype

**Deliverable**

■ Prototype, along with a written set of rules indicating the beginning state, objective, and actions that the player may take

**Suggested Process**

1. **Brainstorm.**
   How do you get electrical current from one side of the screen to the other? What does a "success" look like? Are there any ways to "fail" or does the player simply keep trying until he succeeds?
2. **Create the mechanics.**
   Define the actions that a player can take. What effects do these actions have on the state of the puzzle?
3. **Create a sample puzzle.**
   Using your rules, make a puzzle. Be sure to write down the solution for yourself. If you have time, make two puzzles: one very simple puzzle meant to teach the basic mechanics to a new player, and a more advanced puzzle that shows the depth of your mechanics.
4. **Playtest and iterate.**
   Try your puzzle on some friends, and adjust the rules and difficulty level as needed.
5. **Create deliverable.**

## IRON DESIGNER CHALLENGE 5—PLAY *NEW ELEUSIS* (LIVE)

*New Eleusis* is a game played with two standard decks of cards, for five to eight players. It was originally designed by Robert Abbott and published in *Scientific American* in 1977. Cards are played in order. One player (taking the role of God) creates a rule that determines which cards are legal to play, under what conditions (for example, "always play a red card after a black card"). The other players (playing the role of scientists) attempt to play their cards, and through logical induction try to determine the hidden rule that God created. The role of God rotates so that each player gets to create a rule. At the end of each round, all players receive a score; highest score at the end of the game wins.

The scoring system rewards God for coming up with a rule that is challenging but not impossible to deduce. In particular, God's score is maximized if at least one player at the table figures out the rule (after taking awhile), and at least one player completely and utterly fails to grasp the rule. The designer makes the following suggestions regarding what rules tend to produce good scores:

- Your rule is almost always harder to figure out than you think it is.
- If you give any hints, don't make them misleading. The rule is hard enough to figure out without you actively leading the other players astray.
- At any given time, about half of the cards in the deck should be legal plays. If players are almost always right (or wrong), they will not get enough information to induce your rule.

While this game was originally intended to teach the scientific method, it also happens to teach puzzle design. When a player makes a rule, he is essentially creating a logic puzzle that other players must figure out through experimentation. The scoring system rewards players who create rules of the appropriate difficulty, and it also rewards players for solving each other's puzzles.

Play the game with your fellow puzzle designers. After the game, discuss each rule and what made it too easy, too difficult, or just right.

### Components Required

- Two standard decks of playing cards
- Rules for *New Eleusis*, available online from many locations (as of this printing, the rules can be found at: http://matuszek.org/eleusis0.html but they can also be found elsewhere through a Google search)

### Deliverable

- None

### Suggested Process

1. **Play the game.**
   Play with your fellow puzzle designers. After the game, in a group discuss each rule and what made it too easy, too difficult, or just right.
2. **Write down the lessons learned (optional).**
   Did you learn anything about what makes a good puzzle from playing this game? Write it down and share with any colleagues who did not play with you.

## Non-Digital Shorts

The following list contains ideas for board games, card games, or other games that are free of a digital component. They are ideal for a non-digital design exercise.

1. Create a tile-based game that simulates the process of exploring a dungeon. It should include various items that players require to progress further.
2. Create a tile-based game where the tiles can only fit together correctly in one particular way to solve the game. Create the dynamics that would allow this to happen as a solo- or multiplayer game.
3. Using graph paper and a simple six-sided die, create a map that players must travel through that includes at least two different types of puzzles.
4. Create the rules for a game that uses the following components: a 100-piece jigsaw puzzle (initially unassembled) for use as a game board that's built during play, and uses pawns to represent the players. You may use additional components if desired.

5. Create a game played on the surface of a Rubik's Cube. Assume that there are magnetic pawns, representing the players, which can stick to the sides and bottom of the cube.

6. Take any kind of puzzle that is normally solved by one player (such as a crossword or Sudoku) and modify the rules so that it becomes a two-player competitive game.

7. Take a multiplayer game where the goal is to solve a puzzle (such as the board game *Clue*, the puzzle game *Mastermind*, or the card game *Sleuth*) and modify the rules so that it is a single-player puzzle. Make sure that the player has enough information to solve the puzzle, and that it is playable without a computer or another human providing clues or information.

8. Using pattern recognition, create a game that teaches children how to spell. Note that a correctly spelled word is, in fact, pattern recognition.

9. Create a trivia-based game in which trivia puzzles must be solved by a group in order to progress within the game.

10. Look at the puzzles page of any major newspaper. Select a puzzle and create a mod of it that changes both the theme and introduces or changes at least one mechanic.

## RESOURCES

"Designing the Puzzle," Bob Bates, http://www.scottkim.com/thinkinggames/GDC00/bates.html.

[1] This image was created by Wikipedian User:Michael J. and distributed under the terms of the GNU Free Documentation License, Version 1.2 or any later version published by the Free Software Foundation.

[2] puzzle. Dictionary.com. *Dictionary.com Unabridged* (v 1.1). Random House, Inc. http://dictionary.reference.com/browse/puzzle (accessed: December 30, 2007).

# 4 Converting Digital to Physical

Having just entered their first game-design class, many students are surprised to be tasked with an assignment that they perceive to be working *backward*: making a board-game version of a video game. Though they may not say it, professors can still see the question in their eyes: "Why on earth would I want to do that?"

There are plenty of good reasons. However, the most important reason of all may be this: If you can't design a non-digital game from a digital game, if you can't work "backward," you don't truly understand the nuances of the pure design underneath the art and realized through programming.

As you may have learned, non-digital design is very exposed and tends to reveal bad gameplay mechanics rather quickly. People will have more faith in you, and you'll have more faith in yourself as a game designer, if you can succeed in a non-digital medium, too.

## PRACTICAL APPLICATION

"But this never happens in the industry."

Sure it does. Everything from *Halo* to *Sid Meier's Civilization* to *World of Warcraft* has been turned into non-digital games, and the transmedia popularity of franchises like *The Lord of the Rings*, *Dungeons & Dragons*, and *Pokémon* provide game designers with a virtual arena of opportunity.

Just as great action movies are sometimes made into video games, so too are great video games made into non-digital games. They're also made into movies, but usually that hasn't turned out so well.

Non-digital versions of popular games also make for good portfolio pieces, and may even impress an interviewer if the game is based on one of his IPs.

## HOW TO START

There are multiple places to start a non-digital version of a digital game.

■ Literal conversions attempt to re-create the gameplay experience as closely as possible in a non-digital medium for which it is ideally suited. *Super Mario Kart* is an excellent example of a game that could be converted to a race to the end board game with little modification to the game structure.

- Thematic conversions take the basic theme of the digital game and apply that to a traditional style of non-digital game. For instance, one could make the original *Super Mario Bros.* into something similar to a *Dungeons & Dragons* traditional RPG. One would borrow the storyline from *Super Mario Bros.*, but not the mechanics. Instead, players might roll characters (or get preselected ones), and search for a princess hidden in a castle.
- Mechanic conversions take a particular, common mechanic in the digital game and use it as the basis for a non-digital game.

When doing a conversion, don't force it. Think of a game, and consider how it might work in a non-digital format. A good match doesn't feel forced. Sometimes, it even feels obvious.

## CHALLENGES

The challenges in this section put the skills you learned to the test—your ability to analyze a digital-game IP, determine its strengths and weaknesses, and take into consideration its target market as you create games in a variety of different forms.

Each challenge should result in a board game that takes at least 30 minutes to play and does not involve the roll and move forward mechanic.

### CHALLENGE 1—PICK A GAME, ANY GAME

For this challenge, you have been contacted by Activision/Blizzard and asked to review the current year's releases and create a board-game prototype for one of those games. They are considering simultaneous digital and non-digital releases in the future and want to get an idea of how your group would interpret a video game in board-game form.

#### Components Required

- Internet connection (for research)
- Copy of video game you plan to turn into a board game (optional)

#### Deliverable

- Polished, production-grade board game complete with all components
- Prototype board game complete with all components
- Complete set of written rules

**Suggested Process**

1. **Choose your game.**
   Make a list of the relevant games that you own, or at least have played. There are two ways to approach this. For an easier challenge, choose a game on your list that seems like it would make a particularly interesting board game. If you are an experienced designer (or just feeling a bit adventurous), choose a game that really takes advantage of the digital medium so that a direct conversion to a board game is impossible.

2. **Choose a method.**
   Literal, thematic, or mechanic? Designing a board game based on a single core mechanic is different from starting with a narrative. Is a literal conversion even possible? Most of the time it is, but it may not make for the most compelling choice

3. **Determine player expectation.**
   What will players of the video game expect when they play your board-game version of it? At minimum, they usually expect to see the same signs and symbols of the digital game, the familiar characters, and something reminiscent of the gameplay. List everything you think players will expect in your game, and then determine which of those are actually possible to present.

4. **Scavenge what you can.**
   List all of the elements you can lift immediately from your video game. This provides you with a starting point, either by giving you a narrative, a core mechanic, or an entire set of mechanics and dynamics. For instance, if your video game involves acquiring land, you can probably make the acquisition of land and the mechanics used to acquire it a central point of your board game.

5. **Fill in the blanks.**
   List everything you're missing before you have a complete game. You may need to design additional mechanics, or player goals, or a narrative, or several other things. Grow your game from your starting point in step 4, one item at a time, until you have enough of a game to play it.

6. **Create deliverables.**
   Create a prototype and a tentative set of written rules. Use scrap materials, so that changes are easy to make. (You will be making many changes after your initial prototype, guaranteed.) Play the game a few times and see if you run into any situations the rules don't mention, and make your rules more complete. Also pay attention to the experience. Is the game fun? Are players making interesting decisions? Does the game feel like a solid representation of the source material?

**Variant**

If you have several teams, you can make this an Iron Designer Challenge! Have each team choose a video game from the given company that they think will be very difficult to turn into a board game, and hand that IP to another team. Or randomly choose one video game and have *all* teams compete to see who can make the *best* board-game representation within two hours.

### CHALLENGE 2—MASSIVELY TWO-PLAYER OFFLINE CARD GAME

A popular MMO wants to release a separate stand-alone card game that reflects the thematic content of the virtual world. They are not looking for a literal interpretation, but hope that you'll be able to incorporate some degree of story into the cards and feature at least one of the locations in the game. How you do that is up to you, but they'd like to have at least 50 cards total in the game and have it be for two players.

#### Components Required

- Internet connection (for research)
- Experience playing an MMO (note that there are many free MMOs)

#### Deliverable

- 50-card playing deck based off your selected IP
- One-page rule sheet

#### Suggested Process

1. **Choose a suitable MMO.**
   This challenge will be more meaningful if you choose an MMO that doesn't already have a card game based on it, of course. Selecting an MMO you're unfamiliar with will also expand your knowledge.
2. **Focus on one aspect of the game.**
   Most MMOs have massive amounts of content, storylines, and game worlds, and there is no way you can hope to capture all of that in 50 cards. Instead, consider capturing one part of the larger game that you think will translate well to this new medium.
3. **Create a goal.**
   As with earlier challenges, it often helps to start your design by stating the goal of the game. This may come naturally from the piece of the MMO on which you've chosen to focus.
4. **Create the mechanics.**
   How do players achieve victory in your game? By capturing all the cards? By taking all the other player's hit points? What actions can they take? What effects do those actions have? Given your mechanics, consider what kinds of things must be on the cards. If your game is based on combat, the cards may need to list combat stats. If your game is based on auctions and trade between players, the cards may need to represent items and their costs. Consider all the ways that cards can be used in a game. They can be shuffled to make a common deck from which players draw. They can be held by players in a closed hand. They can be played in front of

a player (face up or face down) to signify ownership. They can be placed in a grid to form a makeshift game board. Think about how you would like to use cards in your game, and what mechanics come from that.

5. **Design the cards.**

   Once you have a general idea of how the game works, create the content on the individual cards. This is likely to be the most time-consuming part of this challenge. Start by writing on index cards with a pencil, so that you can easily make changes if certain cards seem too powerful or weak or confusing. You may find it easier to write the cards on a standard piece of paper or in a computer spreadsheet first, so that you can see all of the cards next to each other and how they compare to one another. You can then transfer them to paper manually or print them out

6. **Create deliverable.**

   Be sure to test your game to make sure that the rules are complete.

### Variant

In hearing about the game you were working on, the marketing guy adds that he would love it if the cards could somehow work into the actual game in the future. He would like you to modify the game you were planning to create, if necessary, and give him a quick write-up on how exactly you might incorporate it into the MMO.

### CHALLENGE 3—WWII: THE TABLETOP RPG

Your group has been selected to create an introductory-level pencil and paper RPG similar to *Dungeons & Dragons*, but using a historical video game as your point of reference. Your game will be used by high-school students to facilitate learning.

There are specific constraints on this project:

1. You should be able to play a full game in one hour
2. Character creation needs to be really quick, but should allow some degree of customization
3. The game should come with one "campaign" for a group of four to six players, with one "referee" (often referred to as the "game master," or "GM") who runs the play session, interprets rules, and resolves player actions. A campaign is effectively the video-game equivalent of a mission or a quest.
4. The game will need rules to handle the situations in which players may find themselves during the campaign. So, what do players do, and how can you determine their success in those tasks?

### Components Required

- A historical video game
- Familiarity with a traditional RPG system or the willingness to learn about one

### Deliverable

- Character-generation system
- Confrontation system, if necessary
- Other systems, as necessary
- Campaign
- Game master rules

### Suggested Process

1. **Choose a video game.**
   Games with a strong narrative are easier to convert than games that focus purely on fast-paced combat. Furthermore, games with strong character development (for example, leveling and character progression) have a good chance of surviving the conversion with fun intact.

2. **Choose and design the characters and setting for your campaign.**
   Who are the player characters (PCs)? What are their goals? Are they meant to co-operate with each other or work against each other? Determine which statistics characters need and what these statistics are for. For instance, strength might be used to determine a character's ability to shove open a locked door. For the sake of this challenge, it's recommended you keep it simple.

3. **Create a template for creatures or enemies, if applicable.**
   What stats will your enemies have? If a character went head to head with one of these enemies, how would you resolve the situation to determine the outcome and, if necessary, who wins in violent combat?

4. **Create a template for items, if applicable.**
   What stats will items have? Do they just do damage, protect from damage, or have specific special powers?

5. **Create the mechanics.**
   What kinds of things do you expect the PCs to do in the game world in order to ac-complish their goals? Make a list. For each item on the list, decide if there are any limitations on that action (for example, you might decide that players can only shoot their guns if they have ammunition). For actions that can fail (leaping from one rooftop to another without falling) or be contested (trying to win an arm-wrestling match), decide how these actions will be resolved to success or failure. This could involve luck (such as the rolling of dice) or character stats or some

combination of the two. Can any of the PCs do something that none of the other PCs can do? Consider adding these special abilities to the characters and defining exactly what conditions trigger their use.

6. **Write down the details of the campaign.**
   This probably includes a character sheet for each player, as well as a set of campaign notes and rules for the GM. It may include other things, depending on your specific game.

### Variant

Originally, the teachers asked you to create a game that could be played with a group of five to seven students total (including the GM), figuring that they would divide their classes into small groups that ran the game concurrently. Now they've changed their minds, and they would prefer a game that could be played with an entire class of 20 to 25 students in a single large game, with the teacher as sole GM.

Creating a system suitable for that many players is difficult. You don't want individual students to get bored while they're waiting for other players to take their turns. Can you think of any mechanics that would allow students to take their turns simultaneously?

### CHALLENGE 4—TWITCH BOARD GAMING?

If you're creating a board-game version of an online turn-based strategy game, that's usually pretty easy. But what if you're making a version of an intense real-time action game? At this point, novice designers shrug and say it can't be done. Naturally, this makes it difficult for them to go in the opposite direction—creating a board-game prototype for an action game.

It turns out that converting real-time games to turn-based is not all that difficult. Suppose that one "turn" consists of, say, half a second of real-time play (enough to move or turn a short distance or perform an action like shooting). You can make turns simultaneous (all players declaring their actions secretly, then revealing and resolving one at a time) to give the feel of uncertainty.

What if the real-time game doesn't have a board, but has instead a large map that isn't neatly divided into squares or hexes? All you have to do is divide the map yourself. For reasons that will become immediately apparent if you compare the two, most designers prefer boards where each space is a hex rather than a square.

Several well known real-time games have been converted into successful (and fun) commercial board games, including *DOOM*, *Warcraft 3: Reign of Chaos*, and *World of Warcraft*. So, it can absolutely be done.

For this challenge, choose any FPS, RTS, or MMORPG that does not already have an official board game based on it. Design a literal conversion of that game to a board game.

### Components Required

- Internet connection for research
- Materials for a board-game prototype
- A copy of the video game you decide to emulate (optional, but recommended)

**Deliverable**

- Playable board-game prototype
- Complete set of written rules

**Suggested Process**

1. **Choose your game.**
   Obviously, you should choose a game that you have played and are familiar with, if at all possible. Check boardgamegeek.com to make sure that there is no board-game version.
2. **Choose a suitable goal.**
   For an RTS, eradicating the other player is a reasonable goal in a board-game version. For an FPS, look at multiplayer modes (death match, capture-the-flag, and so on) and choose one game mode on which to base your board game. For an MMORPG, choose one aspect of the game (a single dungeon or a short series of quests, for example) as the focus of your board game.
3. **Mechanics inventory.**
   Make a list of all relevant mechanics in the video game that you choose. If you are not intimately familiar with the game, you may not *know* the mechanics. In this case, consult an official strategy guide (if you own one), play a demo, or look online for a FAQ.
4. **Mechanics conversion.**
   One at a time, convert the mechanics of the video game to your board-game representation. In some cases, the original mechanics will be extremely complicated (computers enable this, after all) and you may want to simplify things by removing or combining some stats and reducing numeric ranges. Feel free to experiment with this, as it will likely streamline your gameplay.
5. **Prototype, playtest, and iterate.**
   Make a simple game board. You can do this by simply drawing on a blank piece of paper, or you can find a hex grid online and make printouts. For pieces, you can scavenge components like pawns and dice from other games that you own, or you can cut up index cards into small squares. If you do the latter, be careful not to sneeze during a game. Play the game and modify the rules as needed. Your objective is to make the game playable and fun and get a complete set of rules.
6. **Create deliverable.**

### IRON DESIGNER CHALLENGE 5—WOULD YOU LIKE GAMES WITH THAT? (LIVE)

The success of the Xbox 360 *Burger King* games has made some other advertisers think that maybe there is something to the whole "advergame" thing. Your client has already created an advergame available online at his Web site, however, and doesn't have the money to fund another team for another digital game's creation.

For this exercise, they want you to create a board game that will be given away at all retail locations that stock their product. Because it will be given away, it needs to be packaged in a 12 × 9-inch manila envelope, and contain nothing other than cardstock paper. However, the design of the product is totally up to you. They do hope, however, that you will integrate some components of their digital game.

If competing against another team, you may choose an advergame for your opponents, and have them choose one for you.

**Components Required**

- Internet (for research)
- Several sheets of letter-size card stock (any weight)
- Manila envelope

**Deliverable**

- Board game or card game
- Final manila envelope packaging
- Written rules that describe the play of the game

**Suggested Process**

1. **Research.**
   If you're unfamiliar with the advergame you've been assigned, go and play it. Make note of what aspects of the game would translate well to a physical board or card game.
2. **Brainstorm.**
   Come up with ideas. Do you attempt a literal conversion of the original game? Are there just a few mechanics you want to translate, while inventing the rest on your own? Or perhaps you want to scrap the mechanics entirely and only preserve the theme? Come up with a set of core mechanics that fit. Keep in mind that all of your game components are cardboard. This will limit some of the things you can do, although you may find clever workarounds (like using a small deck of shuffled, numbered cards to simulate a "die roll" when you have no dice).
3. **Create the rules, prototype, and playtest.**
   Work on a set of game components and mechanics, jotting down ideas on a whiteboard or some scrap paper, until you've got a game that you think is complete and playable. Then create a prototype and take your new game out for a spin. Modify the pieces and the rules as needed.

4. **Create deliverable.**

Since your prototype *is* the deliverable, this mostly consists of placing it in the manila envelope and sealing it. Remember to write up the rules and include them as well.

## NON-DIGITAL SHORTS

The following list contains ideas for board games, card games, or other games that are free of a digital game component. They encourage you to explore very dynamic concepts in a non-digital format. They are ideal for a non-digital design exercise.

1. Create a board game that simulates the production of presents at Christmas time.
2. Create a collectible card game of 100 different cards separated into packs of five that simulates the running of a radio station. Develop some kind of system that allows you to compete for listeners and reach the coveted #1 station milestone.
3. Develop a game in any medium that incorporates something exceptionally non-traditional, like forcing you to take only one turn per day or making certain moves possible only at certain times.
4. Make a card game that simulates the making of a video game.
5. Develop a tile-based game that incorporates a real-time component. For instance, though players may take turns laying tiles down, at some point, there is an event in the game (or something similar) that forces players into a real-time mode. Games like *Slap Jack* work the same way. Players take turns flipping cards until a Jack is revealed. At that point, all players go into a real-time mode to see who hits the Jack first.
6. Create a game in any medium that is designed to incorporate sequels right from the get-go. As such, its medium must allow for expansion and incorporation of expansion components.
7. Develop a game and a set of rules to be played in a public place by up to 50 players. You may incorporate teams into your design.
8. Select any well-known card game and develop a board-game version of it.
9. Select any well-known but ultimately boring board game and create replayability and unpredictably by making it tile-based and by adding or removing mechanics as necessary.
10. Create a game in any medium that simulates the ebb and flow of people during rush hour. The goal of the game, as well as the number of players, is entirely up to you.

# Part II Chance and Skill

# 5 Elements of Chance

Games such as *Chess* and *Go* are purely strategic. All information is available to all players, and the same actions always end in exactly the same results. For the majority of games, however, this is not the case. Most games contain at least some factors that are random or not repeatable. For instance, many card games involve a random shuffle. Combat in most RPGs includes a variable damage range. A game like *Rock-Paper-Scissors* has dynamics that appear random, even without any random mechanics. This chapter explores the random aspects of games and how a designer can use them.

## THE ROLE (ROLL?) OF CHANCE IN GAMES

Why do so many games include an element of chance? In creating a game an entire family could play, for instance, a hard-core strategy game is not likely to work so well. On the other hand, games that include an element of luck are approachable and winnable by a wider audience. Ultimately, there are many reasons, but each is a conscious decision by the designer to create the desired dynamics.

## DELAYING OR PREVENTING SOLVABILITY

A game is "solvable" if the entire possibility space is known ahead of time and can be exploited such that a specific player, playing correctly, can always win (or draw). Part of the reason that *Tic-Tac-Toe* fails to remain compelling for long is that it can be easily solved. Once a player solves a game, that game loses part of what makes it a game in the first place: an uncertain outcome, a struggle toward a goal.

Solvable games are not automatically bad. *Chess* is solvable, but the possibility space is so large that it continues to entertain. For games with small enough possibility spaces to be solvable by a computer (and especially a human), however, something must be done to keep the game fresh. Adding a random element is one way to accomplish this. It prevents us from mastering the game, because making the same exact decisions may lead to different outcomes.

## MAKING PLAY "COMPETITIVE" FOR ALL PLAYERS

In a pure strategy game like *Chess*, a sufficiently strong player will always beat a weaker player. Some people are competitive enough to enjoy this aspect of games, knowing that if they beat another player that they wholly *earned* that victory. Likewise, if they lost, they know it was through their error or another player's skill, not a random roll of the die.

While this might be fine for some players and result in compelling gameplay, people can't always count on two equally matched players being available at the same time and the same place for a game. If all games were all about skill, games between a parent and a child would generally result in tear-laden defeat after tear-laden defeat, boredom, or frustration. The weaker player simply gets up and walks away determined to never play the game again (or at least not with the same person).

Random elements that occasionally allow a less experienced player to win (or at least offer an advantage) keep these players interested for longer in two ways. First, there is always the chance of victory. Second, the sting of defeat is lessened when a player can blame her own bad luck.

## INCREASING VARIETY

Games with no random elements always start exactly the same, and certain patterns (such as book openings in *Chess*) often emerge. As a result, players can have highly similar experiences from one game to another, and they can find themselves making the same kinds of strategic choices.

When a random element is introduced, players must cope with a wider variety of situations. The random setup of *Settlers of Catan* makes each game feel different. Tile-based games often allow players to build in dozens of different ways. The random battles in *Risk* or *Axis & Allies* require players to change their strategies and often play in unconventional or innovative ways when the dice do not act as one hoped they would. Adding random elements in the right ways can increase the variety of a player's experience, thus increasing the replay value of a game.

### CREATING DRAMATIC MOMENTS

When a player carefully crafts a strategy and then has to depend on the roll the dice (or what have you) to see if his plan succeeds, that moment of truth can be deliciously tense. Role-playing games (RPGs), real-time–strategy games (RTSs), and many, many board games rely on this tension for play. Will your healing spell get to your wounded partner before the monster strikes? Will the AI give you two creatures to battle or one? Will the player land on your recently developed Park Place or Boardwalk or just pass it by? Even without strategy, watching a random process play out can be extremely compelling in the right circumstances—witness the excitement at a *Roulette* or *Craps* table. The level of excitement or tension created by chance increases in direct proportion to how much one has riding on the results.

### ENHANCING DECISION MAKING

The essence of most games is the decisions that the players make. In a pure strategy game, players have complete information and know the exact outcome of every move that they make. Since all variables are known, some decisions aren't particularly exciting; if you have the opportunity to capture your opponent's queen in *Chess* for free with no drawbacks, it's not much of an interesting decision because there is a clear "right" answer.

When random elements exist in a game, there is no longer a strategy that is *always* right. Some moves might have a high chance of failure but also a big potential payoff, making them a risky choice; other moves might be safe but with only a small gain. A player thus analyzes the different moves, their relative risks and benefits, and weighs them with respect to their perceived position in the game. Since there are unknown elements, the decisions become more complicated and thus more compelling.

## MECHANICS OF CHANCE

There are many ways to add randomness to a game. A few of the more common ways are discussed here.

### DICE

Dice come in many shapes and sizes. Standard dice have six sides, but some dice have 4, 8, 10, 12, 20, 30 or even 100 sides to them. Rolling a single die creates a random number between 1 and the number of faces on the die, with each number having an equal chance of being rolled. Rolling 1d10 (a single ten-sided die) has an equal chance of producing any value from 1 to 10. As such, rolling a single die is about as random as you can get.

By rolling multiple dice and adding them together, the result is no longer equally random. The numbers in the middle are rolled more frequently while the numbers at the extreme ends are rolled only rarely. The frequency of rolls becomes similar to a "bell curve." For example, when rolling 2d6 (two six-sided dice added together) the most common roll is 7, while the least common are 2 and 12. The more dice involved, the more heavily the result skews towards the center (thus randomness is decreased). The greater the number of faces on each die, the greater the range (thus randomness is increased).

Dice are one of the few random mechanics where previous results do not influence future ones. No matter how many times 1d8 is rolled, the next roll still has an equal chance of being anywhere between 1 and 8. Even if the previous 10 rolls were all 5, there is still exactly a 1 in 8 chance that the next roll will be 5 also—no more, no less. Gamblers often ignore this fact and assume that the dice are "hot" or "cold," a fallacy that game designers cannot afford to make. While this may seem contrary to the "bell curve" discussed in the previous paragraph, keep in mind that an individual roll merely has a *probability* of rolling certain numbers, not a certainty. Previous rolls never influence future ones.

## Cards

Cards are wonderfully versatile game elements. They can be shuffled, randomizing their order. They can be played face-down on the table, making their information hidden from all players. They can also be dealt to players who can only look at their own cards and no one else's, giving each player privileged information.

Cards can be used as resources, either by being kept in a hand, in a pile, or played in an area in front of an individual player. They can also be used to track game information without adding randomness. People have even used them as projectiles to determine a starting location.

Since there is a finite number of cards included with any game, revealing a card affects the probability of other cards. For example, in the gambling game *Blackjack,* a high proportion of face cards in the remaining deck favors the players; fewer face cards favor the dealer. This ratio of face cards to other cards changes over time as more cards are dealt out of a deck. If a player receives 10 face cards in a row, the probability of getting another decreases (unlike dice). The probabilities are reset when all cards are collected and reshuffled. Some card games even include a card that forces the deck to be reshuffled immediately when it is drawn—a way of randomly varying the amount of randomness in the deck! Note that if the deck is reshuffled after every draw, drawing a single card from a deck of *n* cards is equivalent to rolling a die with *n* sides.

## Pseudo-Random Number Generators

For all their processing power, computers are still driven by nonrandom instructions; it is impossible for most computers to produce a truly random number. However, there are plenty of algorithms in common use for computers to produce what is geekily called a "pseudo-random" number—a number that is technically not random, but that is close enough for the purposes of most games.

Computers can generate pseudo-random numbers of every type imaginable, making them extremely versatile if a designer wants to include defined amounts of chance to a game. For instance, to create a pseudo-random number in Microsoft Excel, enter =RAND()*5+1 in a cell and format the cell to show zero decimals. The result will simulate a d6 roll. Care must be taken to ensure that the numbers generated *are* sufficiently random; one of the authors of this book once worked with an online card game only to discover that the card shuffling method used favored certain cards over others appearing at the top of the deck.

## HIDDEN INFORMATION

When nonrandom information is concealed from the players, it is still random from the player's perspective. For example, in the children's card game *Go Fish*, a player must ask another player for a card of a chosen type. Without any further information, this starts out as a random guess, even though the cards in the opponent's hand are not random as far as the opponent is concerned. (They know *exactly* what they have.) RTS games often include a "fog of war" that conceals information about what the opponents are building. Even without any other randomness, the uncertainty of how best to respond to the unknown threats creates random dynamics. Similar dynamics are seen in *Rock-Paper-Scissors*, especially if played against a pseudo-random–number generator instead of a human.

When hidden information is also random (such as a weapon that deals a completely unknown amount of random damage), there is the danger of the player becoming confused or frustrated. Players should be able to understand the consequences of their actions and be able to form some degree of strategy that takes into account the random elements of the game. If the systems are hidden from them, their task of understanding the game is much more difficult. When making a game, especially a video game, designers are careful when including a random mechanic that is not displayed to the player.

## OTHER GAME BITS

Most other forms of randomness are variants of the above. Spinners (often found in children's board games, where you spin an arrow and see what it points to) behave just like dice. Flipping a coin is essentially the same as rolling a two-sided die. A dreidel (see Figure 5.1) produces the same result as a four-sided die. Cardboard tiles drawn from a bag (popular with many European games such as *Carcassonne* and *Tigris & Euphrates*) provide similar randomness to a deck of cards.

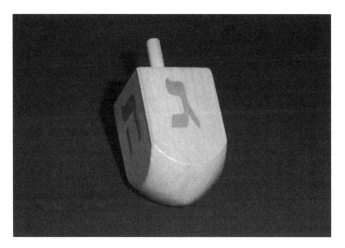

**FIGURE 5.1**
A dreidel. *Photograph by Roland Scheicher.*
*Reprinted from the Wikipedia Commons.*

## ALL RANDOMNESS IS NOT CREATED EQUAL

Consider this question: Is *Poker* a game of luck, or a game of skill? There are certainly elements of both, but which dominates the game? It turns out that the answer depends on how many hands are played.

For a small number of hands, it is likely that one player will be dealt more winning hands than the others, giving them a luck-based advantage. If more and more hands are played, each player will end up with about the same total number of winning hands, and the focus of the game shifts to who can maximize the money that he earns from each winning hand. The same game shifts to a game of skill.

This example illustrates the difference between a purely random game and what is called "measured randomness," where the nature of the random elements are known and can be planned for by the players. Each individual hand (or die roll or spin of the wheel) may be random, but with a sufficiently large number of them, the randomness decreases.

## COMPLETELY RANDOM GAMES

With few exceptions, most games—even those whose winner is primarily determined by luck—have at least some small component of skill. Modifying the mix between luck and skill is covered in Chapter 8, "Chance and Skill: Finding the Balance." Are there any games that are completely random, with no elements of skill at all? Absolutely.

There are two general kinds of games that involve pure chance: children's games, and gambling games. This is not to say that all children's or gambling games involve no skill at all; many of these games contain skill elements as well. But if you find a game that is pure chance, it is probably one of these two types of games.

### CHILDREN'S GAMES

Young children who have not developed the cognitive skills necessary to understand complex decision-making in more strategic games enjoy the games of pure luck—watching what happens as the random elements collide. Ironically, many children will attribute this to their own "skill" in rolling dice or selecting the right cards. Examples include the board games *Chutes & Ladders* and *Candy Land*, the card games *War* and *Old Maid*, and the dice game *Thunderstorm* (see Chapter 6, "Elements of 'Strategic' Skill," Challenge 1 for rules). In these games, the decision making is rather limited. You do what the game tells you to do based on the random outcome.

Luck games that appeal to children tend to have a level of building tension that is resolved by a random event, such as the "wars" in *War*, or the more difficult rolls as the dice get fewer in *Thunderstorm*. They also allow sudden changes of fortune, such as the special spaces in *Chutes & Ladders* that cause a player to advance or fall back suddenly, or when a player draws the one dangerous card in *Old Maid* and is suddenly in a position to lose. Lastly, these games allow the possibility of always coming from behind and winning so that the end result is never certain. This is the purpose for the rule in *Chutes & Ladders* that requires players to land exactly on the final space; no matter how far ahead a player is, there is always a possibility that she'll keep rolling too high and another player will catch up and win.

Compare the use of luck in these games to the use of luck in a game like *Risk*. In *Risk*, three cards of a kind or of a unique kind can provide the player with a progressively increasing number of units to add to her army. At a glance, this seems like a completely random mechanic. While the actual *card* the player receives may be random, when the player uses the cards, and even the means of gaining the cards in the first place, is heavily dependent upon the player's skill.

## Gambling Games

The defining mechanic of gambling games is that real money is won and lost in the process. Without money at stake, pure-luck gambling games quickly lose their appeal. Some gambling games with no skill aspects are *Roulette*, *Craps*, and slot machines.

It's interesting to note that most gambling games, even those that are pure chance, still offer choices. Players can choose a number to bet on in *Roulette*, are offered a choice of betting types in *Craps*, and are even allowed to choose how many coins to play at a time (from one up to three or five) for many slot machines. The game may still be completely random, but the element of choice gives players the *illusion* of control, since different choices lead to different outcomes.

What about games like *Poker*? As noted earlier, the more hands one plays, the less random it is. The substantial skill in *Poker*, however, comes not from the draw but from what the player does with that draw. What cards will he hold? How much will he bet? How good is his bluff? Each of these decisions in conjunction with the decisions of the other players factors in to create a skill-based playfield versus a luck-based playfield.

## Challenges

The challenges in this chapter let you practice working with various random elements. Try your skill at making luck with the following challenges.

### Challenge 1—Luck Tac Toe

Let's start with a simple game, *Tic-Tac-Toe* (better known as *Crosses and Naughts* in some parts of the world). The original game is purely a game of skill—you decide where you want to put the X or the O. Let's add some luck.

Modify this game by adding one or more chance-based mechanics. You may also add other skill-based mechanics provided that the game still resembles *Tic-Tac-Toe* at its core. At the same time, you must make the game *good* for adult players, a significant challenge, particularly since they are often jaded about the game. When's the last time you heard someone over the age of eight say, "Yeah! Let's play a game of *Tic-Tac-Toe!*"

Remember that rolling a d10 to decide where you place your X or your O isn't likely to result in riveting gameplay. However, out there exists some combination of mechanics that can make this old standby compelling again.

### Components Required

■ None

### Deliverable

■ The new game
■ Written rules modification for the new game
■ Analysis of whether your modification makes the original game better or worse, and why (optional)

### Suggested Process

1. **Brainstorm and playtest.**
   There are many ways to add an element of luck to this game. A die roll. Selecting a card. Tiles. Select one and try it out against yourself. Notice the effect that adding luck has on this game. Also notice how different the game plays when you use different kinds of chance.
2. **Create deliverable.**

## CHALLENGE 2—THE GDC CCG

At every game-industry trade show, and especially the Game Developers Conference, there is an economy of business cards. Complete strangers walk up to you and give you one, and you give them yours in a way that's completely normal at a conference and would be completely creepy if you did the same thing to a random person on the street in your hometown.

At any rate, everyone leaves with a stack of business cards they've collected. Most business cards are the same size (2 × 3.5-inch, if you're wondering) so they stack and shuffle well. It's high time someone made a game worth playing with all of these cards. That someone could be you.

For this challenge, design the rules for a collectible card game (CCG) like *Magic: The Gathering.* Your game must adhere to the following constraints:

■ Two players only.
■ Your game must support "constructed deck" format. That is, each player brings her own stack of business cards she's collected, and each player plays from her own deck.
■ Any standard-size business card must be playable in your game. You must therefore make use of the information that is typically found on business cards (names, phone numbers, job titles, etc.). For example, you cannot rely on people putting special icons on their cards just to support your game rules.
■ Since this is a *collectible* game, the cards must be distinct from one another. That is, there should be a reason to include one card over another in any given deck; deck building

should be strategic and not arbitrary. Think of how you might get someone in real life to say to a new acquaintance, "Wow, nice card… can I have an extra copy for my deck?"

Other than that, anything goes.

### Components Required

■  A stack of assorted business cards for play-testing purposes (optional)

### Deliverable

■  Complete set of written rules

### Suggested Process

1. **Find a starting place.**
   For an open-ended challenge like this, it can be hard to know where to begin. This is partly because there are so many places to begin. Pick one:
   ■  Consider business cards and the information contained on them. What attributes can you assign to each card?
   ■  What is the theme of your game? What does a card in play represent?
   ■  What is the object of the game? How do you win?
   ■  How do you set up the game? Do the players do anything special at the beginning of the game (such as shuffling their decks or drawing cards) that is not repeated later?
   ■  What is the progression of play? What is the order that things happen, and how are they resolved?
   If you have never played a CCG before, you may want to do some research on the genre. Play the games, or read some rules online, or talk with a friend or colleague who is familiar with them.
2. **Fill in the details.**
   All of the questions in the previous section need to be answered. After you start with one, work on the others.
3. **Playtest and iterate.**
   Try out your game, either against yourself or with a friend. Continue tuning the game until you have something fun.
4. **Create deliverable .**

### Variant

For greater difficulty, create a game that conforms to the following constraints in addition to those listed above:

■ Since this game should be playable at (or immediately following) a large conference like GDC, the rules should be simple enough to be able to teach another game developer in a short period of time. The written rules should be no longer than a page, and you should be able to explain the complete rules in person in less than two minutes. The rules should also not be the same as GameLab's *GDC 2008* game, which debuted after this book was begun.

For maximum difficulty, add this constraint instead:

■ The written rules must be short enough to fit on the back of your own business card. (In a font size that's readable—no fair using four-point font in order to fit a full page of rules on there.)

### CHALLENGE 3—THE FOURTH WHEEL

When most board games say "for two to four players," what they *really* mean is "for two *or* four players." Three-player games are difficult to design because of their dynamics. If the players have a lot of interaction and can attack or help each other, it's often too easy for two players to join forces against the third player. If there's little interaction, it's common for one player to pull ahead of the others and be uncatchable.

Video games have an easy way of solving this problem: Add a fourth character controlled by the computer (an AI). Implementing a human-like AI in a board or card game, however, is more difficult. Let's take another approach: Add a completely unrealistic, chaotic AI instead.

For this challenge, choose a non-digital game that supports at least two, three, and four players (and possibly more). Examples include *Risk, Monopoly,* and *Blokus.* Create a new set of rules for a three-player game that includes a fourth, randomly controlled nonhuman player. This fake player's actions must be governed by a set of cards that are randomly shuffled, not influenced by the other players in the game. The fourth player therefore adds an element of luck to the game.

### Components Required

■ Copy of the game
■ Index cards to control the fourth player's actions

### Deliverable

■ Set of cards for the fourth player
■ Written set of rules for a modified three-player game using your cards

**Suggested Process**

1. **Choose a game.**
   In keeping with the spirit of this chapter, feel free to choose a game randomly. Play it, or at least read through the rules, to get a feel for the mechanics and dynamics of the game (especially when playing with exactly three players).
2. **Design the cards.**
   What goes on the cards? Simple instructions on which player to attack? Special abilities that break the rules in favor of the fourth player? Random events that affect the rules for *all* players? Remember that all of the decisions the fourth player makes must be written on the cards and not chosen by the human players.
3. **Design the rules.**
   How are the cards played? Does the fourth player simply draw a card and follow its instructions each turn? Are there several piles of cards that are drawn from? Under what conditions are the decks reshuffled?
4. **Create deliverable.**

## CHALLENGE 4—THE ALIEN IN THE DESERT

So many games of chance focus on dice or cards (and spinners are just another form of dice, mechanics-wise). An under-used mechanic in non-digital games is the fog of war, although it's a staple in many video games. If your character can't see it, neither can you. It is this concept you will apply to a new tile-based game, *The Alien in the Desert*. Your game must use or employ the following:

- Tiles similar to those used in games like *Carcassonne* or *Settlers of Catan*
- The name *The Alien in the Desert*, although its interpretation is up to you
- Fog of war

To achieve this effect and create a playable prototype, you may employ any mechanics or bits you want.

**Components Required**

- Tiles of either paper or wood

**Deliverable**

- Playable prototype
- Written rule set

### Suggested Process

1. **Brainstorm.**
   There are many questions you must answer. What does the name of this game mean to you? How do you implement fog of war mechanics in a physical board game? How can you use tiles? Then there are the old standby questions to ask for any non-digital game. What is the object of the game? How many players? What game bits are used? What is the core mechanic?
2. **Playtest and iterate.**
   Throw something together and start playing it. Find the broken parts of the game and fix them. Get something functional, playable, and fun. As with any game, this may involve scrapping everything and starting over a few times if you feel you've gone in the wrong direction.
3. **Create deliverable.**

### IRON DESIGNER CHALLENGE 5—OPEN-ENDED RANDOMNESS

Break into groups of two to four players. Each group is given 100 blank index cards and a pen. Make a game with only these bits, and make it better than the game that the other teams are designing. The game must include an element of randomness, be it through a draw, card flipping, shuffling, and so on. The game may not include any dice, however, or anything other than the 100 cards. The player may shape or alter the cards any way he or she sees fit.

### Components Required

■ 3 × 5-inch index cards
■ Pens

### Deliverable

■ Demonstration of a playable game

### Suggested Process

1. **Brainstorm.**
   It's back to basics. Theme. Object of the game. Setup. Progression of play. Decide on one of these and extend from there.
2. **Create deliverable.**
   Follow the remaining process in Challenge 1.

**Variant**

Instead of cards, use a large bag of dice (with varying numbers of sides) as the only game bits.

## NON-DIGITAL SHORTS

The following list contains ideas for board games, card games, or other games that encourage further creation.

1. Choose a classic card game with a heavy emphasis on skill (such as *Euchre*) and redesign it to be entirely dependent on chance.
2. Redesign the classic card game *War* to incorporate at least three different kinds of chance other than the shuffled deck.
3. In *Risk*, randomness is used to create dramatic moments during battle by incorporating dice rolls. Redesign the game to create these types of moments during a different stage of the game, such as reinforcement or fortification.
4. Identify something that occurs by chance or is heavily influenced by chance in real life. Think of chance meetings or something that would make someone say, "I never expected it!" Then create a game that re-creates this experience.
5. Design a tabletop role-playing game that only uses coin flips to create randomness.
6. Parents the world over are begging you to create a game that involves both skill and chance—skill for them and chance for their kids. Modify an existing kids' game or create your own that fulfills these requirements.
7. Choose a game you have created from a challenge or non-digital short from a different chapter in this book. Redesign the game to be either entirely based on chance or entirely devoid of chance.
8. Design a game based on chance that uses exactly one of each of the following types of die: six-sided, eight-sided, 10-sided, 12-sided, and 20-sided.
9. Design a game using exactly one of each of the following mechanisms of chance: a shuffled deck of cards, tiles dealt and flipped, and tiles blind-drawn from a bag.
10. Use the elements of a well-known children's game (such as *Candy Land*) to create a gambling game.

## RESOURCES

*Dice Games Properly Explained*, Reiner Knizia (book)

# 6 Elements of "Strategic" Skill

Strategy is a very powerful draw for players. In fact, it's what keeps us coming back to games again and again. As Raph Koster notes in his excellent book *A Theory of Fun for Game Design*, we play games and enjoy the process because we are seeking to master the pattern in the game. While mastering a pattern, players are having fun. They are also forming strategy based on their understanding of the game's dynamics. That mastery, that development of strategy, isn't accidental. It's something the designer intended (or at least hoped for) through the use of mechanics that create strategy and tactics.

As noted in the previous chapter, most games have at least a little bit of skill involved. Even games that seem like all luck (like *Rock-Paper-Scissors*) have their own strategy Web sites.

How do we use skill in games?

## THE ROLE OF SKILL IN GAMES

At its heart, a good game is a series of interesting decisions—go right or left, build an offensive or defensive unit, figure out what your unit should do next. The success of decisions—whether a mental or a physical reaction—is a measure of player skill.

Good games cause players to exercise their skills frequently and reward them with immediate and obvious feedback. Throughout play, the player wonders what thing he should do next, and next, and next. Soon, he has entered what's known as the "magic circle"— when he has fallen through the monitor or TV and into the game world. The effect is similar to the one we enter when we watch a movie or read a particularly good book, but good games have a stronger pull because they integrate players and their decisions into the experience.

When the player is constantly making decisions, he enters a state that psychologist and noted researcher Mihaly Csikszentmihalyi called "flow." It is an optimal play state and one designers work hard to achieve. Csikszentmihalyi wrote a whole book on the topic, *Flow: The Psychology of Optimal Experience.* The book isn't limited to games, but covers this state from a wide perspective.

## TYPES OF DECISIONS

How much does player skill influence the outcome of a game? It depends on the decisions the game lets the players make, as well as the weight of those decisions. The extent that the player's actions affect the outcome of the game is broadly classified as "skill" (as opposed to factors outside of player influence, called "chance" or "luck"). The player experience largely involves making decisions that influence the game state. Therefore, a game designer focusing on the player experience should give a great deal of thought to what these decisions are, and why making them is fun or interesting or compelling. If you make a choice, and it has no effect on the game state, what's the point?

There are many kinds of decisions found in games. Some decisions are more interesting than others, and therefore offer more compelling play.

### OBVIOUS DECISIONS

Here's a silly two-player game called the *Highest Number Game*. The first player chooses a number, any number at all. Then, *after* hearing the first player's choice, the second person chooses a different number. Whoever says the highest number wins.

This is not much of an interesting decision for the second player. A higher number wins, a lower number loses. The winning decision is obvious, so it's not much of a decision at all. These choices are not particularly compelling because there is no reason to make any choice other than the optimal one.

Think this doesn't happen in *real* games? Consider the board game *Talisman*, where the primary mechanic is rolling a die and then moving along a track that many spaces, either clockwise or counterclockwise. The direction to move is certainly a choice, but much of the time one space harms the player and the other space helps. So it is an obvious decision. Or consider an "on-rails" RPG or FPS where the player is constantly told which direction to move. The player may be making many decisions, but where to go next is not one of them. These games are fun for many other reasons, but not because of these obvious decisions. Some games even offer no decisions at all. Roll the die, land on Park Place, and pay your friend lots of money. It's often at this stage of *Monopoly* that people begin waiting for the game to end.

In most cases where the decision is blindingly obvious, a designer can remove the choice and make it automatic. For example, modern RPGs rarely require players to rest and eat in order to replenish their stamina, although many RPGs from the 1980s and early 1990s did. Instead, the games do this automatically by replenishing stamina over time and eliminating the need to eat entirely. Some FPS games automatically reload the weapon when it's empty. By automating the trivial decisions, more focus is given to the interesting ones.

Another option is to take an obvious decision and add time pressure, changing it from a strategic decision to a test of dexterity. See Chapter 7, "Elements of 'Twitch' Skill," for more information on these fast kinds of decisions.

## MEANINGLESS DECISIONS

The only thing more frustrating than a choice with an obvious right answer is a choice with no right or wrong answers at all. Though the choice is seemingly present, it has no effect on the game's outcome. Early RPGs were notorious for this. "Dost thou wish to see the king?" a servant would ask, and the player would be given a yes/no choice. If the player said yes, he went to see the king. If the player said no, the servant would respond, "But thou must!" and the player would see the king anyway. The player was treated the same whether he said yes or no, so the choice itself was irrelevant.

If decisions are interesting because they affect the outcome of the game, then meaningless decisions are not interesting because they don't affect anything. Again, it's usually better to eliminate these from the game entirely.

There is one caveat to this, however, and that caveat is player perception. Many modern games offer players a choice in narrative that doesn't actually affect the overall outcome of the game. However, the player certainly perceives that it does, due to the way the game responds to them. Only upon replaying the game is it obvious to them that the route they took the first time—the one that seemed so crafted toward their choices—wasn't actually all that crafted after all. However, on that first play, the *perception* of choice makes those choices meaningful.

## BLIND DECISIONS

In *Roulette*, the player has a real decision of what number to bet on. The decision is not obvious, because it is not clear ahead of time what the correct number is. This decision isn't meaningless, as it affects the outcome of the game. But it's also not an interesting decision, because the player has no information to base her choice on. It's entirely random; one number is as good as any other. The game is still compelling because it offers cold, hard cash as a reward; remove that, and the decisions themselves aren't entertaining in the least.

More strategic games can inadvertently include these decisions as well. If a player approaches an NPC in a game and is given a choice of how to introduce himself (with a secret handshake, a standard greeting, or by showing a badge, etc.) without any additional information, the choice must be made blind. The decision becomes not only interesting but rewarding if the player heard some rumors about this NPC earlier, or if the NPC introduces himself/herself/itself first.

In general, blind decisions can be turned into other kinds of decisions by giving the player enough information. This does not mean *complete* information, by the way. As long as the player has *some* information on which to base a choice, the decision is not blind. In fact, some ongoing decisions are quite interesting because they change as more information is revealed over time.

## TRADEOFFS

A tradeoff happens whenever a player doesn't have enough resources to accomplish all of his goals. There's enough gold to either buy a better weapon *or* some better armor *or* a new spell. Pursue the escaping evil wizard *or* save the princess from the dragon. Hire an army of footmen *or* build a gryphon hatchery and add some fliers. Pack a sniper rifle *or* an AK-47.

Use the Wand of Explosions on this boss fight *or* save it for a later, potentially more difficult battle. None of the choices is clearly "right" or "wrong" but all have advantages and disadvantages. All of a sudden it feels like a real choice, and an important one.

These kinds of decisions can easily become obvious, if one choice is better than another. A game is called *balanced* if the choices are weighted so that there is no single best method that always wins. When games offer several viable paths to victory, and players must choose between them based on their personal styles and environmental factors in the game, the decisions made are quite interesting.

## DILEMMAS

A dilemma is similar to a tradeoff, but occurs when *all* choices will harm the player. For example, in *The Legend of Zelda*, players could encounter a room where they had to either pay some money or permanently lower their maximum health.

A special case is the Prisoner's Dilemma, a famous problem from game theory. In the Prisoner's Dilemma, two players have to independently make a choice: attempt to cooperate with the other player or defect (i.e., stab your partner in the back). If both players cooperate, they each pay a minor penalty. If both players defect, they each pay a much heavier penalty. If one player defects while the other cooperates, the one who tried to cooperate pays a maximum penalty while the one who defected gets no penalty at all. The reason this is a "dilemma" is that no matter what the opponent does, a player can reduce his personal penalty by defecting. However, by following this "optimal" strategy, players end up in the suboptimal situation of everyone defecting, which is worse than if everyone cooperated.

Instances of the Prisoner's Dilemma can be found in many games, especially turn-based strategy games. For example, in the board game *Diplomacy*, there are several locations on the board that give a large strategic advantage to any player who controls them, but the locations start out right in the middle between two opposing players. If both players cooperate, they can leave the area alone and do not have to waste resources fighting each other, but the threat of not fighting and just letting their opponent walk in unopposed is enough to keep both players tied up in a meaningless battle for the first part of the game.

The Prisoner's Dilemma has many variants. If players encounter a series of these decisions instead of just one, the dynamics change greatly. Adding multiple players (so that a small number of players defecting gets an advantage, but too many hurts everyone) changes things as well, especially if players have the ability to seek retribution against those who defected. If players *don't know* who cooperated and who defected, that can likewise change things, bringing in feelings of paranoia.

## RISK VERSUS REWARD TRADEOFFS

A form of tradeoff, a risk versus reward tradeoff happens when the player finds herself faced with a situation that has multiple outcomes, but whose level of risk is different. It's not so much a question of "Which one of these right things do I want" but rather, "Am I willing to risk it all for a potentially huge payoff... or death?"

For instance, in the *Civilization* series, players make many interesting choices, and there are many tradeoffs to be had. Will you pursue a military victory or an economic one? At some juncture, the player may want to attack a neighboring civilization. In evaluating whether or not to launch the attack, the player considers the risk of the mission along with its potential reward. In attacking the Americans, will the player gain some technology that she desperately wants?

These kinds of tradeoffs are common in board games with dice, cards, or other random mechanics. Players often have the option of making a safer move with a smaller reward, or a risky move with a greater reward if it succeeds (and a penalty if it fails). For example, in *Backgammon*, a player might have a choice of whether to leave a piece exposed. If the opponent rolls well, the piece could be captured and the player is set back; otherwise, the player has greatly improved board position on the following turn. Another example is *Spades*, where players can bid null (attempting to take no tricks in a hand). This bid is worth a lot of points if it succeeds, and it has a large penalty if it fails. It is also difficult to make, meaning that it is generally bid only when players have unusual hands, or when they are far enough behind that they must take huge risks out of desperation. In these games, typically, a player who is behind tends to take more risks in order to catch up, while a player in the lead prefers to play it safe in order to preserve his lead. Players exhibit similar behavior on the television game show *Jeopardy*. This tension between risk and reward can lead to some wonderfully tense dynamics.

Players also frequently encounter risk versus reward in RPGs and MMOs. "If I try to take this creature out, there's a possibility that he will smear me into the ground. On the other hand, man, he could have some awesome loot."

## FREQUENCY OR ANTICIPATION OF DECISIONS

In creating decisions in games, designers sometimes forget that the frequency with which the players make decisions is paramount. The quality of a game is affected if the player is only making decisions every 20 minutes versus every second, even if those decisions at the 20-minute mark are significant. A designer's goal, at its lowest level, is to keep the player's brain busy with possibilities. Games like *The Sims* or the *Civilization* series are excellent at providing the player with a constant series of positive choices. Which one of these good things will I do next? Granted, the player can deliberately decide to do things not conducive to good gameplay, but he always has multiple positive paths forward.

There are some cases, naturally, where decisions are not frequent, but the anticipation of a known pending decision sustains the player with thoughts of what she *may* do when decision time rears its head. FPS games with elevators or lifts provide a perfect example of this. Although the player cannot make a choice while in the elevator, the anticipation of a pending series of decisions is enough to hold her over. Likewise, the tunnels that sometimes lead up to boss battles serve to build player anxiety and narrative tension and thus sustain a state of flow.

## STRATEGY AND TACTICS

Gamers and developers have borrowed the terms "strategy" and "tactics" from military jargon, although they are often misused—for example, many so-called "real-time strategy" games have more of a focus on tactics than strategy.

Technically, a "grand strategy" is the overarching means to achieving an ultimate, long-term goal (for example, a victory in a game). A grand strategy consists of several supporting strategies, intermediate goals that must be performed in order to achieve the grand strategy (for example, in a large war, the choice of whether to fight a particular battle is a strategic choice). "Tactics" are the lowest-level micro-decisions made when carrying out a strategy: infantry maneuvers, whether to order an air strike, and when to start firing are tactical decisions made during a military battle. Sometimes, game designers refer to these as macro- and micro-choices.

Informally, players in a game make *strategic* decisions when they are planning for the long term (where "long" is relative to the length of the game), and *tactical* decisions when they are achieving short-term goals.

Tradeoffs make for interesting strategic or tactical decision-making. Fast decisions ("twitch" mechanics) are limited to tactics. This suggests that games that focus more on strategy—generally turn-based games like *Chess* and *Go*—do better to focus on decisions that involve tradeoffs. Games that focus on tactics can use either tradeoffs or fast decisions (or a mixture of both), resulting in very different gameplay. An example of a kind of tactical game that uses mostly tradeoffs is the tactical RPG, popularized by *Final Fantasy Tactics*. Most first-person shooters and other action games are examples of tactical games that focus mostly on instinctive decisions.

## COMPLETELY SKILL-BASED GAMES

Games that focus on strategy and tradeoffs tend to have at least some elements of chance. When these games are purely skill-based, like *Tic-Tac-Toe* or most adventure games, they can be solved, and the decisions that were once interesting can become obvious decisions when there ends up being a single known "right" move. Designing a game like this requires that there be enough depth of choices in the game that it cannot easily be solved by humans… and preferably not even by computers.

Most games that are entirely skill are physically based action games. This is probably because, unlike tradeoff decisions, it is not about getting the right answer but getting it *quickly*. Human reaction time can continue improving over time forever, especially in games where humans play against each other.

## MECHANICS OF SKILL

So far in this chapter, things have been a bit abstract. It is all well and good to say that tradeoff decisions involve limited resources, but there are so many kinds of resources in games: number and abilities of pieces, number of turns, board position, overt resources like gold or lumber, to name a few. What follows, then, are examples of some mechanics that lead to interesting decisions:

## TRADEOFF MECHANICS

A tradeoff puts players in a situation where they must choose between things. In order to keep their money, they can't have the armor they have their eye on. Designers use a variety of mechanics to put players in this situation.

### Auctions

In an auction, players bid some resource (usually money) in order to earn an item. The winner of the auction pays his bid and takes the item.

There are many kinds of auctions.

- In an "open auction," players call out bids at any time, each one being higher than the last, until everyone is silent. (This is the form most people are familiar with—it ends with "going once, going twice, sold!")
- A "sequential auction" involves players each making a bid in turn order, one at a time. There are many variants on this kind of auction: it may only go around once, or it may continue indefinitely, players may or may not be allowed to pass without bidding, and passing (if allowed) may or may not prevent the player from bidding again in a later round (if there is one). Sequential auctions often occur in card games where players bid on the number of tricks they will take. The highest bidder is left to prove his prowess.
- A "silent auction" or "closed auction" involves players each making their own bid, simultaneously and in secret, and revealing their bids at once.
- In a "fixed-price auction," an item is offered at a named price, and the first player to accept the named price buys it. (You can see this on eBay with the "buy it now!" options on some items.)
- A "Dutch auction" offers the item at an initial high price but the price falls slowly over time; the first player to accept the current price wins the auction.
- In a "reverse auction" the item up for bid is a disadvantage or negative event, and players bid to avoid getting stuck with it.

Designers can vary auction mechanics. Instead of auctioning a single item, items can be auctioned in lots (groups). Multiple auctions can be performed at once, with players allocating their resources between them. Players can all lose their bids, instead of just the auction winner. Or the player with the second-highest bid wins a lesser item (or gets hit with a penalty, making high bids dangerous). Instead of the resources being removed from play, the winner can pay his bid to some or all of the losers.

Games that use action mechanics include *Pitch*, *Bridge*, *Modern Art*, and *Monopoly* (though few actually play using those mechanics in the latter).

### Purchases

Instead of players competing in an auction, they have the ability to purchase items, abilities, or actions at fixed prices. The choices come from which stuff to purchase, given that players will be limited in the currency used to make purchases, and when to purchase, particularly if the resource is limited and players may be unable to purchase it later in the game.

### Limited-Use Special Abilities

Special abilities give players the ability to break the standard rules of the game in specific ways. This mechanic was originally popularized with the board game *Cosmic Encounter.*

If players can gain some advantage but only once per game (or twice, or what have you), the choice of *when* to use the ability becomes a compelling decision. A player knows what advantage he will get by using the ability right now, but it is unknown whether a *better* use will make itself available later.

### Dynamic Limited-Use Special Abilities

By varying the strength of special abilities based on space, time, location, or some other factor, the strategic nature of the decision is amplified. For instance, the longer you hold the item (or the longer you hold the button down), the more powerful it may become. Using it now or saving it until later presents the player with an interesting decision. In *Risk*, players face this decision when they try to decide when they should use the cards in the game. Players get an immediate bonus when they use their cards, but they also increase the bonus when their opponents subsequently use *their* cards. Weighing the immediate benefit against larger future rewards isn't always an obvious decision.

### Explicit Choices

Sometimes, a game gives a choice to a player, making clear the effects of both choices. Perhaps the player draws a card that says "Choose one: gain 10 gold, or heal 5 life points." The player must then weigh the relative values of those choices.

### Limited Actions

In games where players have one avatar, all of their actions are taken through that avatar. Where players have multiple avatars, choosing which one takes which action becomes a difficult decision (assuming that the player cannot give orders to every avatar simultaneously). This is more common in board games (think of games where players have multiple pawns on a board and can choose which to move, like *Backgammon*), but can be done in video games as well. (An example would be *The Lost Vikings*, where the player has three characters but can only control one at a time, leaving the other two vulnerable.)

### Trading and Negotiation

Whenever multiple players are working together toward mutual goals, a whole host of social choices come into play. There's the mix of cooperation versus competition. Alliances can be forged and broken. Promises of future considerations in exchange for help at present can be made. (Based on the rules of the game, these can either be formally binding, non-binding, or else with a penalty when the contract is broken.) There are even the metagame considerations of the social relationships of the players outside of the game itself; one plays the board game *Diplomacy* differently with close friends than with total strangers.

## STRATEGIC EVALUATION

How do game designers assess the success of the strategy and tactics they hoped to create? By interviewing players or watching them play, a designer can gather a lot of information. Remember that not every player likes a game of *Chess*, *Go*, or *Risk*. The level of strategy in your game should be commensurate with the audience's desire for the same. Here are some questions you might ask.

### Do players care when other players are taking their turn?

If a game has a high degree of strategy, players are reluctant to leave the table, let alone the room. To illustrate, consider how likely you would be to leave your friends alone with a game of *Monopoly* versus a game of *Risk*.

A strategic game requires players to care about the outcomes of each player's move, because those moves will, in turn, affect their move. They are constantly reassessing the play state as each player takes his or her turn.

### Are players making long-term plans?

Strategic games invite the player to form strategies that can be carried out over multiple turns. If players are stifled by the existing mechanics of the game or allowed too much latitude, they may be unable to see how their strategy could be sustained or achieved over multiple turns. When playing a game, ask the players what they plan to do or how they think they will win the game. These answers usually reveal a strategy or lack thereof.

### Are there multiple strategies for multiple games?

At the beginning of any given game, the player should have an idea of how he will approach the play of the game. The more rich the strategic opportunities are, the more diverse the answers will be. In *Risk*, for instance, a player may have literally dozens of different strategies to play against different players or to compensate for different starting states.

## CHALLENGES

The challenges in this chapter let you practice working with various skill-based elements. Try your luck at making skill…

### CHALLENGE 1—SKILL FROM NOWHERE

Here are the rules for the dice game *Thunderstorm*, a traditional children's game from Germany:

- One player is chosen to begin and then play proceeds clockwise.
- On the first turn, the player throws six standard dice (6d6).
- If a player rolls any 1s on his turn, those dice are set aside and the remaining dice are passed to the next player. In this way, players may have fewer than six dice to throw on their turn.
- If a player rolls *only* 1s on his turn, all six dice are passed to the next player.
- If a player fails to roll any 1s, he is penalized. The first five times this happens to a player, he draws five lines on his paper in the shape of a house. On the sixth failure,

lightning strikes that player's house (draw a sixth line through the house), and he is eliminated from the game.

■ The object of the game is to be the last player remaining in the game. When all players but one have been eliminated, the remaining player is the winner.

This game has no decisions and is all luck. It is fine for a children's game, but adults may tire of it quickly.

Create a variant of this game that involves at least some skill. Your goal is to make this game more palatable to adults (such as the parents of the children who like the original game), while still keeping it close enough to the original that the children are themselves interested in playing.

### Components Required

■ Six standard dice, for playtesting

### Deliverable

■ Written rules modification for the new game
■ Playable game
■ Analysis of whether your modification makes the original game better or worse, and why (optional)

### Suggested Process

1. **Brainstorm and playtest.**
   Consider possible ways to add an element of skill to this game. Could you add an auction? An outside ability to bet on the outcome? What else? Brainstorm various possibilities no matter how odd and try them out against yourself. Notice the effect that adding skill has on this game. Also notice how different the game plays when you use different kinds of skill-based mechanics.
2. **Create deliverable.**

### Variant

Create a variant of a different luck-based game, such as the gambling game *Craps* or the children's board game *Candy Land*.

### CHALLENGE 2—GAME SYSTEMS

A "game system" is a set of components that can be used to play a variety of games, rather than a single game. The best-known game system is a standard deck of playing cards, which can be used for hundreds of games.

The Piecepack (available at www.piecepack.org) is a public domain game system that can be used to create board games. A Piecepack contains the following:

■ 24 tiles: Each contains a unique combination of suit (out of four differently colored suits) and number (zero to five) on one side, and identical back sides that contain a cross, suggesting a division into four small square quarters.

■ 24 small circular tokens: Each contains a unique combination of suit and number, with the suit on one side and the number on the other. Tokens can fit on one of the small squares on the back of each tile, and both front and back side contain a small tick-mark to indicate direction/facing.

■ 4 pawns: One of each suit color, each small enough to fit on one of the small squares on the back of each tile, and each containing a small tick-mark to indicate direction/facing.

■ 4 six-sided dice, numbered 0 to 5: Each one corresponding to a suit.

For this challenge, design a Eurogame that uses only the game bits found in a single Piecepack. Eurogames are discussed in detail in Chapter 11, "Targeting a Market." For the purposes of this challenge, a Eurogame is defined as having the following constraints:

■ Playable in roughly 60 to 90 minutes
■ Short setup time
■ Simple rules, short learning curve
■ Cooperative, not confrontational
■ Contains strategic decision making along with measured randomness, as described in the last chapter
■ Minimal player downtime

In creating your game, you do not need to use all of the bits in the Piecepack, nor do you need to use all of the capabilities of the bits you use, but you cannot use any bits that are not contained in the Piecepack.

#### Components Required

■ A printed Piecepack set

#### Deliverable

■ Complete set of written rules

## Suggested Process

1. **Find a starting place.**
   Find the constraint listed above that scares you the most or feels the most restrictive. Start there and brainstorm some potential core mechanics, something you can build around. Choose a mechanic that seems as if it works well. Another approach is to consider the Piecepack components themselves, as they are quite versatile. The tiles can be placed face-down to form a makeshift game board, or they can be used like a deck of cards. The tokens can be used like playing pieces on a game board, or they can be placed suit-side up to conceal number (or vice versa) to keep some information hidden, or they can be flipped like coins. Dice can be used to track score or other variables in the game, they can be used as pawns, or they can be rolled to produce random numbers. Each game bit can serve a single role, or several.
2. **Build from there.**
   Flesh out the details. Create a playable set of rules.
3. **Playtest and iterate.**
   Try out your game, either against yourself or with a friend. Fill in the holes that you find in the rules. Continue tuning the game until you have something fun.
4. **Constraint check.**
   Verify that your game meets all of the constraints listed above. If it doesn't, ask yourself how to modify your mechanics. Note that you should do this only *after* finding the fun in your game; it is much easier to add a constraint to a fun game than to add fun to a constrained game.
5. **Create deliverable.**

## Variant

Use a different game system. Some suggestions:

- *Icehouse* pieces (by Looney Labs, online at www.looneylabs.com). Contains five each of large, medium, and small pyramids. The pieces are hollow, allowing them to be stacked (with smaller ones being completely covered by larger). They can stand on their base facing up or tilted on an end. Each set of pieces is painted a different color; use one set per player.
- *Stonehenge* (by Paizo Publishing, online at www.paizo.com). Marketed as a "board game anthology," this is a Stonehenge-themed game system containing a board, a deck of cards, and a large pile of plastic pieces.
- Any modified deck of cards. Remove a few cards from each suit, or add an extra suit, or combine several decks, or add some special cards that aren't part of *any* suit (other than the Jokers). You can create a custom deck of your own by purchasing several decks with the same card back and modifying the cards as needed, or you can search for published card games that come with nonstandard cards.

### CHALLENGE 3—STRATEGY ON THE RUN

Design a game that, like a Eurogame (described in the previous challenge), has short setup time, has simple rules, minimizes player downtime, and contains at least some strategy and interesting decisions. You may use any collection of game bits that you want.

Your game should have a playtime of 15 minutes or fewer.

Due to the short play time, you are expected to iterate and polish your game to very high quality.

### Components Required

■ Collection of game bits

### Deliverable

■ Prototype with all game bits included
■ Complete set of written rules

### Suggested Process

1. **Review some Eurogames with short play times.**
   What are these games all about? *Dragon Parade* is about where to put your vendors on a parade route. *Hey, That's My Fish* is about which tile to land on next. A quick trip to a local game store can help you broaden your understanding.

2. **Choose a decision.**
   Short games typically only have a small number of mechanics that players repeat many times. In a longer game, it's preferable to give players more variety so that they don't get burned out on a small set of mechanics, but in a short game it's better to keep things simple. Simpler rules also have the advantage of shortening the learning curve and setup time. Consider the different kinds of strategic decisions that can be made during a game, either listed in this chapter or of your own devising, and choose one as the basis for your game.

3. **Create the mechanics.**
   From the primary decision players will be making, create a core mechanic to support it. Think about what happens when players make this same kind of decision several times in series. From there, fill in the remaining details required for a complete game: rules for setup, progression of play, and victory/end conditions.

4. **Playtest and iterate.**
   With a game that plays so quickly, you can play many times in a short period of time. Each time, try making a small change and see how it affects play. Do this at least 20 times (five hours' worth of playtesting).

5. **Create deliverable.**

### Variant

Instead of creating a game from scratch, take the game you made from Challenge 2 and reduce its play time to 15 minutes or less. Make any changes to the mechanics that you feel are appropriate.

## CHALLENGE 4—A WHOLE NEW DIMENSION

You were all ready to play a game of *Checkers* (or *Draughts*, depending on where you live), but instead of a normal board, you have this 12 × 12 square board instead. You could just ignore four squares on each side, but that's boring. Instead, design a variant that uses the larger board. You may make any rules changes necessary to support the new larger size. What effect does this have on gameplay?

### Components Required

- 12 × 12 board and a set of checkers or tokens. These will probably be homemade since this *Checkers* variant is not typically sold in stores.
- A computer with an Internet connection, in case you've forgotten how to play *Checkers* (more common than you know)

### Deliverable

- Written list of rules changes you tried and an analysis of their effect on gameplay.

### Suggested Process

1. **Build the game.**
   Create the components. This can be as simple as using coins or cutouts from a standard sheet of paper.
2. **Play the game.**
   By yourself or with a friend, play the game. As you play, take notes on how things have changed. Are the decisions you make more or less compelling than the original? How have the player decisions changed, just by changing the size of the board?
3. **Create deliverable.**

### Variant

Use a 6 × 6 board. How is a smaller board different from the standard game? How is it different from the larger 12 × 12 board? Do there appear to be any trends as size increases or decreases, or is each size its own unique, unpredictable experience?

**Variant**

Use a 7 × 7 or 9 × 9 board. Now the board is symmetrical, which should have a greater effect on game dynamics. How do things change now? Does this fit the size trends you found in the previous variant, or are odd-sized and even-sized boards completely different play experiences?

**Variant**

Instead of *Checkers*, use a different square-based game such as *Chess*.

## IRON DESIGNER CHALLENGE 5—BLACK FRIDAY: THE BOARD GAME

Break into groups of two to four players. Each group names a regularly occurring event. Or use this list:

- "Black Friday" (the shopping day immediately after Thanksgiving in the United States)
- High school class reunion
- Game Developers Conference
- Routine dental cleaning
- Academy Awards
- Toyotathon

Each team is assigned an event (or a single event is randomly chosen for all teams). Make a board or card game based on the event. The game must have a strong element of strategy and interesting player decisions (although some elements of chance are acceptable).

**Components Required**

- Game bits required for the game

**Deliverable**

- Demonstration of a playable game

**Suggested Process**

1. **Choose a perspective.**
   The theme may be decided, but each theme can be looked at from different angles. Who are the players? If the theme is a high school class reunion, is each avatar a graduate of the class (suggesting that the objective is to impress your classmates or have a good time), or a member of the planning committee (so that the objective is making sure *everyone* has a good time), or a janitor (where the objective might be to clean up your area fastest)?
2. **Choose mechanics.**

With a theme and an objective, decide on the core mechanics that allow players to achieve that objective. What decisions will they make, and how do those decisions affect the game state?

3. **Create deliverable.**

## NON-DIGITAL SHORTS

Roll a d10 and consider creating one of these games.

1. Create a tile-based game to be played in multiple rounds or sets that facilitate long-term planning.
2. Choose a simple skill-based board game (such as *Checkers*) and design a "speed" version of it that requires players to make decisions within a set time limit.
3. Design a card game that uses the Prisoner's Dilemma as its core mechanic.
4. Design a tile-based game in which each player records a grand strategy in advance and wins only when it is achieved.
5. Design a card game in which players may purchase the right to make other players' decisions for them.
6. Design a race to the end board game with a hidden objective that requires players to reveal it by a purchase or auction mechanic.
7. Redesign *Monopoly* such that each of the avatar tokens (the car, iron, dog, ship, etc.) has a limited-use special ability.
8. Redesign a classic roll-and-move game (such as *Parcheesi*) to involve trading and negotiation.
9. Redesign the luck game *Craps* to involve at least three skill-based mechanics.
10. Create a game that emphasizes game design as a skill by forcing players to come up with believable (though likely humorous) designs in a short amount of time.

## RESOURCES

www.worldrps.com: The World RPS Society Web site, which includes a number of (serious) strategy articles for playing *Rock-Paper-Scissors*.

# 7 Elements of "Twitch" Skill

In the previous chapter, we explored one type of skill in games, the skill of deliberate, considered decision making (colloquially referred to as "strategy"). There is another kind of skill that sees frequent use in video games, and even the occasional non-digital game. This second kind of skill requires fast thinking, dexterity, and reaction speed. These fast decisions are often referred to as "twitch mechanics," and the games that use them at their core are called "twitch games." Many early arcade games were almost entirely tests of this kind of skill. Some modern games, particularly shooting games, also fall into this category.

## CHALLENGING THE PLAYER

Players play games because they present challenges. Gradually, by responding to a challenge again and again, players become better, ultimately achieving mastery. If a game presents too many twitch challenges too quickly, the player can be overwhelmed and frustrated. At the other extreme, if the challenges are too easy to overcome, the player quickly becomes bored. Finding the balance between them, when the player feels challenged at the peak of his ability, called "tuning," is one of the game designer's most important jobs. To keep the game interesting, designers also have to allow for the game to become progressively more difficult. *Guitar Hero* is an excellent example of this. At first, some players struggle through the song "I Love Rock and Roll." Within an hour, they're blowing through it.

Strategic games also have to deal difficulty progression, but in those games the question is one of depth of decision making, because players typically have all the time they need to consider their options. In twitch games, the problem of overwhelming (or underwhelming) the player with challenge is much more obvious.

## TUNING

One difficulty of twitch challenges is that they must be crafted to challenge the player at an optimal level of difficulty. This would be easy except that every player's ability level is different, so *any* level of challenge is going to be too hard for some players and too easy for others. Luckily, game designers have learned a few ways around this.

### DIFFICULTY LEVELS

You can scale the game to be easier or harder, and then allow players to choose his own level of challenge. Most forms of twitch skill can scale easily: the requirements of how fast a player must react in a pure speed challenge can be modified; the window of opportunity for a timing challenge can be widened or narrowed; a precision challenge can be made more forgiving or can be assisted by some form of automatic aiming; the number of things to avoid in an avoidance challenge can be modified; and a strict time limit for a timed challenge can be changed to ease or increase the time pressure.

### DYNAMIC DIFFICULTY ADJUSTMENT

Some games not only have multiple difficulty levels but also can change them on the fly. If the player is doing too well, the difficulty can increase until the player is sufficiently challenged. If the player is losing frequently, the game can ease up a bit so that the player is not frustrated.

### DIFFICULTY CURVES

Some games, particularly video games that have a sequence of levels, simply start off easy and become progressively more difficult as time goes on. This continues until the player is finally overwhelmed. Many classic arcade games like *Pac-Man* and *Space Invaders* do this, as do puzzle games like *Tetris*.

### PLAYTESTING

When tuning a game, a steady stream of playtesters is indispensable. Designers understand their own games too well to discern the new player experience on their own. Testers who have experience with a game are great for finding bugs, but their skill level has likely increased to the point where they can no longer objectively test for difficulty. Throughout development, find new playtesters on a continual basis and constantly monitor their first reactions to the difficulty of the game.

## TWITCH DECISION MAKING

The decisions a player makes in a twitch environment are of a different nature than those in a slower, more strategic game. The player is still making decisions, but those decisions are being made on a far more rapid basis (many times per second, as opposed to one decision every few seconds or minutes in a pure strategy game).

Most twitch decisions have an obvious correct action that the player should take. The challenge comes from executing that action quickly and accurately. In an FPS, for example, the decisions a player makes involve which way to turn and fire. The information is there on the screen, and the challenge is not just to make the right decision, but to make the decision faster than the enemy. It is not the thinking part of the player's brain that is engaged, as much as the instinctive, reactive part of the brain.

There is a lesson here. Obvious decisions (see Chapter 6, "Elements of 'Strategic' Skill") are not very compelling in a strategic environment, but they can be made more interesting if the player has limited time to make those decisions. A perfect illustration of this is the ShockWave game *No Brainer* [1], where the player is asked a series of extremely easy and obvious trivia questions under extreme time pressure. Before long, most players will find themselves saying that broccoli is made of metal or that limestone rock has a brain, simply because their minds cannot keep pace with the game.

## TWITCH MECHANICS

While twitch mechanics are often lumped into a single category, there are actually several types, each of which has a different effect on play.

### PURE SPEED

Some games ask players to perform a routine task in a minimum amount of time (such as a car racing game), or perform a repetitive task as many times as possible within a set time limit (often referred to as "button mashing," exemplified by the classic arcade game *Track and Field*, which essentially rewarded the player for hitting a button rapidly). Foot races in real life are an example of this as well.

In non-digital games, this mechanic shows up in places the average person might not expect—causal and children's games. The game *Slapjack* tasks players with being the first to slap a jack card when it is flipped face up onto a pile of cards. Winner takes all. Likewise, some trivia games (especially game shows like *Jeopardy!*) award the player with the first right answer.

### TIMING

A common mechanic in video games is to require the player to press the right button at the right time. *Dance Dance Revolution* and *Rock Band* not only require rapid movement, but also precise timing. The objective is not merely to hit buttons rapidly, but to step on the right arrows or hit the right input device at the correct time.

### PRECISION

Sometimes the challenge is not simply to do something fast or to perform an action at a particular moment, but to do something accurately. First-person shooters generally require the player to aim at a target, and players must move the crosshairs quickly but also toward the correct facing (and often a moving target).

Non-digital games that require precision are often referred to as "dexterity games," as they require careful manual dexterity rather than pure speed. Examples include the stacking game *Jenga*, where players must remove blocks from a tower without causing it to fall, the electronic game *Operation*, which requires players to pick up small plastic pieces with a set of tweezers, and the party game *Twister*, where players must place their hands and feet in awkward positions without falling down. The most obvious type of precision occurs in sports games where the player needs to hit the ball at the right time and in the right place, among other things.

## AVOIDANCE

A favorite of side-scrolling games, staying away from harmful enemies or projectile works differently depending on the game. Some games (mostly in 2D) show all of the surrounding area, making this mostly a challenge of keeping threats in view and heading for safer areas. In games where field of vision is limited (as with first-person 3D games), there is an additional challenge of identifying where the threats are. Sometimes, players are provided with an overhead view mini map; other times, they are expected to just look in different directions a lot.

In some cases, particularly when projectiles or enemies are very fast, locating areas of cover is important in avoiding threats. In other games, everything moves slower, and the concept of "cover" is nonexistent.

In non-digital form, this type of skill is most often found in sports and other physical games such as *Tag* or *Dodgeball*.

## TIME PRESSURE

Any task becomes more difficult when a time limit is added. This can be an explicit time limit (such as solving a puzzle within three minutes) or implicit (find and shoot your opponent faster than they can do the same to you). Time limits can be added to all types of skill (both strategic and twitch), changing the dynamics of the game in often drastic ways. Consider the difference between *Chess*, where players are given as long as they want to make a move and *Speed Chess*, where players have a total of five minutes to make all of their moves for the whole game. The rules of both games are identical, but they have an entirely different feel.

## CHALLENGES

What are you doing reading this? Hurry up and pick a challenge before time runs out!

### CHALLENGE 1—ADDING TWITCH TO STRATEGY

The purpose of this challenge is to gain an understanding of how play dynamics change when a strategic element of a game has a twitch mechanic added to it.

Choose any game that is a pure strategy game, with no luck and no twitch mechanics. Examples are *Chess*, *Go*, and *Othello*. Modify the rules to allow some kind of twitch component. Play the game, and note how the new game is different and whether the game was made better or worse (or just different) from the change.

#### Components Required

■    A playable version of the game you have chosen

**Deliverable**

- Written rules modifications for the new game
- Analysis of how the game dynamics have changed, whether your modification makes the original game better or worse, and why (optional)

**Suggested Process**

1. **Brainstorm and playtest.**
   There are many ways to add an element of twitch skill to this game. Time pressure is the most obvious (just add a time limit to how long a player can take to move, as with *Speed Chess*), but you should be able to come up with something more original. Try adding a dexterity component instead.
2. **Create deliverable.**

## CHALLENGE 2—MULTI-BALL

In the non-digital realm, the most common place to find twitch mechanics is in sports. Most sports require speed, precision, and time pressure, and contact sports also contain avoidance.

A majority of popular sports involve the players moving a ball around a field of play, usually trying to put it into some specific area. Let's try something different: instead of *one* ball in play, there must be *two or more* balls in play at once. The balls may be identical, or they may serve different functions, at your discretion.

The design of popular sports games is normally a tricky business, because the designer must consider not only a sport that is accessible and fun to play, but also one that is fun to watch. For this challenge, do not worry about these details. Simply make a game that is fun to play.

**Components Required**

- At least two balls of some kind

**Deliverable**

- Complete set of written rules

### Suggested Process

1. **Choose your constraints.**
   The world of sports includes many different kinds of balls: footballs, baseballs, golf balls, tennis balls, ping-pong balls, and dozens of others. Do you want several balls of the same type or one ball each of several different types? Which types?
   There are many potential fields of play. Do you want your sport to be playable indoors or outside? Can it be played on concrete, or must it be a soft surface like grass or sand? Note how the field of play interacts with the balls. Some balls will only bounce or roll on certain surfaces. Can you use an existing play area, like a local football field or basketball court, for playtesting? How many players? Is each player competing on his own or do players form teams? You do not need to answer all of these questions at once, but any one of them can give you a starting point. Once you've chosen, say, two volleyballs, you can then ask yourself how you intend to use them.

2. **Develop core mechanics.**
   The kinds of balls used in sports are highly interactive. They can be dropped, kicked, thrown, hit with a blunt object, bounced, and so on. What are the ways you want your players to interact with the two balls? Are there any methods of interaction that are not allowed (such as carrying a ball in *Basketball*)?

3. **Flesh out the rules.**
   What is the object of the game? How is it played? When is it over? Take your core concept and develop it to a complete rule set.

4. **Safety and reality check.**
   Your game should be safe to play. If you want players to throw balls in the general direction of other players, those balls should be soft enough not to cause injury. Avoid full-contact sports unless you're prepared to provide sufficient safety equipment. Be sure to prohibit any player actions that could cause injury. Look to other sports as a general guideline, and when in doubt you should err on the side of caution. Your game should also be playable. *Quidditch* may sound like a fun game to design, but you'll have a difficult time playtesting.

5. **Try it out.**
   Get some friends together and play.

6. **Create deliverable.**

### CHALLENGE 3—TWITCH DICE

Design a game that involves only twitch mechanics and luck—no strategic elements—using only dice as your components. You may use anywhere between five and ten dice for your game, and you can choose what kinds of dice from those that you have available.

Your game should be playable in five minutes or fewer.

**Components Required**

- Dice, preferably of several types (d4, d6, d8, d10, d12, d20) and in a variety of colors

**Deliverable**

- Complete list of written rules

**Suggested Process**

1. **Brainstorm or research.**
   What kinds of twitch mechanics are possible with dice? If you can't think of anything, look on the Internet for rules of card games that have twitch components (such as *Slapjack*, *Brawl*, and *Egyptian Ratscrew*).
2. **Consider physical difficulties.**
   Avoid mechanics that might make play difficult. For example, if the dice are rolled and then players must quickly grab certain dice, there is the possibility that the facing of the dice could be changed while players grab them. If the numbers displayed on the dice matter, indiscriminate grabbing or hoarding of dice could cause problems and would need to be avoided or worked around.
3. **Create mechanics.**
   Come up with a preliminary set of mechanics. Decide on an objective, progression of play, and rules for how the game ends.
4. **Playtest.**
   For such a fast-moving game, you should be able to play many times in a short period of time, ending up with a high-quality polished experience.
5. **Create deliverable.**

## CHALLENGE 4—AVOIDANCE UNDER PRESSURE

Avoidance is a common mechanic employed in video games. Arcade games regularly force you to avoid enemies, projectiles, or cars, or be killed. Other games use avoidance as a secondary tactic. In an FPS, avoidance is key to staying in the game. Some games take avoidance to the peak by putting the player in the position where she must practice stealth. Choose any video game that you own or have access to that does not have an explicit time limit (if it's your own creation, so much the better). Create a non-digital version of that game that employs avoidance and gets progressively more challenging through the use of time pressure. You may even use a timer to see whether players complete their tasks on time.

### Components Required

- Playable video game
- Timer (such as a clock, stopwatch, or kitchen timer)

### Deliverable

- Written rule set
- Prototype of game

### Suggested Process

1. **Choose a game.**
   A game where there is something to avoid is necessary. If you're having trouble, look up *Scotland Yard* on BoardGameGeek.com for an example of avoidance done well.
2. **Choose a means of avoidance.**
   What are your players avoiding, and what means will they be using to avoid it? Remember that avoidance should be the primary activity, not secondary to blasting your way from point A to point B.
3. **Choose a means of time progression.**
   What speeds up the time in the game? Why is it that players need to go faster? If there's something believable in the narrative or setting of the game, that goes a long way toward increasing believability.
4. **Test the game.**
   Do you find yourself playing in a stealthy way because it's optimum or because you're trying to make the challenge work for you? How does the inclusion of time pressure affect things?
5. **Create deliverable.**

### Iron Designer Challenge 5—That's Hard!

Back in the day, the goal of arcade games was to make the player lose (preferably in three minutes or fewer) to make the machines as profitable as they could be. These games did not typically have multiple difficulty levels. Today, many players expect a longer and more customizable experience that is perhaps not quite so intense. Maybe it's time we consider how that early arrangement—hook 'em, and then pay for play—could be employed today.

Select any game with which you're familiar and add the necessary mechanics that end the game but allow players to keep playing, provided they can afford it. You may need to also add mechanics that cause the player to be removed from the game before its normal end. You may choose a digital or non-digital game for this exercise (or have someone with a sadistic streak choose a game for you).

**Components Required**

■ A video game or non-digital game for research
■ Components for prototype

**Deliverable**

■ List of mechanics that allow for difficulty scaling
■ Prototype

**Suggested Process**

1. **Select a game**
   Consider picking a game that doesn't offer up an immediate and obvious solution. In fact, the less obvious, the more you'll get out of the challenge.
2. **Brainstorm mechanics.**
   At a minimum, there are three things to be addressed here: a) how the game ends, b) how the player keeps playing, and c) how the player gets the resource (if any) that allows him to keep playing. Experiment with a variety of possibilities.
3. **Create deliverable.**

## NON-DIGITAL SHORTS

These shorts will exercise your ability to make games that cause others to move.

1. Create a game that doesn't involve pain that uses 10 pencils and whose winner is the one to get rid of all those pencils first.
2. Time pressure is usually a factor in a game. Sometimes, though, it's on the designer. Create a game from the first 10 things you pull from your home or office junk drawer or which are sitting on your desk. You have 20 minutes to complete your first iteration of that game. (A similar exercise is commonly used to teach entry-level design students that one can make a game about anything.)
3. Re-envision an FPS as a non-digital art piece where the gun isn't a gun but the basic mechanics of the game remain unchanged. The piece should be political in nature and be designed to make a statement.
4. Create a tile-based game that incorporates real-time play. Think *Slapjack*, but don't do *Slapjack*.
5. Create a single-player game that requires the player to complete a given series of tasks within a certain period of time. You may add a time limit to an existing game or create one of your own.

6. Create a dexterity game using only sticks and stones as game bits. The game must involve no physical risk—no possibility of broken bones.
7. Create a card-based game with the concept that the players must work together to defuse a bomb. Use a time limit, where the bomb blows up and the players lose if they take too long.
8. Take a trivia game like *Trivial Pursuit* and modify the rules in such a way that players must answer their questions quickly, not just accurately. Note how this changes the dynamics.
9. Modify an existing non-digital game that uses primarily dexterity mechanics, changing its focus to pure speed. Or modify a pure speed game to be a dexterity game.
10. Consider any physical contact sport. Modify the rules so that there is absolutely no contact between players at all (not even using touching or flags).

## REFERENCES

1   Available online at http://www.shockwave.com/contentPlay/shockwave.jsp?id=nbrainer&
    preplay=1 (Accessed May 26, 2008).

# 8 Chance and Skill: Finding the Balance

Some games are all chance and have no skill-based player decisions. Most of these are either children's games (like *Chutes and Ladders* and *War*) or gambling games (such as *Roulette* and *Keno*). Children's games are compelling for those who do not have much experience observing random processes. Gambling games are compelling because they offer the possibility of giving the player real money. These games are discussed in detail in Chapter 5, "Elements of Chance."

Some games, by contrast, are all skill. These vary from the simplistic (*Tic-Tac-Toe*) to the complex (*Chess* and *Go*). There are also differences between strategic skill (as with most turn-based strategy games) and twitch skill (found in dexterity games and sports). These games can be fun because of the meaningful decisions that players make. These two types of skill are covered in Chapters 6, "Elements of 'Strategic' Skill," and 7, "Elements of 'Twitch' Skill."

Many games fall somewhere in between. *Settlers of Catan* has many skill-based game-play elements, including trading, building, and resource management. However, it also has random die rolls, a deck of shuffled cards, and a random board setup. *Backgammon* and *Poker* both have strong skill and luck elements. Imagine a game of *Backgammon* without die rolls, or *Poker* without the ability to bet or bluff, and it becomes apparent that some games are better with a mix of skill and chance. Remove either one, and the game fails to be as compelling.

How does a game designer include the correct mix of skill and chance in a game? When is it appropriate to shift a game toward one extreme or the other?

## CONSIDER THE TARGET AUDIENCE

Who is the player?

This is an important question, often the first one that a designer asks. Designing a game for six-year-olds leads to very different results than a game meant for college-age males. Different players have different levels of tolerance for chance and skill. What might be a blast for a young girl quickly becomes boring for an adult, as parents that have played any number of children's games can attest.

## CHILDREN

When first tasked with designing a game for children, many adults assume it's an easy proposition. However, when they start to actually design or playtest the game, they quickly realize just how complicated it can be to make a game that's simple but compelling. Balancing luck and skill is a critical task, and to do this it is necessary to understand the target audience.

First and foremost, children are playing a game to have fun. Teachers may assign them games to learn, but the children's primary goal upon hearing "game" is to have fun along the way. That means that they hope to win and want to have a chance of beating anyone they're playing with, especially their parents. Naturally, for the average child, this requires a lot of luck.

Children younger than five may not yet possess the mental skills necessary to make strategic decisions in a game or to keep track of resources. Games for the young tend to have few, if any, player decisions, and those games have strong elements of chance. Often, these games also allow children to disconnect from turn to turn so that each turn is about immediacy (what do I need to do now?), not permanence and strategy (how will my move last turn and this turn ultimately lead to where I want to be in the end?). As children get older, the number and complexity of skill-based decisions can gradually increase, displacing some of the luck.

Does that mean that children can only play games that are purely luck based? No, particularly if they are playing against each other where they are relatively evenly matched. Physical games like *Baseball* and *Tag* involve skill. So does *Tic-Tac-Toe*.

However, the level of skill involved must go hand in hand with the degree of complexity. Fortunately, the lack of skill and the high degree of luck in many young kids' games doesn't ruin the play experience for most kids. In fact, if asked, most kids will insist they are great at games that involve pure luck. For example, young children often feel that rolling high numbers on dice is a skill.

## COMPETITIVE GAMERS

Players with a competitive streak tend to prefer games with more elements of skill. It provides them with a chance to go one on one with another player, matching brain against brain, reflexes against reflexes, strategy against strategy. The *last* thing a truly competitive player wants is a die roll ruining a perfectly executed and skillful play.

To illustrate this, consider the game *Bowling*. Imagine if there was a 20-percent chance that a strong breeze would push upon the ball causing it to go in one direction or another. Obviously, the average bowler would quit such a game, or at the very least declare that the game was "just for fun" and not a true measure of his skill.

Games like *Chess* are all about skill. *Risk* is partly luck, but only because of its inclusion of die rolls for combat and random card draw. The luck, however, is mitigated by the strategic decision to raid another country in the first place.

Why would designers add luck to skill-based games? Many reasons—it keeps things unpredictable, increases replayability, and it allows players of slightly differing skills to compete. If the better player always wins, then the only games that are interesting are those between two players who are evenly matched. The greater the amount of luck in the game, the greater the potential difference between the players' skill levels while still allowing for a good game. Additionally, even a small random element can take some of the sting out of losing; some highly competitive players play to win, and a part-luck, part-skill game allows the winner to feel like he has superior skill while the loser can feel like it was just an unlucky die roll.

## Social Gamers

There's an interesting discussion that happens whenever lots of people talk about games. Some will vehemently declare that *Monopoly* is a terrible game. Others will insist that it's brilliant. The reason for the difference? We play games for different reasons.

Social gamers—those who like to play games for primarily social reasons—don't care so much about intense strategy. In fact, some may perceive that it takes away from the "fun" of the game. They play *Monopoly* to socialize and to talk with friends. For them, it's all about the play experience, win or lose. These people can tolerate a greater range of luck, although there still needs to be enough interesting decisions (especially those that affect other players, which leads to social play) to create a reason to play in the first place.

The greater the luck in a game, the more even the playing field.

## Professional Players

Games that can be played professionally tend to have extremely strong skill components. Many of these games have no luck at all, such as *Chess* and *Go*. Others do have some luck, such as *Poker* and *Magic: the Gathering*, but the skill elements outweigh the luck (as witnessed by seeing the same people consistently winning tournaments). The skill in *Poker*, for example, is knowing what to keep, when to bet, how much to bet, and when to fold.

## Families

Some games are targeted at families that play games together. These groups may contain a mix of young children, older children, competitive teenagers or adults, and social adults. Designing a game that can appeal to all ages is challenging (but not impossible—witness the commercial success of *Settlers of Catan*). Generally, family games tend to have certain traits:

- Short playing time, so as not to outlive the attention span of youngsters
- Relatively simple rules, so they can be taught to children
- Some elements of luck, to allow children and social players to have a chance of winning against the more competitive players
- Some elements of skill with interesting decisions, to keep the adults entertained and engaged

Note that some luck-based children's games promote themselves as "family" games, even though they do not have enough interesting decisions to keep adults interested. That's where some designers confuse "family games" with "children's games." Designing for the lowest common denominator does not make for a better game; it leads to a game that makes young children happy at the expense of everyone else.

## PLAYTESTING FOR LUCK/SKILL BALANCE

How do game designers know if their game has too much luck or not enough? This is something that becomes apparent when observing playtesters who are part of the target audience.
Some common warning signals:

- **The players are bored.** This can signal that there is too much luck in the game, or that the frequency of interesting decisions is too low. To fix this, convert some random elements to player decisions, or else shorten the length of the game.
- **The players are bored on all *but* their turn.** Find a way for players to engage with other players through gameplay. If your players don't care when other players are taking their turn, odds are your game isn't as immersive as it could be. Alternatively, make player turns short enough that no one has to wait long for her turn.
- **The players never become engaged, or seem confused about what to do.** This can mean that the game is too complicated, or that there are too many decisions, or there is too much information for the players to process. Consider removing some decisions, either by automating them or making them random, and perhaps reducing the complexity of the rules in general.
- **One player beats all of the other players by a wide margin.** If your players have varying levels of skill, this suggests a game that has too many skill elements. Add some randomness to the game. Another possibility is to add a negative feedback loop, some mechanics that make it easier for players who are behind to catch up (see Chapter 2, "Game Design Atoms," for more information on feedback loops).

## EXCHANGING LUCK AND SKILL

There are many specific ways to alter the mix between chance and skill in a game, but they all ultimately come down to adding or removing random elements and adding or removing player decisions that affect the state of the game.

Adding randomness (die rolls, shuffled cards, and so on) increases the amount of luck in the game. Random elements can either be removed by automating them ("All players move forward one space on their turn" instead of "Players move forward 1d6 spaces") or replacing them with a player decision ("Players choose to move from one to three spaces forward on their turn").

Decisions can be added by replacing automatic rules. For example, in the printed rules of *Monopoly*, the player always rolls the dice and moves forward that many spaces on the board. If this were replaced by a decision (say, "You may choose to pay $50 before rolling, and if you do then you roll *three* dice and choose any two for your roll"), then the game gains an actual player decision.

Remember that "player decisions" can involve thinking decisions, but this also includes the split-second dexterity ("twitch") elements that are common in digital games. Games like *Guitar Hero, Dance Dance Revolution*, or the classic arcade game *Track and Field*, while requiring little in the way of strategy, are still considered highly skill-based. Interestingly, when a twitch game exceeds a player's skill, it becomes "luck" for that player. For example, in an FPS like *Halo*, shooting an enemy in the head is an automatic kill. For good players, these "head shots" are part of the skill of the game. For beginners, a head shot only happens occasionally, and only by accident, so it is an element of chance. Ironically, this means that adding an extremely difficult twitch element to a game can actually *widen* the gap between beginner and expert, because experts can exploit it while beginners can't.

Also, remember that there are elements of chance beyond simple random die rolls or shuffled decks of cards. Information that is concealed from the players involves chance, even if that information is not random. This may include things such as the location or combat strength of enemy units, or whether the opponent is planning to throw rock, paper, or scissors next.

## COMBINING LUCK AND SKILL

At their heart, all games are dominated by chance, twitch skill, or strategic skill. Games may have elements of two or even all three of these, but one always has the strongest influence on the game's outcome.

### GAMES OF CHANCE

Games that are primarily chance tend to fall into one of two categories: children's games and gambling games. For children's games, adding elements of strategic skill is acceptable in small amounts, and can even make the game into more of a family game that's palatable to adults. Adding twitch skill is also possible, but if the game is meant to be played between children and their parents, then care must be taken not to give an unfair advantage to the adult. For example, a game that requires players to pick up as many cards as possible in a short period of time gives an advantage to a grown player with large hands.

For gambling games, adding elements of skill (either kind) is quite possible, and if those elements are strong enough, they can even convert the game to being primarily skill-based. *Billiards* is a twitch-based game. *Poker* is a strategy-based game. Both are often played for money.

Additionally, even the illusion of skill is enough to make some gambling games more interesting. Casino games like *Roulette* and *Keno* are pure luck, but they involve the player decision of choosing what numbers to bet on. Some players feel that winning or losing is always in their power, since they have free choice, and this adds a compelling element to an otherwise dull game.

### GAMES OF TWITCH SKILL

It is difficult to add much luck or strategy to a primarily twitch-based game.

The fun of twitch games comes from the mastery of a difficult dexterity challenge. Think of some of the more challenging painting puzzles in *Okami*. Any elements of chance serve to remove control of the outcome from the player, which reduces the ability of a player to master the game, which in turn makes the game less fun. Imagine if you just lined up the perfect shot in a shooting game and then your gun jammed; would this be fun, or would you feel like you were robbed?

Tactical elements are common in twitch games, especially those that involve shooting. However, heavier strategy (especially of the turn-based variety) can be disruptive and can remove the player from the flow of the game. Twitch games are an adrenaline rush, and stopping the action so the player can strategize is a bit like going on a five-mile run and then stopping every few minutes to do a crossword puzzle.

### GAMES OF STRATEGIC SKILL

Ironically, while adding strategy to a twitch game is unsettling, adding minor twitch elements to a strategy game can be a pleasant way to break up long stretches of strategy with a bit of action. Consider the popularity of twitch-based mini-games embedded in epic RPGs.

Adding luck to a strategy game can widen the audience by allowing players of differing skill levels to play, while still allowing the weaker player to win occasionally. On the other hand, too much luck can take the thrill out of winning, if a player feels that he only won because of favorable card draws or die rolls. Ultimately, the amount of luck that is acceptable to add depends on the target audience. Competitive gamers will generally tolerate only a small amount of luck, while social and family gamers can accept larger amounts.

## CHALLENGES

In the following challenges, you are asked to take existing games and modify the mix between skill and chance. Good luck. Or, good skill, depending on how you look at it.

### CHALLENGE 1—*RISK* FOR KIDS

The strategy board game *Risk* is appropriate for older children and teenagers, but has enough strategic decision making to overwhelm younger children. This is a shame, because it has many colorful game bits that would be enticing to a young player (provided the kid is old enough not to eat them).

Create a rules variant for this board game that removes many of the strategic elements and replaces them with chance, in order to make it playable by children ages five to eight.

**Components Required**

- Copy of the board game

**Deliverable**
- Written rules variant

**Suggested Process**

1. **Read the rules.**
   Break down the rules into skill and chance elements.
2. **Systematically change skill into chance.**
   Think of ways to remove decision-making elements or introduce elements of chance.
3. **Simplify, simplify, simplify.**
   Remember the target audience. Reduce the complexity of your rules wherever possible. Look at the complete rules for other children's games, like *Chutes and Ladders, Candy Land*, and *Sorry!*. Try to get your rules to a similar complexity and about the same number of paragraphs. Feel free to add or remove components that would help you achieve this.
4. **Shorten the playing time.**
   The original game lasts longer than a typical child's attention span. Modify your rules further to keep the playing time around 30 minutes or so.

**Variant**

Use a different strategy board game. Some examples are *Chess, Stratego*, and *Othello*.

For additional challenge, instead of making a children's game, make it a family game that can appeal to all ages.

## CHALLENGE 2—ADULT CHILDREN'S GAMES

*Pretty Pretty Princess* is a children's game with virtually no skill involved. The game comes complete with princess attire for each player—earrings, a ring, a bracelet, and a necklace. There is also a single crown. The person to collect all her pieces first, as well as the crown, wins the game. Players move around the board by using a spinner that tells them where to go and what item to pick up. Some spaces list a specific item to pick up, while others give the player their choice of items. The game also comes with a black ring, which prevents the player from winning until someone else is forced to take the ring from them. Players periodically take things from each other and put things back in the pot, too.

Modify the rules of this game to make it a family game, so that it is more interesting to adults, too. You are free to change the overall narrative of the game, but the basic structure of play must remain the same.

**Components Required**

■   Copy of the original game

**Deliverable**

■   Written rules variant

### Suggested Process

1. **Change chance into skill.**
   As in the previous challenge, identify the individual mechanics of the game so that you know what could be modified to add decisions or remove randomness.
2. **Don't go too far.**
   Remember that the modified game should still be enjoyable by kids, as well as adults. Keep the playing time short, keep the theme, and keep some elements of chance. Don't add so many rules or such deep decision making that it's impossible for kids to play.
3. **Create deliverable.**

### Variant

Use a different children's game. Examples include *Chutes and Ladders*, *Candy Land*, and the card game *War*.

For a change of pace, instead of making this into a family game, make it a game targeted at competitive adults. (Doing this requires adding much deeper strategic elements and removing most of the chance.) In this case, your modified game is likely to be extremely different from the original.

## CHALLENGE 3—FOG OF STRATEGY

For this challenge, choose an entirely skill-based, non-digital game with no elements of chance at all, such as *Connect Four*, *Chess*, or *Go*. To adapt this game for less competitive players, you're going to add some chance. Specifically, add "fog of war": your opponent's pieces are hidden from you (and vice versa) except under certain conditions. In video games, when a fog of war is used, it means that you can only see what your characters in the game see. So, if your character's sight is blocked by a mountain or a house, you can't see what's there either. Some games employ cloud cover to give this effect. Others just don't show enemies or objects until they are in the character's line of sight. In this non-digital challenge, maybe you can see your opponent's pieces if they are within a certain number of squares of yours, or maybe you can choose to look at a specific square on your turn. It is up to you how "visible range" is defined in the context of the game.

You may change the rules of the game as needed to support fog of war, but try to keep the spirit of the game intact otherwise.

### Components Required

- Copy of the game that you are modifying

**Deliverable**

■   Written set of rules for the modified game

**Suggested Process**

1. **Interpret "fog of war."**
   Fog of war is more common in digital than non-digital games, because the computer can keep track of hidden information. In non-digital games this is more difficult without using a person who is not playing to be a moderator. Think of ways to hide information from one player or the other, without requiring the players to verify each other's moves or provide information that they don't know themselves.
2. **Try it out.**
   Play your modified game. What effect does hidden information have on the gameplay? Do you feel it is more luck-based? Do you find the modification more fun than the original?
3. **Create deliverable.**

## VARIANT

One well-known non-digital game that features fog of war as its primary mechanic is the board game *Battleship*, where players take turns guessing a location on a grid in an attempt to locate the opponent's hidden ships. However, this game would offer little strategy if the fog of war were removed. It is essentially a guessing game, thus containing more luck than skill.

Instead of taking a strategy game and adding fog of war, try taking the fog of war game *Battleship* and adding strategy elements. Modify the rules so that, even if you *could* see your opponent's board, it would still be a valid strategy game (but the game is still playable even if you can't see your opponent's board).

## CHALLENGE 4—CASUAL *QUAKE*

First person shooter games like *Doom*, *Quake*, and *Halo* are often considered the realm of the "hard-core" gamer. Someone who has never played a game like this can get absolutely crushed by an experienced player. Let's try to even the playing field.

For this challenge, create a concept for an original FPS (or a mod to an existing FPS) that is more accessible to less skilled players. Decrease the impact that player skill (primarily physical skill, in this case) has on the outcome of the game. You're also free to modify the narrative to make it more palatable to these players.

**Components Required**

■   At least one game in this genre or an Internet connection (for research)

### Deliverable

■ Concept doc that includes a list of gameplay features

### Suggested Process

1. **Research the genre.**
   If you're unfamiliar with the FPS genre, play some games of this type, or read reviews of FPS games, or interview friends or colleagues who play them heavily. Are there some FPS games that are considered more "newbie-friendly" than others? Which FPSs carry more prestige for people who win tournaments, because the games are considered more skill based? What mechanics differ between the "casual" and "hard-core" FPS games?
2. **Identify the elements of skill.**
   Where does the skill in FPS games come from? Think of ways to modify it.
   Note that simply making the game more difficult to play (such as having the crosshairs sway back and forth unpredictably, or allowing head shots to be an automatic win) actually make the game *more* skill-based, not less. Extremely skilled players quickly learn to compensate for the added difficulty, while less skilled players remain handicapped by the system.
3. **Brainstorm.**
   Make a list of every way you can think of to make an FPS more accessible to a wider audience, without removing the key features that make it an FPS in the first place.
4. **Create deliverable.**

## IRON DESIGNER CHALLENGE 5—HARDCORE/CASUAL

For this challenge, choose a game that is marketed as a "casual" game. Examples include *Bejeweled*, *Peggle*, and *Chuzzle*. If you are doing this challenge with enough people to form several teams, have each team choose a game to inflict on someone else.

With the game you're assigned, propose a modified version aimed at the competitive, hard-core gamer market. Most casual games are one player, and the game can remain so, as long as it is assumed there is a high-score list or leaderboard. Consider ways to support tournament play that remove as much luck as possible, so that the more skilled players can consistently win.

### Components Required

■ Copies of some casual games or an Internet connection (for research)

### Deliverable

- Description of new game design/modifications
- Written paragraph describing additional metagame elements that could be added to support a healthy competitive environment

### Suggested Process

1. **Play the game.**
   How much of it is skill? How much is luck? How much is skill but *feels* like luck, or vice versa? If the game is unavailable, read reviews or player comments about the game, or interview someone you know who has played it.
2. **Brainstorm modifications.**
   What elements could you add to increase the skill of the game? Note that this doesn't necessarily mean *removing* random elements. For example, *Tetris* uses a random series of blocks, but if the player is notified of what the next block will be after the current one, it allows for better planning and the game is more skill-based as a result.
3. **Create deliverable.**

### Variant

Instead of a digital game, use a card or board game that is often played in a social or family setting. Examples include *Hearts*, *Scrabble*, and *Settlers of Catan*.

## NON-DIGITAL SHORTS

Mixing up skill and luck and playing with the various levels of each produces interesting play dynamics, sometimes resulting in odd play that you hadn't expected. These shorts encourage you to explore the different ways to bring these elements to games.

1. Take any traditional children's game and modify it so that it is enjoyable to adults.
2. Add a bidding mechanic to any children's game of your choice. Consider, for example, what would happen if you added bidding to *Candy Land*.
3. Create a tile-based game based on the current CNN.com headline that primarily uses skill, but still has some random element. The game may not be made with anything other than tiles.
4. Select an incredibly dangerous job and make a game about it that integrates both skill and luck.

5. Watch children playing. Then make a game about their play that replicates the skill and luck involved in their play.

6. Every rule has exceptions. Create a family game that has no luck elements at all.

7. Take a primarily luck-based game and modify the rules so that it is instead dominated by twitch skill.

8. Try to create a card game that has equal elements of chance, twitch skill, and strategic skill without any single one outweighing the others. Playtest your creation and keep modifying the mix whenever it seems dominated by one type of chance or skill.

9. In *Poker*, repeated play makes the game more focused on skill than luck. In *Candy Land*, no matter how much you play, it's still luck. Consider the differences between the two games, then add one or more rules to *Candy Land* that keeps it luck-based on a single turn, but skill-based over the play of an entire game.

10. Try this game-design game with two or more players. First, select any non-digital game that you have available. Then, have one player choose a mechanic and roll a die (1,2 = chance; 3,4 = strategic skill; 5,6 = twitch skill). Roll again if your die roll matches the mechanic already. Another player then must modify the mechanic to use the new kind of chance or skill based on the die roll, while still keeping the game playable and fun. See how many rules you can modify in this way until something in the game breaks.

# Part III

# Writing Game Concepts

# 9 What Is Intellectual Property?

Mario. Madden. Master Chief. Duke Nukem. Lara Croft. Each name is video game gold and simultaneously nurtured and fiercely protected by its owners.

In the game and other industries, that gold is referred to as "intellectual property," or IP. In a nutshell, intellectual property is an idea or a collection of ideas that is owned by someone or something and is the result of creative work. A quick scan of the shelves of any game retailer or online site reveals just how pervasive IPs are in games. In fact, in any given year, the majority of best-selling game titles are derived from pre-existing IP. These games are either sequels to previous games in the series or licensed titles usually coinciding with a major movie release.

The preponderance of licensed IPs leads some to say innovation in games is dead. They reason that when using IP, it's impossible to leave a mark all your own. Others find room for innovation even while using an IP. After all, when it comes to games, innovation isn't found in the name, but rather in new game mechanics. The one thing that everyone seems to agree on is that, for better or worse, IPs are part of the reality of making games professionally.

## Types of IP

IP comes in several forms, from amazingly valuable to utterly worthless. In the game industry, three basic types of IP are frequently discussed:

- Original IP is developed by or for the IP holder and, in the case of the game industry, is owned by the publisher or developer. The IP has yet to be attached to any other game or any product in any medium. Successful original IPs like *Warcraft* or *Halo* are very profitable for the IP holders since no licensing fees need be paid. We tend not to hear from unsuccessful IPs again unless they are embarrassingly unsuccessful, in which case they show up (usually heavily mocked) on YouTube.
- Licensed IP is pre-existing IP that is licensed for use in a video game by the publisher or developer. *Spider-Man*, *Dungeons & Dragons*, and *NBA* are all examples of licensed IP. Publishers pay a fee or a royalty to use IPs in their games.
- Sequels are subsequent releases of either original or licensed IP. Sequels are covered in full in Chapter 10, "Creating Sequels."

In a nutshell, any collection of ideas that represents something of creative value is IP.

## Why IP?

Publishers and developers gravitate toward licensed IP for one reason above all others—risk mitigation. By partnering with known successes—whether a sequel, a licensed title, or both—publishers hope to maximize the sales of the title and minimize the expense required for it to gain recognition and sales.

Consider the IP spectrum of the *Madden* series by EA Sports:

- John Madden
- NFL
- Football teams
- Individual players
- EA Sports
- Previous *Madden* titles

The game is fully loaded with IP. While the *Madden* series has long since carried its own weight, in the early days, the fact that it featured the real players, the real teams, and John Madden himself had a tremendous effect on its success. Players recognized the title, the teams, and the players, and they understood what the game was about all without opening the box. The IPs alone carried a certain amount of built-in player trust.

It's the same reason advertisers use celebrity endorsements for their products. Publishers hope that players will want to purchase the game based on the IP alone, regardless of the game's quality. The Infogrames PC title *Survivor: the Interactive Game* was universally panned by critics, but sold well based on the strength of its IP alone.

In contrast to *Madden* and other licensed titles, developers and publishers create their own IP whenever they put a name on a game. If the IP develops into a successful series, it can bring its owner an incredible return on its investment. For instance, IPs like *Blood-Rayne*, *Silent Hill*, and *Resident Evil* have made it to the big screen, becoming licensed IPs in another industry. Mario himself has appeared in over 100 games and been featured on everything from lunch boxes to clothing to books.

## WORKING WITH AN IP

While most professionals would like to work on their own original IP—there's not a game developer out there, real or potential, who doesn't have an idea for a game—the reality is that most in the mainstream game industry will be working on games attached to a license for at least part of their career. Generally, developers don't get to choose what license they work with, either. Rather, you are given a license and told to make a game with it as best you can. Sometimes, you get to work with *Star Wars*; other times you get *Barbie Horse Adventures*.

How does this happen? In many cases, a publisher will approach a developer and that developer will in turn approach the design department. "BigName Publisher is looking to get a proposal for [insert IP name here]." It might be a television show, a movie, or a book. The designers will then be tasked with creating a proposal—known as a "pitch"—for the company to hand over to BigName Publisher. Usually, designers aren't alone in this effort, either. BigName Publisher has likely approached five or six developers, hoping to cherry-pick the best of the lot.

It's not all big publishers and big names, though. With the growth of the serious game market, the range of IPs has become somewhat dizzying for developers and requires all game designers to become exceptionally versatile. Corporate training games, advergames, flash games, online games, board games, and ARGs all contribute to the IP landscape. It's quite conceivable that one could be designing a *Home Depot* game just as easily as one could be working on the third game in a series, similar to the way Neversoft completed *Guitar Hero III*.

Fortunately for designers, the skills required are the same: research, know your constraints, honor the player, and develop a solid core mechanic.

## RESEARCH

The late Marlon Brando was often said to be a method actor. He threw himself wholly into his roles and lived them. It's no accident that he's credited as being one of the greatest actors of all time. For designers working on IP, the "method" process works well, too.

How does it apply?

When designers first begin working on an IP, whether new or pre-existing, odds are they know little about it. Even if they *think* they know a lot, when it comes to putting these thoughts on-screen, designers often find they know a whole lot less than the licensor. The viewpoint of a fan is different from the viewpoint of the designer. As a fan, you're enjoying the experience. As a designer, you're actually trying to figure out what about that experience is exciting to others. Even for new IPs, this holds true. If your new game IP *Boru* is based on the Irish High King Brian Boru, there are many fans of Irish history that will be attracted to your game and expect a certain amount of authenticity from it and from you as its designer.

So designers need to do research—a lot. Naturally, the amount of research you do depends on the amount of time that you have before the publisher or IP holder expects to see a proposal. You may have several months to prepare the proposal, particularly for serious games that issue "RFPs" (requests for proposal), or only several hours. If it's your own IP you're developing, you have all the time you want or until you run out of money to finance your research, whichever comes first.

Designers must throw themselves into the player's role and develop excellent research sources *before* a proposal hits. Knowing where to go for that research or whom to contact is key, particularly when developing a new IP. For an existing IP, it's important to take into account previous games that have been developed using the same IP. No one appreciates a reinvented wheel, and learning what went right and wrong in previous games can be invaluable. Comparative products are also analyzed. If someone's made something very similar to your intended product or with a similar IP, take a look.

For students, Wikipedia is a regular starting place. However, it's often little more than that. Since Wikipedia is community-generated knowledge, it can't be relied upon for accuracy. In fact, the listing for a former employer of one of this book's authors is filled with errors and missing much critical information. Many professors also don't consider it a credible, citable source. In any case, the IP holder itself is a far better source of information. Any IP worth the time has a Web site devoted to it, usually created by the IP holder itself. Furthermore, most IPs have all kinds of articles written on them, and college libraries, particularly online libraries, are excellent reference sources.

If you're lucky, someone on your team may be a huge fan of the TV show that's up for a pitch. It might be a serious game and require one or more on-site visits. Often, the most important research you do will be a series of simple questions directed at those who asked for the proposal. The answers will become your constraints.

## KNOW YOUR CONSTRAINTS

When someone approaches a developer with a licensed IP, the constraints conversation usually goes one of four ways:

- They already know the game they want you to make, know the fundamentals of game design, and have made a credible suggestion.
- They already know the game they want you to make, have no idea about the fundamentals of game design, and have suggested a game that borders on horrifying.
- They already know the game they want you to make, and it's just like a recent hit, only "better" or "different."
- They have no idea what they want to make, and are relying on you to tell them.

Seriously.

Once the IP in question has been disclosed—whether it's a game sequel, a movie tie-in, or a book license—it's up to the designer or team of designers to ask the right questions during that initial meeting to nail down the constraints for the project (See Chapter 1,

"The Basics," for more information on constraints).

With the key questions out of the way, there are other questions that designers should ask their client that are particularly important when working with licensed IP:

- What is the target audience for the game?
- What is the desired rating for the game? (Although the game won't be rated by the ESRB until it's nearly finished with production, if at all, publishers have an ideal rating in mind and strive to develop a game to fit that rating.)
- Do you have any particular genre or type of game in mind?
- Are there any features that you'd like to see in the game?

In addition to these constraints, each IP may have its own particular set of do's and don'ts. For very famous IP characters, there is a whole set of behaviors that the IP holder routinely disallows or demands. If the game involves real-life celebrities, similar stipulations may apply. For instance, the celebrity might not want players doing to them what they've seen done to other video game characters (like being blown to bits by a rocket launcher, flung off a building, run over by a car, trapped in a room until they wet themselves, and so on).

Similarly, sometimes an IP holder may not own the rights to use the likenesses of all the people that we commonly think of as part of the IP. For instance, *Star Trek* is owned by Paramount. However, Paramount doesn't own the actors' likenesses. As a result, developers of at least one *Star Trek* game had to secure the rights from each individual actor who appeared in the game. Conversely, the WWE pro wrestling group owns all the IP rights to its moves, personas, and everything else. So it was not necessary for the same developers to individually secure those rights.

Above all things, developers must honor the IP and decide where it fits best within the room left by the constraints. Consider a license like *Dora the Explorer*. The IP alone suggests certain constraints—an E-rated game targeted at children, for instance. It's also highly unlikely that the IP holders would welcome a game in which the characters were run over one by one or put up as gun fodder in a FPS.

Developers will also want to see what previous games bearing the same IP have been done, if any exist.

### HONOR THE PLAYER

In all the talk of what the IP holder, publisher, and developer want from the game, don't forget the player. After all, it's who you're making the game for. If the player doesn't like it, *no one* will like it. Ask yourself and your fellow designers what key things the player expects from a game bearing your assigned IP.

If your game is about Disneyland, what will players expect to see and do? How about Wal*Mart or The Marines? Different IPs raise different expectations. These expectations generally hold true whether it's a tycoon game or a massively multiplayer RPG. What actions would the player take in these situations or places, and what possible roles could the player play?

The MDA framework, available online at http://algorithmancy.8kindsoffun.com, also provides a great reference to analyze the player's expectations. What is the overall aesthetic (or feeling) evoked by the IP? What about it evokes that feeling? Players will generally expect to feel the same when they play the game. If the movie scares you, so should the game.

### THE CORE OF THE GAME VERSUS THE CORE OF THE IP

Like games, every IP has its own core, which is the message that the marketing department of the IP wants to get across. However, that core may not translate so well into the video game world.

For instance, consider an IP like the classic and award-winning book *A Clockwork Orange*. The book contains an incredible amount of sex and violence, and both of these things are central to the theme of the book. This content would very likely earn it an Adults Only (AO) rating if that "core" were directly transferred to a video game world.

- [Game name] is about ultraviolence.
- [Game name] is about sex.
- [Game name] is about ultraviolence and sex.

While it's workable, it's not likely *profitable*. No AO-rated game would be sold in the great majority of retail stores.

So the IP's designers need to find a way to preserve the intent of the IP if they are unable to translate its core perfectly from one medium to another.

## CHALLENGES

IP. Love it, hate it, and torture others with it. The challenges in this chapter are meant to perfect your ability to work dexterously with IP.

### CHALLENGE 1—CARE BEARS IP

Congratulations! Your development team has been approached by Hasbro. They are planning on revitalizing Kenner's Care Bears series of toys with major media promotions, and they want part of that rollout to be a new video game created by your development team.

They want a game that goes back to the origins of the license: the original 10 bears. The bears that were added later (and the Care Bear Cousins) will be reserved for sequels if your game is successful.

Your game concept should be true to the license. No blood or decapitation, for example. Keep it rated E for Everyone.

One additional constraint: As part of the release, Hasbro wants the game to target young children (and nostalgic older children) of both genders.

#### Components Required

- Internet connection for research

**Deliverable**

- Pitch, including at least the following: game genre or brief description of gameplay, list of major game features, and list of major characters (playable characters and villains, if any)
- Sample screenshot

**Suggested Process**

1. **Identify important examples.**
   Take a moment to think about the licensed games that you have played that were either really good or really terrible. Write them down in two columns, like so:

   Licensed Games that r0x0rz        Licensed Games that suxx0rz

   Pay particular attention to groups of games that use the same license, where some of those games were good and others were bad. Highlight those groups.
2. **Identify design rules.**
   Look for common themes, trends, and patterns in your list. What is it about the good games that make them work in a way that the bad games just don't? What is the difference between a good and bad use of a license? After comparing, you may want to come up with your own list of design rules when making use of a license.
3. **Research the license.**
   Learn about the Care Bears license. (Because you just know that no one else on your development team will admit to being a guru on the subject.) Answer the following questions:
   - What is the appeal of the license? You may not like it yourself, but why would a fan of the IP like it?
   - List the main characters and briefly describe their characteristics.
   - List the "rules" of the world—what happens in this license that is different from the real world, and what kinds of things never happen there?
4. **Research the market.**
   Learn about the limits and desires of your target market. If your game is to be developed for children under six, then reading is likely out of the question. For even younger kids, use of a controller might be beyond them.
5. **Brainstorm.**
   In a group, discuss potential concepts.
6. **Create deliverable.**

### Variants

Choose a different license for both the research and game-design challenges.

Choose an IP that you have heard of, but do not understand how it could possibly be as popular as it is. Licenses for children (especially those of the opposite sex from you) tend to be the most instructive.

Choose a good IP, like an Academy Award–winning movie of old that's yet to be made into a video game. Select your own target market and rating level.

### CHALLENGE 2—ADD AN IP

Most game developers (especially designers) have a pile of game concepts that they would love to make some day. Every now and then, they get to pitch one of their concepts to a publisher that responds by asking if they can adapt the concept to fit a particular license. For the purposes of this challenge, you will pretend that Clarence Darrow never existed, that the game *Monopoly* was never published, and that you have just come up with an idea for a real-estate game. You have pitched the concept to Electronic Arts; they are excited, but they don't see this game going anywhere as an original IP. Luckily, they have just secured the *Dukes of Hazzard* license, and they are asking you to redo your pitch to incorporate the license.

Take the classic board game *Monopoly* and change it to include this license. Also suggest at least one change to the game rules to make the game a better fit for the license.

### Components Required

- A copy of *Monopoly* for reference (optional)
- An Internet connection to research the license
- Sheet of posterboard and 2d6, if making a functional board game

### Deliverable

- Prototype-level functional board game or
- Production-grade functional board game

### Suggested Process

1. **Read over the rules to *Monopoly*.**

### *Monopoly Mods*

*Keep in mind that most people do not play this game by its original written rules. Money on free parking and double money for landing on "Go" are all mods to the original Monopoly (which was, by the way, a mod in itself). Similarly, almost no one employs the auction mechanic, which comes into effect if someone refuses to buy property when he lands on it.*

**NOTE**

2. **Research the license (refer to Challenge 1, step 3 ).**
3. **Research the market (refer to Challenge 1, step 4 ).**

   Remember to honor the player and include the features, individuals, and settings they'd hope to see.

4. **Brainstorm.**

   Dukes of Hazzard is a fun license with lots of possibilities for cool gameplay. Think of the things you wish you could do if you were playing the game, and make a list of these actions. In a group, discuss the similarities and differences between the core of the game and the core of the license. Also, discuss changes in the game rules to increase the similarity.

5. **Create deliverable.**

### Variants

Use a different original game, like *Carcassonne,* or a different license. If working in groups, it's fun and occasionally mean to select a random license and a random game for the opposing group.

Take an idea that you actually have for a game and apply it to a non-digital game or a mod of an existing non-digital game.

## CHALLENGE 3—FIND THE IP

Occasionally, to make a game concept more appealing to a publisher in a pitch, a designer decides to propose a suitable license. For instance, a game about people stuck on an island struggling to survive could adapt itself to the television shows *Gilligan's Island, LOST,* and *Survivor,* or even the movie *Castaway.*

For this challenge, choose a game (this can be either a digital game or a board game) that is an original IP and modify it so that it accurately reflects another popular IP. For instance, consider a *Star Trek* version of *Carcassonne* or a *Transformers* version of *Risk.* In fact, the latter was actually created, as were other famous IP versions of *Risk.* Ideally, find a license that would not require significant changes to gameplay or seem an odd fit for the game. Going back to a previous challenge, a *Care Bears* version of *Risk* seems unlikely.

### Components Required

- Internet connection to research proposed IP (optional)
- Board game to apply found IP to
- Components for a prototype game

### Deliverable

- Prototype game of any medium

**Suggested Process**

1. **Decide on a game.**
   Select a non-digital game that you currently enjoy playing. It can be any game at all, so long as it is non-digital. It's recommended that you don't select *Risk*, though, since we've used it heavily in this challenge already.
2. **Brainstorm possible IPs.**
   Consider IPs that might be a fit for the game selected in step 1. It helps to identify the core dynamic of the game and then search for IPs with similar core dynamics. If the dynamic in your game is about exploring new territory with risk, it might be a good fit for *Star Wars* or *Battlestar Galactica* or even *Ice Road Truckers*.
3. **Research the license (refer to Challenge 1, step 3).**
   Remember to honor the player and include the features, individuals, and settings they'd hope to see.
4. **Create deliverable.**

### CHALLENGE 4—SHAKESPEARE

Some games take advantage of the vast pool of IP that is already in the public domain. Usually, this is in the form of ancient Roman, Greek, or Japanese mythology, but there is no need to limit the range of our designs to these. There is vast potential in more recent public-domain works that have not even begun to be explored in the medium of games.

For this exercise, you will create a game concept based on any Shakespearean play. Naturally, familiarity with said play will be of great help in creating a concept.

**Components Required**

- Internet connection for research
- Components for prototype game
- Shakespearian play

**Deliverable**

- Prototype board game or
- Pitch for a digital game

**Suggested Process**

1. **Decide on a play.**
   Select a play that you're familiar with or that seems interesting to you. If it's been a long, long time since you and the Bard spent anytime together, Wikipedia provides

quick summaries of each of his plays. Select one that feels like a good fit for your desired difficulty level.

2. **Brainstorm possible approaches.**

   How you implement Shakespeare's work into game form is entirely up to you. Will you try to follow the major acts and the feeling it creates as Knizia did with *Lord of the Rings*? Will you focus on a small component of the story, like Romeo and Juliet's desire to be together or their parents' desire to stop them? Will you perhaps select a unique viewpoint, like that of a sympathetic guard? Wait until you get one that really appeals to you, no matter how difficult it initially seems.

3. **Mull mechanics and features.**

   Exactly how would your approach work from a gameplay perspective? If you're planning to create the pitch deliverable, consider the features that a player would expect in the game. If you're creating a board game, what actions will the player be able to perform? What's standing in their way? Consider your approach versus various dynamics such as territorial acquisition or race to the end.

4. **Create deliverable.**

   A pitch should include the following:
   - Brief summary of the game's storyline
   - Game genre or brief description of gameplay
   - List of major game features
   - List of major characters (playable characters and villains, if any)

### Variants

Use a different public-domain IP. Consider Renaissance artists and their works; famous deceased people of long ago like Brian Boru, Strongbow, and Mary Reid, an Irish pirate; widely celebrated religious holidays; and famous buildings with significant history (for example, the Tower of London). The past is literally filled with video games waiting to happen and excellent IPs that many, many people already know.

### CHALLENGE 5—IRON DESIGNER CHALLENGE (LIVE)

With an IP challenge or two under your belt, the Iron Designer Challenge is an excellent project to take on. The IDC gets you thinking about potential IPs and exploring possibilities you hadn't previously considered. This challenge will require at least two teams of individuals.

For this challenge, write the numbers 1-6 in two columns on a whiteboard or a piece of paper. For one column, ask people to provide you with IPs that would be phenomenally challenging to make into a game. Next, for the other column, ask people to provide you with IPs that would make excellent games, but have not yet been made into a game for one reason or another.

Typically, the list looks something like Table 9.1:

Table 9.1  Example IP List

| Challenging IP | Good IP |
| --- | --- |
| 1. Radio Shack | 1. Psycho |
| 2. Harper's Magazine | 2. Pulp Fiction |
| 3. Paris Hilton | 3. Air Force |
| 4. Eggo Waffles | 4. [Current Popular TV Show] |
| 5. CNN | 5. [Current Popular Movie] |
| 6. U.S. Postal Service | 6. Samuel L. Jackson |

Each of these IPs is undoubtedly valuable and recognizable. However, the IPs in the right column seem to suggest better games to the average designer. If you find that people are having a difficult time coming up with good or bad ideas, start putting up your own bad and good ideas. That almost always gets them moving.

Once your list is created, each team rolls a die. Teams that roll 1-3 get on the challenging list. Teams that roll a 4-6 get on the good list. Next, they roll a die to determine which IP they get. The process is fun and occasionally terrifying, particularly to those teams who end up on the challenging list.

**Components Required**

- Internet connection for research
- 1d6

**Deliverable**

- Pitch

**Suggested Process**

1. **Acceptance and research.**
   When awarded an IP, particularly a challenging IP, some designers feel stuck. "What am I supposed to do with the Radio Shack license?" they say. It's important at this point to think of the full range of video games. Games are much more than the latest console hit. The Radio Shack IP could easily be used to create a training game or an ARG to promote a new store's opening or an advergame to promote the store's diverse collection of electronic components. So, think range, and do your research. By researching topics, you may find things out about the IP that easily shape themselves to a video game world.

2. **Explore the genres.**

   Explore the IP from a variety of viewpoints. Imagine it as a serious game, a casual game, an FPS, or an RPG. In addition to opening your eyes to the possibilities, it's almost always worth a laugh, since some IPs are horrible fits for some genres. Decide on the genre.

3. **Create a feature set.**

   With both IP and genre in mind, consider the requirements of the genre, as well as that of the IP holder. While certain IPs might seem to be particularly funny when manhandled into a particular feature set, the IP holder is unlikely to approve such a list. Take the challenge in the spirit in which it is offered—try to actually make a good game out of the hand you've been dealt.

4. **Create deliverable.**

   The pitch should include the following:
   - Brief summary of the game's storyline
   - Game genre or brief description of gameplay
   - List of major game features
   - List of major characters (playable characters and villains, if any)

### Variants

Ask each team or individual to think of the worst IP possible. When everyone's decided, tell them to pick someone to receive the undesirable IP. That team or individual must come up with a possible design.

## NON-DIGITAL SHORTS

The following list contains ideas for board games, card games, or other games that are free of a digital game component. They encourage you to explore very dynamic concepts in a non-digital format. They are ideal for a non-digital design exercise.

1. Design a card game based around one of your non-game-related hobbies that uses a well-known IP within that hobby.
2. Design an advergame for an activity or organization in which you participate.
3. The target audience is a critical part of any IP. Take an otherwise mature IP, such as *Law & Order*, and design a game based on it but targeted to children age six to eight.
4. Choose a design you have already created from a challenge in this book and add an IP to it without changing the core mechanic. You may add other mechanics to it, however.
5. Choose a classic card game like *Spades* and invent an IP for it; then design a sequel to the game based on that IP.
6. Choose a board game based on IP from a video game and design an expansion for it.

7. Exceptional IPs regularly spawn new IPs based on their content—TV "spinoff" shows are examples of this. Invent a spinoff for one of your favorite video-game IPs and design a board game based on it.

8. Using IPs is all about securing rights. Imagine you're given the IP of a well-known film to make a board game, but you were unable to secure the rights to the lead actor's likeness. Design the board game with that limitation.

9. As an alternative to #8, choose an existing board or card game based on IP and re-design it without some critical element of the IP, such as a major setting, character, or signature move.

10. Select a famous character from a western TV show or film and create a game based on this character.

# 10 Creating Sequels

Licensed IPs aren't the only thing you'll find in major retail stores. You'll also find sequels to licensed IPs!

Sequels to successful, moderately successful, and sometimes downright awful games are a staple of the game industry (and many other industries, for that matter). While players bemoan their very existence, saying that there's no innovation or original mechanics in today's video games, there's a very good reason why publishers still order, ship, and sell sequels: because gamers buy them, no matter what they say.

*Psychonauts* by DoubleFine Productions was an incredibly innovative title. So was *Katamari Damacy*. Both products were praised as "sleeper hits," the polite way of saying, "They should have sold more." The latter, of course, eventually produced a sequel.

## WHY SEQUELS?

As with IP, publishers and developers publish sequels to mitigate risk. With sequels, though, there are a few additional benefits to a developer that may not be immediately obvious to someone not in the game industry. For the sake of discussion, let's say that we're talking about a game called *Bazooka Bomb* (which is a terrible name for a game, so feel free to steal it).

### WE CAN MAKE IT BETTER

With the release of the original *Bazooka Bomb*, the developers did reasonably well. The publisher was pleased, and the game earned out its advance and even began to pay a few royalties. Posts have started appearing on game forums complimenting particular features, complaining about others, and wishing still more features were there. All of this gives developers ideas for the sequel.

Before you go thinking that this is the surefire road to your career in game design, rest assured it's not. The ideas developers get on these boards will, more than likely, only validate the knowledge they already have, or raise issues to which they need to find design solutions. Information that developers collect from reviewers, critical analysis (an emerging field), and fan forums are only a part of the puzzle. Odds are, there were at least 10 things they wanted to get in the game if only they'd had time to do so.

With all this knowledge in hand—having created the game at least once and run, in essence, an enormous pay-for-play focus test—the developers are well equipped to make the next game even better than the one before, particularly given all the feedback they've received. They know what works, and they know what doesn't.

For every great sequel iteration out there, like *Final Fantasy VI to Final Fantasy VII*, there's usually a sequel gone wrong as well. *X-Com: Terror from the Deep*, an award-winning title, was followed up by the somewhat tragic *X-Com Enforcer*, a game that some say broke all the good things about its predecessor. Other times, the sequel can be better than the game that inspired it. Consider games like *Warcraft 2: Tides of Darkness, Mega Man 2*, and *Street Fighter 2*. Most people had never heard of the original games in these series, at least not until after they'd played the "hit" sequel.

## WE HAVE THE TECHNOLOGY

Another benefit of sequels is proven technology, particularly if it's a second or third game in a series on a particular generation of consoles. Things like saving and loading, combat, networking, engine speed, and the like may be improved—sometimes dramatically—but the benefit of starting with a stable code base can't be understated.

So, sequels that share technology sequel-to-sequel save not only time, but money, too.

Sometimes, sequels don't share technology, though. During the 1990s, many longstanding game series made the switch from 2D worlds to 3D tile-based worlds to full 3D smooth scrolling worlds. In the industry at that time, it was not uncommon to hear that a particular game had been "developed from the ground up." It wasn't a feature—it was a necessity.

## WE MAY EVEN HAVE THE CONTENT

Our game example, *Bazooka Bomb*, has lost one of its level designers to another company. As a result, it took the team three months longer to finish the project than expected, and they also delivered it three levels short of what they'd intended. While it certainly wasn't an ideal situation, the game design was scalable, and the net result wasn't noticed by players. If there were supposed to be three more levels in your current favorite level-based game, how would you know?

The designs for the levels had all been completed, but the loss of the level designer left them unpolished. Similar things happen all the time in games—narrative potential that wasn't realized, art assets that were created but not implemented, and cut features that might still have potential, if only they were done a slightly different way or could have slightly more development time devoted to them.

This content has the potential to be used in a sequel or an expansion pack, covered later in this section.

## TYPES OF SEQUELS

Although the term "sequel" is used relatively loosely in the game industry, there are actually different kinds of sequels.

## EXPANSION PACKS

Expansion packs require the player to own the original game from which the sequel came and are designed to expand upon the original play experience. They frequently contain additional narrative, missions, and quests, as well as new weapons and NPCs. The game *World of Warcraft: The Burning Crusade* was an expansion for the MMO *World of Warcraft*.

## MODS

Mods usually take the form of new levels, new missions, and new items. While it's a stretch to call mods "sequels," they are more or less expansion packs made by external groups. *Counterstrike* is arguably the most famous mod, and was created by two college students.

## SEQUELS

When people refer to a "sequel," they are usually referring to stand-alone products that are good to go right out of the box and require no additional software to play. Sometimes, these games allow you to import your character from previous games or to load in your saved game from the previous game in the series. Full sequels may resemble the game upon which they are based, or the designers may have kept the name only, changing much of what was under the hood.

## YEARLY RELEASES

Like clockwork, these games ship with the same basic play set and abilities, but fill the game with new content. The *Madden* series is a perfect example of a yearly game. While similar to expansion packs, yearly releases don't require ownership of any previous game to play.

## SPIRITUAL SUCCESSORS

Spiritual successors are not truly sequels, but are given special recognition among game players and developers for various reasons. For instance, they may be developed by the same group that worked on a previous game together, but with no access to the IP. The indie game *Laser Squad Nemesis* is often called the spiritual successor to *X-Com* and is, in fact, made by the same team of developers.

## CLONES

"Make it just like the *Garden of Eden*, only with a 'live' mode. And two snakes. And a bigger apple."

Whenever a technological or gameplay leap occurs in the game industry that results in significant sales, you can rest assured that some marketing department somewhere is asking for the same thing, only different and better. In the game industry, we (somewhat derisively) call these games "clones." They're not true sequels to a game, but are designed to target the same audience and hopefully achieve the same success as the title that inspired the clone in the first place. Older games like *Myst*, *Doom*, *Ultima Online*, and *Grand Theft Auto 3* (which moved the series into 3D) made marketing departments everywhere ask for something that would target the same audience.

## WORKING ON SEQUELS

Working on sequels to successful games is, in some respects, easier for designers than working on a brand new product. A solid core is already there, and the feature set has been critiqued by the public at large. At the same time, working on the sequel to a popular game can be daunting. Expectations are high, the fans are loyal, and things can go wrong just as easily as they can go right.

In working with sequels, the pattern to successful design is fourfold:

- **Exploit:** Know what made the original game good, and don't screw it up.
- **Expand:** Improve upon many of the features in the game, checking each to make sure that it still strengthens the core of the game in some way.
- **Explore:** Survey the genre overall as compared to your game and try to innovate in some way—be it an online feature or a new play mode such as co-op.
- **Exterminate:** If there are features that make the game's core weaker or detract from features that make the game core stronger, remove them. If your players hate it, it's a safe bet that it should go, too.

This is a simplistic view of sequel game design, and discussions can go back and forth for weeks deciding what needs to be implemented, left alone, or ripped out entirely. Nonetheless, this framework is generally the one that designers follow.

As with any game design, constraints also factor in. If you have three months to make the sequel, getting the garbage out and adding in some new content may be the best you can do. (Believe it or not, some sequels have had three-month development times.)

Here are some common constraints in a sequel:

- **Minding the story:** Some sequels have an added responsibility of carrying on a detailed narrative in addition to a style of gameplay. In the heydays of CRPGs, stories sometimes carried across five, six, or seven games. For the *Wizardry* series, the document that analyzed the story, all its loose ends, and potential future paths was over 70 pages alone. The series spanned 20 years and nine games with two trilogies among them.
- **When what's old is new:** Publishers sometimes farm out sequels to other development teams to work on. For instance, while Harmonix worked on the first two *Guitar Hero* games, *Guitar Hero III* was developed by Neversoft. It's not uncommon in the industry at all. In cases like this, although the game may be quite familiar, its design and technology might not be.

## HONORING THE PLAYER

Player expectation factors into every game design. Designers must think through what players will experience, feel, and learn from their game-to-be and figure out exactly what combination of mechanics can deliver that. When players already have a preconceived notion about what the game is and, furthermore, what the game *should be*, it becomes something the team must devote exceptional attention to.

This is why research is so important in sequel development.

## RESEARCH

There are multiple ways to monitor fan and critical reaction to previous games in a series. One could, of course, just Google the game's name, but that's just going to give you a massive list of reactions, starting with the game's official site. At that official site, you're unlikely to find, "This is the worst game ever made and should be buried." After all, the site was designed to market the game, not steer people away from it.

Instead, explore aggregator sites that collapse many reviews into a single figure:

- GameRankings.com provides an average rating for reviews appearing in online and print media. It is not comprehensive, but covers all the larger bases. A fault of the list, however, is that it rates Joe's Crappy Game Blog the same as it rates the larger, more established game review sites.
- Mobygames.com provides its own mobyscore for each game on its site and has an amazing database that contains everything from screenshots to credit information.
- GameFAQs.com provides FAQs (frequently asked questions) for many games. Looking at a couple of the top FAQs, you're likely to encounter things like bugs, exploits, and game balance issues in the first game. Often, the FAQ writer can't help but to interject his commentary into the FAQ.
- GameSpot.com, IGN.com, 1Up.com and other sites offer both the reviewer's and players' ratings.

Instead of just taking things at face value, read a good collection of reviews from the top, bottom, and middle of the spectrum.

Another good place to gain information about the game is at community boards supported by the company as well as those maintained outside the community. These generally vary from series to series.

## CHALLENGES

As a budding game developer, the odds are good that you'll work on a sequel to a game before you work on an original game, unless you enter the indie game or serious games space. Far from a bad thing, it's actually one of the best ways for a developer to start in the game industry. Let's face it—*any* way you get your start in the game industry is a good way to start.

### CHALLENGE 1—LET'S DO IT RIGHT THIS TIME

Choose a game with a GameRankings or MobyGames score of 65–75 percent—that is, not terrible but certainly not great—and that has no sequel. First, research the original game by reading multiple professional reviews to get a consensus on what the game's best and worst features are. Then brainstorm what an ideal sequel would be like. Finally, write a one-page proposal for a sequel, giving a short core description and a feature list (assume the same ESRB rating and target audience as the original game). If problems exist with the interface, you're encouraged to include a concept sketch of the new interface in your pitch.

#### Components Required

- Internet connection (for research)
- The original game and a machine to play it on (optional)

#### Deliverable

- List of the strengths and weaknesses of the original game
- Proposal for a new game giving a short core description and a feature list
- Discussion after completion

#### Suggested Process

1. **Identify important examples.**
   Think about sequels you've played that were either significantly better or significantly worse than the original game. Separate the franchises into two groups (better sequels and better originals). What do the pairs of games in each group have in common? What are the common differences between the two groups?
2. **Identify design rules.**
   What do the pairs of games in each group have in common? What are the common differences between the two groups? After discussing, come up with your own list of design rules when making a sequel.
3. **Research your original game.**
4. **Brainstorm.**
   In a group, discuss potential concepts. Agree on a single concept and flesh out some basic details.
5. **Create deliverable.**

## CHALLENGE 2—CREATING MONOPOLY 2

Design a full board game sequel to the classic *Monopoly*. This should not just be a thematic update (like *Monopoly: Here and Now*). Instead, update the game mechanics.

### Components Required

- Tokens of various sizes and shapes, posterboard, index cards
- A copy of the original game (optional)

### Deliverable

- A complete, playable physical game prototype
- Written rules

### Suggested Process

1. **Brainstorm ideas for what to keep, what to improve, and what to remove.**
   Start by thinking about the original game. What are the greatest gameplay moments, the ones that make playing worthwhile? What mechanics are the root cause of those aesthetics? Make sure that you keep those mechanics. Are there any things you always wanted to do in *Monopoly*, but couldn't do because the rules prevented you from doing so? What are the most boring or frustrating parts of the game? Can you think of a way to improve those parts to make them more fun? Can you think of a way to remove them entirely without ruining the rest of the play experience? Are there any aspects of the game that players will expect to be in a sequel? Make sure you don't remove anything that is an audience expectation. For the desired length, do you think the game needs more strategy or more luck? Can you make any changes to shift the balance one way or the other? (See Chapter 8, "Chance and Skill: Finding the Balance," for more information on the tradeoff between chance and skill.)

2. **Write a tentative set of rules.**
   Bring together the results of your brainstorming into a coherent set of rules that all of the designers in your group understand. The rules may not be complete or well organized yet—in fact, they probably won't be—but you should have a rough draft. Agree on a few changes and run with them. Remember that games are an interactive medium, and no matter how much we talk about the rules and what *might* happen during play, you can't be sure until it actually *does* happen.

3. **Build a prototype.**
   Create the components for your sequel. Do not put very much time or effort into your prototype at this point; you will surely find rules that need to change, and it is much harder to force yourself to make needed changes if you created "the perfect board" right off the bat. Prototypes should be quick and dirty, but playable, and ready to change at a moment's notice.

4. **Playtest in your group.**

Play your prototype. Take notes as you run into rules clarifications, balance issues, or parts of the game that are not as fun as you thought they'd be. Don't be afraid to change the rules as you play. This playtest isn't about winning; it's about figuring out if the game itself "works." Continue revising and playtesting until your group can complete and enjoy a game without running into any major issues. Completing a game is one thing—enjoying it is another. Make sure that your game is fun to play. If people don't want to play it again, that's a sign that it's not a good game. Also revise your rules document as you play, making sure that all of your rules are contained in the document and that it is organized in a logical, readable fashion.

5. **Create professional-quality prototype (optional).**

At this point, it is worth creating a professional-looking prototype. Make a copy of your game components with final-quality artwork. Create nice-looking tokens, and print any cards you may have on cardstock paper. (You may need to visit a professional printer to do this.)

### Variants

Choose another classic board game to modify, such as *Risk* or *Parcheesi*.

### CHALLENGE 3—RETURNING FROM THE DEAD

Remember that great game *Shadowrun* for the Sega Genesis? Neither do we, but we hear it was really fun from everyone who was a gamer in the 1990s. Let's call it a "sleeper hit."

Suppose this game was made available for download on the Wii™'s virtual console, and it took off with a new generation of gamers that rediscovered this old classic. And suppose that with all the hype, your studio (and several others) was contracted to propose a modern sequel on the Wii.

Create a concept pitch for the sequel.

### Components Required

- Internet connection (for research)

### Deliverable

- One-page concept pitch for the sequel or
- Three concept sketches *each* of a potential interface and a main, updated character for the game (each concept sketch should differ from the others and show an attempt to explore possibilities) or
- Discussion after completion

### Suggested Process

1. **Research the original game.**
   If you are unfamiliar with the game, read reviews and FAQs to familiarize yourself with the game's genre, strengths, weaknesses, and overall mechanics. If you happen to be lucky enough to own an original Sega Genesis and *Shadowrun*, so much the better. It's not necessary, though.
2. **Brainstorm.**
   In a group, discuss potential concepts. What did players like? What should remain the same? What should be improved? What should be removed? What new innovations in the action/RPG genre (ever since the original game was released) could be adapted to enhance the gameplay of the original?
3. **Create deliverable.**

### Variants

Do this challenge with a different game. Choose a game that is more than 10 years old, that was well received (high review scores, or at least a general sense of nostalgia among gamers that were around when it was released), but that never launched a true sequel or launched its last sequel more than 10 years ago.

Select a recently released game that you've played, and create its spiritual sequel. Be sure to include your own design touch and features that the original game's fans would enjoy without stealing the original game's design outright.

## CHALLENGE X+1: THE SEQUEL

Throughout this book, there are many game-design challenges. If you're working through these challenges as a group, you've likely created some game ideas that you'd rather not admit you created. It happens to most designers at some point or another. For the sake of this challenge, though, we're going to ask that you not only remember that less-than-stellar effort, but do it right this time. Create a pitch for a sequel to a game that you or your teammates proposed or created in a previous challenge.

### Components Required

▨  None

### Deliverable

▨  Informal presentation after completion or
▨  Prepare a "sequel" to whatever deliverable was previously created

### Variants

Select an IP that one would not naturally associate with an entertainment software project, such as stamp collecting, the United States Postal Service, or Canadian immigration. Spend 10 minutes trying to create a core and feature set for the IP you've selected. Next, select another designer or another team, and task them with creating the sequel to the project that you have created.

## IRON DESIGNER CHALLENGE 5—INFAMOUSLY BAD (LIVE)

After you're comfortable making sequels, try this exercise. Split into teams of two to four individuals.

Have each team choose a really horrible game, one that was critically panned (score of 40 percent or less on GameRankings or MetaCritic) and that thankfully never had a sequel.

Or use this list:

- *Big Rigs* (PC)
- *Trespasser: Jurassic Park* (PC)
- *Fight Club* (PS2) (M-rated)
- *BMX XXX* (GameCube) (M-rated)
- *25 to Life* (PS2) (M-rated)
- *Superman* (N64)

Each of these games is infamous within the industry (and within the gamer community). Each lucky team gets assigned one of these games (by any means that your group chooses: for example, randomly assigned by die roll; leader's choice; or each team gets to choose another team to inflict their game on). Your mission is to create a serious concept pitch for a sequel, a pitch so inspiring that you might actually convince a publisher to let you have a go at it.

### Components Required

- Internet connection for research

### Deliverable

- Informal presentation after completion or
- Formal product pitch
- 3–5-page concept document

**Suggested Process**

1. **Acceptance and research.**
   After you've selected your game, go online and research it. Read some of the bad reviews. Look for game footage on YouTube. Have fun enjoying the bad.
2. **Brainstorm a core.**
   Whether the game is good, bad, or anywhere in between, the rules are still the same. No matter how bad a game is, it is sure to have some tiny nugget of fun in it somewhere (even if accidentally). Even if not, you can at least look at it and decide for yourself where the original designers thought the fun was *supposed* to be. Decide not only what was so bad about the original game, but also where the potential was: Why was the game so disappointing, and what *could* it have been? This is the direction you should be thinking about for your sequel
3. **Create a feature set.**
   Create a list of four to five features that support the core of the game. Remember that people have certain expectations of a sequel, so completely jettisoning everything that made the previous game distinctive won't work. After all, if you didn't plan to use anything from the previous game, why would you be using the IP?
4. **Create deliverable.**

## NON-DIGITAL SHORTS

Sequels and expansion packs are big in the non-digital market. Just ask anyone who's ever played *Magic: The Gathering*. These shorts give you an opportunity to work with existing games to find expansion solutions.

1. Expand: Design an expansion pack for *Risk*. Include a smaller board with at least five new nations than extends the original board.
2. Explore: Choose a successful territory game (such as *Settlers of Catan*) and redesign it to include a popular feature from another territory game.
3. Exterminate: Choose a mediocre board game (such as *Sorry!*) and identify at least two weak mechanics. Redesign the game by eliminating or replacing these mechanics.
4. Design a sequel for *Chess* based on WWII combat instead of medieval.
5. Choose a lengthy, thematic board game (such as *Axis & Allies* or *Betrayal at House on the Hill*) and redesign it as if it had been created as a trilogy of three separate games.
6. Create a clone of a classic card game (such as *Hearts*) that incorporates "new" technology —tradable/collectible cards, multi-sided dice, or a tile-based board.
7. Create a mod for *Monopoly* with the theme "slum lords and mob bosses." Note: as a mod, you *must* use the original board and all original tokens.

8. Choose a theme that happens annually or bi-annually (such as political elections or holiday seasons) and design a tile-based game intended for yearly release.

9. Design a sequel to *The Game of Life* based on progression of story—what happens after the players reach retirement at the end of the original game.

10. Design a first draft of a collectible card game incorporating 100 cards (two packs of index cards). Use a unique IP or theme that others haven't explored or aren't expecting.

# 11 Targeting a Market

If you get into the game industry and stay long enough, you will work on a pitch that targets a demographic other than your own. Suppose that you're a well educated, student-loan poor person from a small Midwestern city; you may be asked to design a game for the New York Republican Caucus, an expansion pack to a first-person shooter, 10 new missions for an MMOG, or an online casual game for young girls that frequent a specific social network.

"But I'd never work for a company that made games like that."

Yes, you would. The company you join and its current products are not a guarantee of future projects. Companies diversify and create new revenue streams. They are sold off, purchased, asked to work on smaller, special projects, or create functional prototypes for one thing or another. Sometimes, design teams within companies stretch their mental muscle by performing design exercises just like the ones in this book. The ability to rapidly design within any set of constraints is the hallmark of a good designer. Learn to really dance in the medium, no matter what it throws at you, and you'll be much better off.

Some demographics are used quite frequently in the game industry (age, gender) and others practically not at all (race, religion, income level, occupation, political affiliation). Note that the latter categories, while mostly ignored or sadly stereotyped in entertainment games, can quite definitely come into play for serious games.

## WHY DO I CARE? ISN'T THIS FOR MARKETING PEOPLE?

Unlike IP and sequels, targeting a market is not done to mitigate risk (it specifically *limits* the market to the chosen demographics, after all), but to break into an underserved market where the publisher senses an opportunity or has a purpose.

For example, both the ill-fated Purple Moon and the more recent Ubisoft Imagine are making "games for girls"—not because this isn't risky, but because there are a lot of girls out there who are interested in playing video games, and a game that sells to all (or most) of them would be immensely profitable.

On the one hand, a game targeted at a specific market increases "market penetration" (the percentage of people within that market who will buy the game) while decreasing "mass-market appeal." This is a tradeoff, and deciding whether it is worthwhile is indeed what we pay marketers to do.

Once a publisher's marketing people have done their research and determined that a certain target market is worth pursuing, they might issue an RFP (request for proposals) to several developers (just like they do with an IP), and it is up to you, the designer, to create a product proposal targeted at the given market.

In the serious games space, software is often designed not with the goal of selling a zillion units, but instead with achieving a specific purpose. In fact, the software may be given away! For instance, the goal of a particular project may be teaching students how to save money for a college education. Other times, a game's sole purpose may be editorial. In 2007, in fact, the *New York Times* incorporated games as part of its editorial coverage.

## LEARNING ABOUT YOUR TARGET MARKET

Unlike a game based on IP, you do not usually start with a body of knowledge about your target market. In fact, unless you are part of the target market yourself, you probably know very little about what kinds of things will appeal to the market. If you were tasked with creating an exercise game for senior citizens, would you know where to start?

Occasionally, you can find scientific research (most often in the fields of psychology or advertising) that describes individual things that appeal to certain demographics. But a demographic literature search is much more difficult than playing the previous game in a series, as in the case of a sequel, or watching a bunch of television shows, as in the case of IP. It is far more time consuming, and the results of the research may not apply directly to your game.

In some cases, the publisher may have already done this research and will pass it on to you. Sometimes, they do not have this information either, or else they will not make it available to you until after they've accepted your proposal. Other times, you will work with outside subject matter experts. Experienced game designers cultivate connections like these.

No matter how much information you're given, though, do some research yourself by contacting people in your target market and *asking* them what they'd like to see in this game. Don't assume you can figure it out on your own by looking at other content targeted at the same market. Many targeted games (and other entertainment) fail miserably, often because they have (say) a development team full of middle-aged males trying to make a game for eight-year-old girls, and they get it wrong. Even for the products that are successful, it is not always clear why they are successful, and if you copy the wrong parts while missing that one subtle thing that makes those products *work*, your project is dead.

## ABILITIES OF THE TARGET MARKET

"Different strokes for different folks."

There's truth behind every common saying, and this one is no exception. When designing games for different target markets, it's important for a designer to take into account the whole picture.

## READING ABILITIES

One of the most common mistakes made by designers creating indie software designs for children is overestimating their ability to read. In general, children start reading at age four or five, but even then, it's more likely common sight words such as "yellow," "the," "away," and "a," not exactly the stuff of riveting game narratives. Even games without narratives can stop a young kid in his or her tracks with options like "Save Game," "Load Game," or "Start New Game." Some games echo game text with voiceovers to help children follow along.

Young children aren't the only ones who have difficulty reading, of course. One of the authors of this book worked on a serious game project which targeted inner-city teens and young adults. As a mandate of the project, in-game text was off limits, though spoken dialogue was perfectly permissible.

## LEARNING CURVE

For a game-savvy six year old, a video-game controller might be as common as (or more common than) a fork. For older individuals, however, a game controller might be "for kids" and something they just don't understand. No matter how fun a game looks, if the controller's perceived learning curve is too high, people will dismiss it as not worth the effort. It doesn't matter if your controls are actually easy to learn. They won't know that unless they try, and since people often dismiss things *before* they try—that's the perceived learning curve—you won't have that chance to change their minds.

Both the Nintendo DS, whose controller resembles a pen, and the Nintendo Wii, whose controller resembles a remote control, used perceived knowledge to their advantage. Many games that target a larger market even offer a practice mode where players can get familiar with the game without feeling pressure to perform perfectly.

The learning curve goes beyond the controller. Common conventions in games that provide useful feedback for experienced players, like life meters, hit points, subscreens and heads-up displays may be unfamiliar and confusing to someone who has never played a video game before. If you include these elements in a game that targets certain demographics, you may have to take great care to explain what they are and how to use them, without initially overwhelming the player.

## COGNITIVE ABILITIES

There's a reason many six year olds don't play *Risk*. It's the same reason that most serious board game players find *Monopoly* boring as dry white toast—both games fail to challenge the player cognitively. For average six year olds, the level of strategizing necessary to succeed in *Risk* is more than they can muster, so they give up, disinterested or frustrated. Games like *Monopoly* also fail to challenge older players cognitively. As more than one player has said, if the outcome of the game is largely based on luck, what's the point of exercising any mental muscle?

The cognitive challenge present in the game is dependent upon the target market… or will define it.

## LEARNING STYLE

In her book *Gender Inclusive Game Design*, designer Sheri Graner Ray points out that men and women have different learning styles. Men use explorative learning while women use modeling behavior. Men grab the controller and go. Women want to watch first, or at the very least read the manual. Graner Ray advises designers to take these different learning styles into account when creating game tutorials.

## PHYSICAL ABILITIES

When Microsoft released the original Xbox, the controller that shipped with the North American units was too large for many children's hands. Lots of people without "man hands" also found the controller challenging to use. Microsoft later replaced that controller with the "S-type" controller, which was standard in Japan. The lesson is an important one: In creating your product, consider the motor skills of your target audience.

Young children have yet to establish good motor control, and as such, a game that requires precision, provided that's not the main goal, might cause more frustration than fun. The VTech V.Smile console was specifically created for children and features big color-coded buttons that can't possibly be missed. Similarly, older individuals, particularly those with arthritis, may have difficulty with the repetitive pressing and clicking required by many games. The stylus for the Nintendo DS is much easier for many to use.

Physical abilities aren't limited to use of a controller, of course. On the PC, a game that requires a lot of mouse-clicks may prevent someone with arthritis or carpal tunnel syndrome from playing entirely. Requiring extreme precision with the mouse (for example, moving to within a pixel or two of the target) will be impossible for the very young or the very old, or even a normal, healthy adult who just happens to have a cluttered desk or a dirty mouse ball.

## TACTILE DESIRES

From the minute the box is opened, players begin to touch the various parts of the game. Things are labeled "quality" or "cheap" almost instantly, and small touches are noticed. In some games, there is a cloth bag to hold the game bits; in others, there is a plastic bag or no bag at all. From the thickness of the tiles to the quality and weight of the wood used in the tokens, all of it factors into a player's overall opinion of the game. In children's games in particular, the tactile components are extremely important. It is through these pieces that children experience the game. They touch them, put them in their mouths, and sometimes even use them as toys outside of the game.

These tactile considerations are not limited to non-digital games. Unpacking the Xbox 360, many players commented upon the cables that connected the unit to the televisions. Though these cables never entered directly into play, players were impressed by their quality and therefore, impressed by the system as well. Likewise, the Wii, shaped like a remote control, was also familiar to players and therefore failed to set off alarm bells (or the same amount of alarm bells) that a traditional controller otherwise would have.

## FOCUS GROUPS

Focus groups are invaluable to game designers, particularly those targeting a market outside their own experience. By bringing together a group of individuals that represents the product's desired target market, focus groups give designers an opportunity to solicit questions, test theories, and watch their game being played or considered as a concept before the game is released to the general market. The experience often illuminates unanticipated problems, suggests improvements, and validates design decisions you've already made.

Encourage your testers to give feedback by responding positively and not defending your ideas. Nothing can shut down a good feedback session like a developer who defends her ideas, even if they are good ones. Remember, what you hear helps you to refine. It's not a mandate to change things.

For at least one of the challenges in this chapter, we suggest you consider incorporating a focus group as part of the exercise.

## THE MASS MARKET

Targeting a specific market, such as a limited demographic, is in opposition to the "mass market," meaning a game with the goal of selling to as wide a range as possible across *all* demographics. Intuitively, it would seem that mass market games are not targeted at all. In fact, the reverse is true—designers of these games have an understanding of a broad range of demographics in order to avoid excluding anyone.

Eurogames are an interesting case study in mass-market appeal. Also known as "German games" or "designer games," Eurogames were given their name because of the area where many of them were designed and played. In general, they are family games that can be enjoyed by all ages, male and female. *Settlers of Catan* was the first game to popularize the genre in North America; other well-known games include *Carcassonne* and *Puerto Rico*. For the purposes of this book, a Eurogame is a non-digital game defined by the following characteristics:

- **Playable in roughly 20 to 90 minutes.** If a game is too short, adults feel it's over too quickly. If it takes too long, children get bored.
- **Short setup time.** Game setup is busywork required in order to play the game. It's not part of the fun of the game because no decisions are being made.
- **Simple rules, short learning curve.** Children—and many adults—don't enjoy sitting still and listening attentively for 20 minutes while all of the rules are explained.
- **Cooperative, not confrontational.** Eurogames frequently use mechanics that involve player cooperation, such as trading and negotiation, over purely destructive mechanics where one player actively harms another. Confrontational mechanics can cause bitter fights among younger children, and also tend to steer adult targeting decisions in non-optimal directions in order to avoid that same issue. The beauty of co-op play lies in its ability to make everyone feel comfortable regardless of their skill level. New players and expert players can work with one another, each able to take up the others shortcomings. Note that this does not mean the game can't be competitive; cooperative games can still involve intense competition.

- **Contains strategic decision making along with measured randomness, as described in Chapter 5.** Too much luck or unstructured randomness fails to give adults the meaningful decisions that keep them engaged. Too much strategy and children can never win unless the adults let them.
- **Minimal player downtime.** Eurogames, when they have turns at all, often allow players to take actions on other players' turns, or else keep the turns short enough that no one is just sitting around waiting for *their* turn. Players of all ages tend to dislike a game where most of their time is spent waiting.

## CHALLENGES

All games have target markets. Usually, that target comes with the license. At some point in your career, however, you may be asked to create a game targeted toward a specific market. You may be familiar with it, or you may not. If you work for a bigger publisher or in serious games, then learning how to target your games to a specific market is a key skill.

### CHALLENGE 1—GEARS FOR GIRLS

First-person shooters already appeal to a great number of females (witness the Frag Dolls and PMS Clan). But suppose a publisher had the idea of taking the FPS genre and targeted it *exclusively* at females ages eight to 16, and suppose that (against your will) you have been tasked with creating a proposal. Remember that FPSs don't have to involve big, nasty guns, either. Expand the game's horizons, particularly since part of your market is only eight years old.

**Components Required**

- None

**Deliverable**

- A convincing discussion on the target market, including a list of game styles, features, mechanics, and so on that would be desirable—and why.
- Feature list of the product
- Concept sketches or mock-up of the game's HUD (heads-up display)

**Suggested Process**

1. **Bring together a focus group.**
   Find some people in this demographic. (In a class, the instructor may bring some people to the lecture for a group Q&A session, or it may be left to individuals or

groups to find a focus group on their own. For people not taking a class, you're on your own for this.) Keep in mind the difference between asking questions of a group and doing individual interviews. Consider doing a mix of both, to avoid "groupthink."

2. **Identify design rules.**
   Tell your group a little about the kind of game you'd like to make, and ask them what they'd like to see. Start with open-ended questions and get more specific after you've identified broad areas. If the group says they really *like* or really *don't* like something, find out why. (This may be difficult if the group is young enough that it's difficult for them to express complicated emotions; it will be up to you as a designer to draw inferences.)

3. **Brainstorm concepts.**

4. **Create deliverable.**

### CHALLENGE 2—BEYOND DDR

Konami, the makers of *Dance Dance Revolution*, want to expand their current market. However, they don't want you to just create a sequel—they want you to analyze their current hardware, the dance pad, and come up with at least five different uses for it, each of which targets a different market. They'd be even more impressed if your new designs have nothing to do with dancing, or dancing, or revolution. They've hinted that they'd like to see something for senior citizens or disabled individuals, but other than that, they're relying on your ingenuity.

**Components Required**

- A dance pad, or an Internet connection for an image of one

**Deliverable**

- A game proposal using the DDR pad in an innovative way that targets a new audience. The proposal should include an overview, demographic breakdown, feature set and interface mockups, or
- List of five potential markets along with a core and brief feature set for that market, or
- Informal presentation after completion

**Suggested Process**

1. **Brainstorm actions.**
   Aside from dancing, what different things could you do with a dance pad? Think of people you know with varying levels of physical ability and ages. What could they possibly use a game pad like this for?

2. **Determine the feature set.**

   Select one or more possible target markets for your game idea. Next, pause to consider that target market as you create your feature set. If your target market includes young children, having a big "help" section with diet information and recipes may not be the best thing. Your feature set should incorporate three to five different things that are designed specifically with the target market in mind.

3. **Create deliverable.**

## CHALLENGE 3—TARGETING THE EVERYMAN

*Deer Hunter* was a tremendous success with Wal-Mart shoppers. What's surprising to many, however, is that this product was made to order by Wal-Mart itself. They were looking for a game that would appeal to the everyman who shopped in their stores. Now, and for the sake of this challenge, let's assume Target wants something similar but new. Your target market is the 35+-year-old male who's not interested in video games. *Deer Hunter* got him to buy, and this retailer is willing to bet something else will, too.

### Components Required

- Internet connection for research.
- Men's magazine such as *GQ*, *Sports Illustrated*, or *Men's Fitness*
- Focus group (optional, but recommended)

### Deliverable

- A formal pitch presentation to the powers that be at our fake Target. Select several individuals to make up a mock review board, ideally not involved with another design team also working on the same challenge. (Finding actual retail executives is not necessary, probably not advisable, and definitely not as entertaining.)
- A concept document
- Informal discussion after completion

### Suggested Process

1. **Break into groups of three to four people.**
2. **Analyze your market.**

   Who is this "everyman" and what exactly does he like? What does he do in his spare time? What would he do in his spare time if only he had time to do it? For this challenge, you must push yourself beyond the bounds of who you are and what you know (unless you *are* that everyman who is not interested in video games that somehow got his hands on this book). Sports games immediately come to mind, but remember, your everyman hasn't been hooked by *Madden* or the racing games that are out there.

3. **Do market research.**

   Find the most popular magazines for this demographic. What they read could be an indication of what they might play. Explore your local newspaper's "Events" column. Most every city has a variety of events going on. Which events are likely to attract that audience?

4. **Find a focus group.**

   In person, over the phone, or online, establish a focus group and solicit their opinions on hobbies and interests. Each of these might be a possible game. You will return to this focus group with ideas you have for a game. Be sure to ask them what it is they like about a particular event or sport or hobby. These are features you may want to reflect in the game.

5. **Brainstorm.**

   Brainstorm on the research you've done. What games suggest themselves?

6. **Determine the feature set.**

   Select one or more of the ideas and develop a feature set for your game idea. Review the notes or comments from your focus test to develop features that your players thought would be interesting. Your feature set should incorporate three to five different things that are designed specifically with the target market in mind.

7. **Return to focus group (optional).**

   Return to your focus group to discuss the ideas you have for a game with them.

8. **Create deliverable.**

## CHALLENGE 4—CARIBBEAN TARGETED TOURISM

In an effort to expand knowledge of its culture beyond tourism, several Caribbean countries have banded together to create a game series that focuses on the history, culture, people, and art of the individual islands. They want the products to go well beyond the traditional stereotypes people think of and highlight the unique island experiences. In the end, they hope these projects will spur new business opportunities and investment on the individual islands. The products should target middle- and upper-class African Americans in their forties, a lucrative market familiar with West Indian tourism and previously targeted by numerous countries' tourism boards. The nonprofit organization is quick to note that you must do your homework. Previous developers neglected to include other islands, and let the well-known culture of Jamaica speak for the Caribbean as a whole.

### Components Required

- Internet connection for research
- Magazines that target African Americans such as *Ebony* and *Black Enterprise*
- Focus group (optional, but recommended)

**Deliverable**

■ A research analysis report that would be provided to a developer who could, in turn, use this research to develop the game or

■ A formal pitch presentation to the "representatives" of three selected countries. Each ambassador will be traveling with a person from the country's economic development authority. For the sake of this challenge, select three to six individuals to make up the review board, ideally not involved with another design team also working on the same challenge. These individuals need not be from these countries, but should at least read an overview on the country before the pitch. Their goal is to give you feedback on the design.

■ A mock-up of the main gameplay screen and a list of at least five missions, if applicable, and a collection of concept art for the project.

**Suggested Process**

1. **Break into groups of three to four people.**
2. **Select three islands to target.**
   It will be easiest for you if you select islands that speak the same language.
3. **Analyze your market.**
   What attracts people to the Caribbean? What opportunities for businesses are there? If the ultimate goal is to attract people to the islands for investment and business opportunities, explore things someone would invest in, and what businesses make sense. A low labor cost, very high literacy rates, and fluent English speakers have already caused some businesses to set up shops there. Don't forget the amazing beaches and the quality of life. Do your research and take advantage of research that the economic development offices of the target islands have already done for you. Be sure that the game reflects your target market. A quick look at games in game stores shows that the great majority of games do not.
4. **Do market research.**
   When people in the target market are planning a vacation or planning for investment, where do they look? What makes them consider these opportunities? Compare how other countries market themselves to this specific market.
5. **Find a focus group.**
   In person, over the phone, or online, establish a focus group and solicit their opinions on business and investment. Ask them their thoughts on the Caribbean and find out what their initial impressions are. Encourage them to speak about their game-playing habits, if any, and don't neglect to mention casual games.
6. **Brainstorm.**
   Take all the information in and brainstorm possibilities. Will you create one game featuring all the islands or an engine into which each island can be molded?

7. **Determine the core and feature set**

   Determine a core for the project. Due to its very nature, it seems to have several different possibilities. Establish a priority for your project, and focus on that. Develop a feature set with four to five different features *per island*. Islands may share some features with one another.

8. **Return to focus group (optional).**

   As in the previous challenge, return to your focus group to discuss the ideas you have for a game with them.

9. **Create deliverable.**

### Easier Variant

Use all the steps above, but create a deliverable for your home state or country that targets people in another state or country.

### Variant

Create a game for the Irish government that targets Irish Americans. Don't exclusively focus on things like St. Patrick's Day, however. Instead, focus on the reasons why someone would want to visit and invest in Ireland the other 364 days of the year. Ultimately, as with the previous challenge, the game must foster investment and business opportunities in the Green Isle. Feel free to target particular subsets of people, such as Irish-American artists or game developers.

## IRON DESIGNER CHALLENGE 5—THE EDUCATIONAL MMO

Online environments provide a perfect learning environment for people from all over the world. At the same time, they also expose people to players from all over the world. You have received a grant from the U.S. Department of Education to develop an MMO that targets middle-school students and teaches them about a topic of your choice. They also want you to incorporate some kind of mechanic that encourages player retention and maybe even character growth. However, there can't be any violence.

Communication is another issue. Obviously, exposure to other cultures and being part of a positive social network is desirable for this age group. On the other hand, if you have a standard chat interface, anything can (and has and will be) said, including profanity and offensive slurs and epithets. Therefore, you are not allowed any kind of freeform text communication (such as unrestricted chat or message boards). Still, players should be able to communicate with one another and be social... somehow.

### Components Required

■ Internet connection for research

**Deliverable**

- Mock-up screenshot that shows your plan for non–freeform-text socialization
- One-page plan for player retention (what will keep them playing once they try it?)
- One-page design spec for a character-development system sans violence (what do they do to make their characters gain levels?)
- A two-page summary that describes the player experience (what do they do in the game?)
- A formal pitch presentation on the project

**Suggested Process**

1. **Break into groups of three to four people.**
2. **Choose a topic.**
3. **Analyze your market.**
   What types of games do children in grades six to eight play? What are they learning during those grades? Your MMO should incorporate similar learning principles. However, bear in mind that games are excellent teaching tools, and as such, have an opportunity to pull students into the experience.
4. **Consider potential mechanics.**
   Your publishers have asked for two challenging things—socializing without text chat and character development without violence. Spend some time on both of these requests and consider how a game's mechanics could create them. How can you incorporate a social atmosphere without unrestricted text chat? It exists, believe it or not. Explore social networks beyond games and see how other spaces have become exceptionally social without any form of chat at all. For this challenge, however, think of a way that players can communicate through something other than text.
5. **Create deliverable.**

**Variants**

Select a disturbing event or time that happened in the past. Keeping that disturbance in mind, create an MMO that allows people to actually walk in the shoes of those who experienced the topic you've selected.

## NON-DIGITAL SHORTS

Each of the following shorts deals with a different market or a need of the same. The shorts can easily be modified by changing the market requirement for even more options for design.

1. Design a card game in which all the rules are learnable through observation and imitation within the first five minutes of play.
2. Choose a game with a heavy emphasis on text (such as *Monopoly*) and redesign it to require no reading at all.
3. Choose a game with a steep learning curve (such as any miniature game) and redesign it to be playable by children aged 8-10 without adult supervision.
4. Identify one issue or interest that appeals to the middle-aged female demographic and design a game using that as the core.
5. Choose a common video-game time-saving convention, such as the life meter or the inventory screen, and design a tile-based game that teaches non-gamers how to understand this convention.
6. Create a territorial acquisition board game targeted to high-school girls.
7. Create a persistent turn-based strategy game to be incorporated into the curriculum or recreation of an elementary-school class.
8. Create a tile-based game intended to introduce your home country to potential immigrants. Assume the players don't speak your national language.
9. Choose a card or tile game targeted to children (such as *Ruckus* or *Go Fish*) and redesign it for use in a casino, offering challenge and reward on the level of *Blackjack*.
10. Create a game in any medium that's designed to assist some population as it reenters the community from a halfway-house living situation.

# 12 Learning an Unfamiliar Genre

Most of the time, a publisher approaches a developer with a request for a proposal (RFP) with a specific genre in mind. "Give us an MMO targeted at kids," they'll say. "That market's growing more every year."

In a way, this is somewhere between making a sequel and targeting a market. You are, technically, targeting the market of people who like games of a particular genre, and it's expected that the game will conform to that genre in the same (if less restrictive) way that a sequel will conform to its predecessors.

If you've designed dozens of RPGs and played hundreds more, and you're asked to create an RPG, this is not a problem. If you're asked to create a social simulation or a sports game, and you've never designed one, then you'd better find a way to learn... and fast.

## WHY START WITH GENRE?

Publishers often request a specific genre. Genres, like markets, are easy to track; the industry keeps numbers on how well genres are doing (in terms of how many different games are produced, and how many purchased, each year). Publishers can detect certain market trends by genre that signal a financial opportunity. For example, if they know that there are 25 million RPG players in the world and that no other RPGs have been announced for Q4 of next year on the leading console, they might decide to finance one on the theory that fans of the genre will buy *anything* if it's their only choice. Such opportunities are what allow games like *Summoner* to be highly profitable, in spite of mediocre review scores (and, to be fair, games like *Baldur's Gate: Dark Alliance*, which have outstanding review scores, but might have done less in sales if they didn't also have a monopoly on their genre for at least six months in either direction).

## HOW TO START

Learning a new genre well enough to design a game in it is among the most difficult things a designer can be asked to do. The basic principles of research are present here in all their glory, but the research is more demanding than usual if you want to honor the player.

## Play, Play, Play

If you're new to the genre you're designing in, immerse yourself within the genre's world. Play every game you can get your hands on, paying particular attention to the latest games in the genre. Play first as a player, trying to find the fun. If it's not fun for you, at least try to figure out why it *might* be fun for enough other people to support the genre (but seriously consider whether you're the right designer for the job). After playing as a player, play as a designer, figuring out what mechanics create the fun. It is easy to say "we should include feature X because well-known Game Y has it" and equally easy to say "we shouldn't include feature X in order to differentiate our game from well-known Game Y"; knowing when to say each is critical.

Play a number of games in the genre and compare them. What are the similarities? What are the differences? What are the genre conventions that your players will expect to be there, and what are the superficial similarities that you could get away with changing in the name of innovation?

## Hit the Books

Hint guides offer a lot of information to gamers and game designers. Often, these books expose the inner workings of a game, showing you item statistics, play strategies, and the like that are helpful in trying to analyze how a system works. It's not the same as looking at the code or design doc of a product to be sure, but it's more information than you'd get by merely playing the game.

In addition to hint guides, many books have been written on game design, and some specifically target particular genres like MMOs and RPGs. If you're literally at a starting point with the genre, the time you spend with a book helps you to understand the genre's fundamentals from another perspective. Typically, such books are written by industry professionals, or those who have extensively studied the genre.

## Playing Versus Designing

Playing a game, of course, is different from designing one. In theory, anyone who can drive can hop into a BMW and drive it down the road. However, few people could design or build the engine that powers that same BMW. This metaphor extends itself to games. Just because you can play a game—and even play it well—doesn't mean that you understand the design decisions that made that game what it was (or is), let alone replicate its success.

## Review the Reviews

Look at professional reviews of the games you've played, especially those written by reviewers who are fans of the genre. What kinds of things are they looking for in a game, and what kinds of things do they criticize when a game in the genre is not up to par?

Ideally, by the time you're done researching, you should be a major fan of the new genre… or at least you should have a new-found appreciation for that genre that you never had before. This will make it much easier for you to choose an appropriate core.

## CHALLENGES

It's best to repeat the challenges in this chapter for *all* genres that you're unfamiliar with (including new ones as they are created) in your own time… *before* you are called upon to make a game in a new genre. Every time you work in a new genre, you learn a palette of new techniques that can be applied to other genres, and you strengthen your skills as a designer. The time spent now will also be paid back a hundredfold later if you ever *are* asked to design a game outside of your comfort zone.

Some actors and musicians are known for their range of roles or styles. Be like them and expand the range of games you understand and can design. By doing so, you broaden your ability to work in unfamiliar territory, and you also increase your chances of getting hired. (For example, a studio looking for an RTS designer will be asking interview questions about that genre, and if you can answer them well—even if it's not your favorite genre—you'll make a much better impression.)

In reality, if you are asked to design a game in a wholly unfamiliar genre, try to mentor under someone who's successfully made games in that genre before you. Trial by fire is rarely a good thing. Fortunately for you, stuff like this normally happens when you change jobs. In that case, someone else hopefully shows you the ropes before they give you an opportunity to hang yourself with them.

### CHALLENGE 1—SPORTS GAMES

Due to your incredible luck, Electronic Arts has hired your studio to do a remake of the classic *Mutant League Football* and *Mutant League Hockey* games on a modern console with updated graphics, a new game mode, and a new sport—cricket.

If you're like many game developers, you're not a big sports fan. However, many game players *are* big fans of sports and like to play games based on those sports. Since exposure to and understanding of a sport is heavily influenced by the culture in which you live, there's a chance you might not have played cricket before… or even know what it is. Most Americans aren't rabid over soccer, rugby, or cricket, while many people in the Caribbean can easily live without American baseball and football. Working in a new genre with a possibly unfamiliar sport creates quite a challenge.

#### Components Required

- Internet connection (for research)
- At least one modern game representing the sport you have chosen and a machine to play it on (optional)
- *Mutant League Football* or *Mutant League Hockey* and a machine to play it on (optional)

#### Deliverable

- Rules summary of the chosen sport (you will need to be very brief instead of being complete) and

■ "Market research" summary on the sport, detailing where the "fun" of the sport is
■ Summary of a video game(s) based on the sport, detailing the game mode(s) available and whether each was good or bad and why (you may either play the games or read professional reviews) and
■ Screen mockups of all major screens during the play of a two-player game and a list of controls on that screen and
■ Proposal and informal presentation on your game concept

**Suggested Process**

1. **Research the sport.**
   You can find information for new fans on Wikipedia, but a better source will be the professional sports association's Web site. (Many of them have a place to go for newcomers.) Many sports can be watched on TV, and watching a game or two (especially if you can watch it with a friend or colleague who is already a fan, as they can explain the game's finer points to you) will help you to understand its appeal.

2. **Research the modern games.**
   Play a modern game based on the sport you chose. Pay particular attention to those aspects that a designer needs to be aware of: the game modes, the play experience, and (optionally) the user interface. The artificial intelligence (AI) is also important, but is beyond the scope of this exercise (or indeed, this entire book).

3. **Research the old games.**
   Find the appeal of the *Mutant League* series of games. They are not perfect copies of a sport and therefore may not appeal to purists, but they do appeal to many sports gamers, and even a few gamers who *aren't* fans of the sport. Play the games if you can; if not, read reviews and FAQs to familiarize yourself with the difference between the *Mutant League* games and the sports they represent.

4. **Brainstorm.**
   In a group, discuss potential concepts. Allow two hours to agree on a single concept and flesh out some basic details.

5. **Create deliverable.**
   Include a description of all proposed game modes and the differences between the mechanics of your game and those of the actual sport.

6. **Design the user interface (optional).**
   In your research and in your design, look at the screen layout and controls again and again. Sports games offer numerous challenges for designers, including the following:
   ■ How does a player choose how and when to swing?
   ■ How does a player decide his or her pitch? How can he do this without the other playing seeing his choice?
   ■ How does a player decide when to pass the turn to the other team?

■   What camera angles are available for viewing the game, and how are they controlled? Is it better in two-player mode to have a single camera view or a split screen view (horizontal or vertical)?

■   What kinds of information should be displayed on-screen (HUD) at all times during play (and at breaks in the action, if any)?

■   What is the best way to control multiple people at once? Do you control one player at a time and have some intuitive way to switch between players, or direct the entire team concurrently?

If you do not own a game to do your research, looking at screenshots included in professional game reviews will be necessary.

For your deliverable, include screen mockups (these can be crudely drawn by hand and labeled to show the screen elements) of all major screens during a two-player game (for example, it is not necessary to show the main menu or saving/loading screens). For each mockup, clearly show the different parts of the screen, and what information is shown in each part. Also include a controller on a modern console for each screen and show what controls map to what in-game actions.

### Variant

For this variant, choose a different sport. Ideally, select a sport that you already find boring or pointless. This will help you build the empathy skills you'll need to do all kinds of other market research. *Your sport must have at least one published video game that is based on it.*

## CHALLENGE 2—MOLDING THE MOB

Movies, televisions shows, and books that feature the Mafia are ever popular. The Mafia is also a popular subject in games, although social simulations aren't the first genre that comes to mind when one thinks of a "Mob game." Your publisher believes this is an oversight. Given the amazing success of *The Sims* series, the publisher figures it's only a matter of time before someone explores a darker side well. They hope you'll be the team to do it. They expect you to create not only a concept for a potential game, but also an original IP for them in the process. As such, you may not use any existing Mob-related IPs.

### Components Required

■   Internet connection (for research)

### Deliverable

■   One-page summary of the defining hallmarks of a simulation game

■   One-page summary of your new IP

■   Informal pitch featuring the game's core, potential for emergent narrative, and feature set

**Suggested Process**

1. **Research the Mob.**
   Select a means to research the organizational structure of the Mob. Research everything you feel might be relevant to the topic when expressed as a social simulation. Make a list of things players will expect to see in a game that features the Mafia.

2. **Research social simulations.**
   What features make a game a social simulation? How do these games work? Find an online hint guide or FAQ and study the structure of these games.

3. **Research modern Mob games.**
   Play a modern game based on the Mob. What topics did they highlight? Were those topics a requirement of the genre or of the topic?

4. **Brainstorm.**
   In a group, discuss potential concepts. Allow two hours to agree on a single concept and flesh out some basic details.

5. **Create deliverable.**

### Challenge 3—Idea Exploration

A publisher has contacted you with a not-so-odd request: They want to reach that elusive "everyman" again (see Chapter 11, "Targeting a Market," Challenge 3) and are seeking proposals from innovative developers able to see beyond the shelves of first-person shooters. First, they want you to find a game premise that everyone can understand at a single glance without even flipping over the box. For this product, they're not interested in someone who knows what a "frag" is—they want to grab the average Christmas shopper going through the PC aisle. During your initial meeting, they suggest topics like cooking, barbecuing, and vacations—topics that practically every person—young or old, rich or poor—can understand and identify with.

For this challenge, it's your task to develop an IP that someone can understand at a glance (like *Deer Hunter*). Once you have developed the IP, develop a spectrum of potential applications for that IP in a variety of genres: tycoon, RTS, FPS, RPG, MMO, casual games, and so on.

Go down the list of video-game genres to see what the possibilities are. The publisher would like to see at least six different applications of the IP across a spectrum of genres.

**Components Required**

■ None

**Deliverable**

- Summary of the IP and
- A write up or discussion on the IP applied to at least six different genres. For each, discuss one or two key features and summarize gameplay in a few sentences.

**Suggested Process**

1. **Brainstorm.**
   Consider the request of the publisher, and brainstorm a whole list of ideas, no matter how little they seem to relate to video games. Note hobbies, likes, dislikes, material goods, and jobs everyone understands. Narrow your list down to 10 different possibilities.
2. **Think genre.**
   Subject each idea you come up with to a series of genres to see if any game ideas rise. Some will suggest games easily—cooking tycoon, for instance. Others will provide more laughter than possibility (like the barbecue FPS). Don't feel the need to limit yourself to mainstream genres, either. For this challenge, it's all open. Consider 4X games, adventure games, 2D platformers, and tactical RPGs. For a good idea of different genres, visit a popular indie games site where games are listed by these genres.
3. **Think names.**
   In 2005, *Caterpillar Construction Tycoon* was released. You may never have heard of the game, but you already know exactly what it's about. Try to title your potential games similarly. Remember that this is a component of your deliverable for this project. Can you brand a game such that it tells you what it's all about in the title alone?
4. **Create deliverable.**

## CHALLENGE 4—CLUELESS

In the previous challenge, you've probably played it relatively safe by selecting a genre that made you feel, at the very least, comfortable. For this challenge, though, you must select a genre about which you know nothing, define its hallmarks as a genre (what makes it what it is), and attempt to design a game for it.

**Components Required**

- Internet connection for research
- Game of selected genre (optional)

### Deliverable

- Three-page concept doc or
- Five-page proposal document listing the game's demographics, features, and gameplay overview or
- Non-digital paper prototype of the game. You may choose any medium you like, including a traditional RPG.

### Suggested Process

1. **Find a genre.**
   Ask others for genre recommendations or review Wikipedia's listing of game genres (search under *video game genres*). Select one that's not known to you. Likely candidates are 4X games, adventure games, shmups, turn-based fantasy games, or text adventures. Visit any good indie game site, like ManifestoGames.com, to see the variety of genres offered outside the mainstream industry.
2. **Explore the genre.**
   Play multiple games in the genre to get an idea of the basic gameplay style, as well as player expectations. After you play a few shmups, for instance, you have a basic idea of what to expect in one of those games. Think through the games as you play them and make note of the basic mechanics of the genre, as well as how it rewards its players for progress.
3. **Brainstorm.**
4. **Create deliverable.**

### Iron Designer Challenge 5—Genre Change

It seems everyone's playing the latest game—no matter who you talk to, it's the game on the tip of their tongues and the one that's keeping them up half the night. Its online play or storyline or AI or *something* is second to none. It might be an MMO or an FPS, but whatever it is, you know it already.

Its publishers are keen to maximize the game's potential revenue, and have approached you to design something new—a collectible card game (CCG) version of the IP. Naturally, they hope to replicate the success of the *Magic: The Gathering* or *Pokémon* cards. They want the CCG to take advantage of the IP and be playable online. However, it must provide a different play experience altogether. Players need not have played or own the main product to play the CCG, but it would be ideal if the CCG incorporated some components of the main product that players will recognize and appreciate if they had. How the game incorporates these ideas is up to you.

### Components Required

- Internet connection for research
- Copy of selected game (optional)

### Deliverable

- Non-digital card prototype of game in question
- Written rules that describe the play of the game
- Feature list for CCG with analysis of how these features are representative of the CCG genre and incorporate the IP you have selected for this exercise.

### Suggested Process

1. **Research the game.**
   If you've only been hearing about the latest new game that everyone's talking about, take some time to actually play it, first as a player and then as a designer. If there are practical reasons that prevent you from doing so, at least read enough reviews and FAQs to get an understanding of the game.
2. **Research the genre.**
   If you've never played a CCG before, play some games in the genre, read some rules and card lists that can be found online for a selection of CCGs, or find several people (in your local area or online) who are fans of the genre and can explain it to you.
3. **Brainstorm.**
4. **Create deliverable.**
   Creating an entire CCG is a massive undertaking; most basic sets have over 200 unique cards. You only need to make a playable prototype: a single starter deck (perhaps 60 cards total, with some duplicates) printed twice. The game does not need to be extensively playtested and balanced for the purposes of this challenge, as long as the basic mechanics are there.

## NON-DIGITAL SHORTS

Each of these shorts encourages you to explore a genre or a new genre in a different way.

1. Analyze a territorial acquisition game (such as *Carcassonne*) and identify three defining mechanics. Design a card game using those same mechanics.
2. Design a game and write two sets of rules, one using tiles and the other using cards, that maintain the same core and dynamics.

3. Choose a classic card game (such as *Spades*) and expand it to incorporate at least three mechanics common to tabletop role-playing games.
4. Design a tabletop role-playing game, playable without dice.
5. Create a card-game version of *Risk*.
6. Redesign *Monopoly* to operate like a sim game using all the original pieces.
7. Design a tabletop miniature game using only a standard deck of playing cards and a tape measure.
8. Choose your favorite video-game genre and then choose one of your favorite games within that genre. Create a board or card game based on the video game. If one already exists, choose a different video game.
9. Similar to #8, choose the genre you selected for Challenge 4 in this chapter, and create a board or card game based on that. You may either make an original game or one based on an existing video-game IP.
10. Take the combat mechanics from any digital RPG and modify them to be used in a tabletop RPG. This may involve finding a hint guide or FAQ that explains how the combat mechanics work and then simplifying them so that they don't require hundreds of calculations from a computer.

# 13 Designing a Game to Tell a Story

In a sense, all games tell a story, even if that story is emergent and develops as a result of the player's actions in the game. Stories of sports victories are told nightly on the evening news, and increasingly, fans of sports have turned players themselves, relating successes in *Madden* and *Tiger Woods Golf* to their friends. These are stories, too.

When designers create a game to tell a specific story, however, it's a different matter, and a challenging one. Many newly minted designers have grand plans to tell epic stories in their games, but they forget the most important feature of all—games are about players making meaningful choices that affect the outcome of the game. If the "game" is only about moving through one narrative branch or another, there's really no choice at all, and therefore, there's also no game. "Interactive dramas" might be a better term for what these writers and designers are creating.

Since games are about making choices that affect gameplay, telling a structured story presents a paradox of sorts. Think of how a movie would seem if you were able to interrupt it 10 different times to make meaningful decisions—for example, whether a character lives or dies, gets his wish, leaves his partner, or whatever the twist may be. It might be fun and novel the first time, but after a while, viewers might prefer something more structured.

In games, there are a variety of ways that stories are incorporated. We'll cover some of those ways here.

## WRITER, DESIGNER, OR BOTH?

Game designers create games. Game writers like Lee Sheldon, Bob Bates, Mark Nelson, or Susan O'Connor create stories. In many cases, the game writer is also a game designer, but the two jobs are distinctly different and require different skill sets. There are many brilliant systems designers in this industry that should be kept at arm's length of a game story for the good of everyone. In professional video-game development, the best results are achieved when a game writer is involved from the beginning of the game. Those interested in game writing should explore the book *Character Development and Storytelling for Games* by Lee Sheldon.

# STORY ARCS

Like taking a long road trip, having an idea of where your story is going results in a better execution than slapping a story together on the fly. To do this, game writers create story arcs. A "story arc" is the path that a story takes from beginning to end. In games, two kinds of arcs are commonly used: the classic three-part story arc, as identified in Aristotle's *Poetics* and Joseph Campbell's five-part arc, as defined in *The Hero with a Thousand Faces*.

## THE THREE-ACT STORY ARC

In the three-act story arc, the story follows this path:

- **Act 1:** The story begins with an inciting moment. An "inciting moment" is a problem that fundamentally changes or affects the character. It's something he feels driven to pursue. There may be hours of gameplay before this inciting moment (a prelude or an opening), but all play leads up to this key point. If a game doesn't start with the inciting moment, it should, at the very least, start the player with a problem. Arriving in a game world with no goal, no sense of direction, and no issue to resolve leaves players feeling confused, frustrated, or bored. A common problem in games, in fact, is that the alleged inciting moment fails to motivate the player at all or seems completely unbelievable, even in an imaginary context. Following the inciting moment, the player progresses for some time toward his ultimate goal—destroying the villain, restoring his family name, etc.
- **Act 2:** A dramatic reversal occurs. For instance, perhaps the hero realizes that the person he thought was his friend is actually his enemy and has been working against him this whole time. The dramatic reversal should seem logical and possible, not what Aristotle calls a "deus ex machina," an impossible or improbable "machine of the gods" created to help the writer achieve his needs.
- **Act 3:** The goal presented in the inciting moment is resolved. The hero gets what he is looking for or resolves not to get what he is looking for. Either way, an irreversible resolution is achieved. Sometimes, a second reversal may occur.

Numerous game designers have written about the three-act structure as applied to video games. A search through Gamasutra.com's archives will provide numerous references to assist you in understanding this story structure.

## THE FIVE-PART HERO'S JOURNEY

In 1949, Joseph Campbell published a seminal work, *The Hero with a Thousand Faces*. In his book, he asserted that although stories may be told about thousands of heroes, there really is only one path that they follow. Therefore, as Campbell saw it, there is but one hero and one path told in a thousand different ways. He called this the "monomyth."

Campbell's five-part story arc is as follows:

- **Part 1:** The hero receives a "call to adventure" and begins a journey.
- **Part 2:** The hero passes through a series of challenges (a "trail of trials").

- **Part 3:** The hero confronts the final evil and achieves the goal.
- **Part 4:** The hero returns to the everyday world.
- **Part 5:** The hero applies the lesson or object learned in the adventure to that everyday world.

As with the three-act structure, game designers have also explored the use of the hero's journey as applied to video games. Numerous articles can be found on game-development Web sites.

## THE SCREENWRITER'S MASTER CHART

Screenwriter Mary Shomon expanded upon Aristotle's classic story arc in her "Screenwriter's Master Chart," which includes 14 separate acts, as well as script page numbers that suggest where a writer should be in the script when these events happen. The full chart may be found online on Shomon's site at http://members.aol.com/maryjs/scrnrite.htm.

## NARRATOLOGY AND LUDOLOGY

Though primarily discussed in academic circles, an understanding of narratology and ludology is useful to those learning about storytelling in games.

"Ludology" is the study of games as rules (or mechanics). Ludologists believe that a game is first and foremost a collection of rules that give rise to the dynamics of play when a player sets the game in motion through an interface of some sort. From this perspective, modern-day games are an extension of ancient games like *Go* and *Chess*. Story is not a part of a game, but rather something layered on top, much like *Lara Croft* and other innumerable narratives are layered on top of the mechanics of third-person shooters. At the core, the third-person shooter rules remain unchanged.

"Narratology" is the study of games as a storytelling medium. Just as a theatre, camera, seats, and a setting are necessary for a movie to play out, so too are the rules of a game necessary for a story to be told. Those who study games from this perspective have been called narratologists.

These two divergent schools of thought are, for the most part, exactly that—thought. In the life of a work-a-day game designer, the topics are rarely discussed in as black-and-white definitions as they are above. Rather, the designer usually focuses on what's not up to snuff in the game, whether it's something whacked with the balance or an untested story path he has yet to implement.

Furthermore, these two schools of thought aren't in a "versus" situation as many portray them to be. One of the authors of this books is a staunch ludologist, who believes that game writers are essential in order to bring today's generation of video games to their next level. The two schools are complementary.

## TYPES OF STORIES IN GAMES

When designing games to tell a story, designers typically have several models from which to choose. The model the designer chooses is usually dictated by the story in question. Adventure games, for instance, usually use linear or branching narratives. Larger, modern RPGs feature nonlinear or branching narratives. MMOs typically feature instances or emergent stories. There is no one perfect story type for any game.

### LINEAR STORIES

Linear stories progress from point A to B to C and frequently have periodic, optional side quests. Games like this are often referred to as being "on rails" like a train; players start at one point and go straight to the end. The benefit of a linear story is that it shares the most in common with other storytelling media so it is familiar. Linear stories can be emotionally powerful (just ask anyone who played *Planetfall* or *Final Fantasy VII* what they felt when their companion died). They are also the only narrative structure that does not *require* players to play through the game several times just to see all possible outcomes; for stories that are not linear, the player may miss much of the game content on their first playthrough.

### BRANCHING STORIES

Branching stories present the player with multiple ways to get through a story with a possibility of multiple endings. The play paths change in response to choices the player makes. Branching stories take advantage of the interactivity offered by games as a medium, and they leave a lot of room for the storyline to respond believably to player decisions. However, depending on the medium, they can be expensive, as the writer must create several related stories instead of just one. In a video game, each of these branches could mean unique art assets.

One variant of a complete branching story, a parallel path, forces the story to fold back on itself at certain critical points. In this way, players can branch several times but will always find themselves facing the same key dramatic moments, although they can reach these moments in a variety of ways due to the branching. In this way, the cost of branching is kept manageable because the overall story arc is still linear.

### OPEN-ENDED STORIES

Open-ended (or multilinear or threaded) stories start players in a particular place or a variety of places and allow them to progress is many different directions, each of which affects the outcome of their play. The *Elder Scrolls* series, particularly *Oblivion*, are excellent examples. These kinds of stories are difficult to write because the player may take any number of paths in any order, and the story still has to make sense. The number of possible paths through the story is even greater than that of a branching story. Designers are careful to prevent situations where the story makes no sense because it is told out of order, either by limiting the player's choices through fact trees (for example, if they don't know about X, don't tell them about Y), or writing different stories for different paths that the player takes.

Open-ended games tend to have dedicated game writers or teams of game writers whose job it is to create and implement these vast stories.

### INSTANCES

Instances are a special case of open-ended stories. They are commonly used in MMOs and present the player or group of players with an "instance" of a particular story thread. For example, it might be as simple as "Go get object Y, bring it to Mr. X, and then return here." Players can choose which instances they attempt and in what order. Like episodes in a TV series, instances don't usually affect the overall story arc that much. Rather, they are complete, self-contained mini-stories. This makes them easier to write, and it also allows new instances to be added at a later time.

### EMERGENT STORIES

Emergent stories arise purely from the play mechanics of the game. The stories are created by player experience or player-created content and are not placed within the world by the game's designers. *The Sims* series is an example of a game that makes heavy use of emergent stories. Players even post gameplay movies of their Sims adventures online.

### THEMATIC SETUPS

Thematic setups, called "opening cutscenes" in the industry, paint a picture for the player in the game's beginning, but integrate no further story components once the game has begun. Many board games, action games, and early 8-bit games use this setup. In this case, the story is little more than window dressing to set context for the rules.

### ALGORITHMIC STORIES

Algorithmic stories such as the one found in *Façade* are constructed by computer AI and respond to player inputs to determine the story's direction. While all the writing is still done by a human, the AI is still given a set of predetermined plot points. It's similar to an act-based structure where each "act" has multiple entry and exit points, and within each act it's kind of open-ended. So, it's like having a bunch of self-contained, small, open-ended stories linked together in a larger, open-ended macro-story.

These stories share the advantages of parallel paths (nonlinear, expressive story without the explosive complexity and cost of full branching). The disadvantage is that this form of story is very new. *Façade* itself took over five years to construct, and its story plays out in a mere 20 minutes or so.

## STORYTELLING METHODS

Take any game down from the shelf or, better yet, download an indie game with a story component. Within an hour of play, it's generally obvious what methods the designers are using in order to tell the story of the game. Games often use a combination of methods.

### CUTSCENES AND CINEMATICS

"Cutscenes" are movies that set up or continue the narrative of the game, but occur outside of the game's engine.

"Cinematics" (or scripted events) occur within the game using the game's engine in order to set up a scene or otherwise advance the story's narrative. In some cases, the player is able to control some of the action or make a choice or two during the cinematic.

Note that these two terms are occasionally used interchangeably.

Cutscenes and cinematics are a popular way to present a game's story in an emotionally engaging way. Many games have rich back stories or are based on vibrantly detailed universes, but this information can be difficult to convey through gameplay alone. As a result, game writers sometimes turn to the conventions of a familiar medium—film. Like mini-movies, cinematics and cutscenes are unbound by the technical or interface demands of the regular game, and they can thus be truly spectacular. Many players feel that well-crafted, beautiful cutscenes add a great deal of depth and holding power to their favorite games. Games such as *Diablo* and *Final Fantasy* are renowned for having stunning cutscenes.

These story events can also be used to break the tension after a particularly tense moment (such as a boss fight) as a way to allow the player to relax.

## In-Game Events

While similar in some respects to a cinematic, scripted in-game events often do not remove control from the player, but trigger when the player does something within the game. For instance, as the player arrives on a level, she may interrupt other characters talking about a particular event. They turn to see her and attack. During this process, the player never loses control.

## Dialogue

Dialogue is spoken by the avatar or the NPCs in the game. Sometimes, this dialogue isn't heard but rather appears as text on the screen. When the player is given the option to respond, dialogue can become interactive. Other times (such as during cutscenes), the dialogue is fixed. In any case, games with purely spoken dialogue typically allow text display as an option for the benefit of gamers who are deaf or who are playing with the sound off.

## Text

Text is contained in in-game descriptive messages, notes, books, etchings on the wall, or whatever else the writers may choose. Such methods are particularly useful for conveying back story. Remember, though, that text is not inherently interactive. In short bursts, it most certainly has the potential to be, much like a conversation in an instant-messaging window is interactive. Forcing the player to read through pages and pages of text just to continue playing the game can make the player bored, of course, and players who skip the text end up missing critical information that they need later.

## A Note About Interactivity

With the exception of dialogue that allows responses, each method listed above presents the story to the player in a passive way. In a medium crafted to elicit meaningful choices out of the player, how do you tell a story, something that by its nature requires players to passively digest information given to them?

## TELL, SHOW, DO

In an article in the July 2005 article on Gamasutra titled "What Every Game Developer Needs to Know about Story," writer John Sutherland twisted the familiar storytelling maxim "Show, Don't Tell" into "Do, Don't Show".[1] Later, in January 2007, *Game Developer* magazine's Noah Falstein, himself a veteran game designer, emphasized the point.

Rather than *tell* the player what he or she needs to do, or *show* them information in cutscenes or cinematics, Sutherland and Falstein challenged designers to allow the player to actually take part in the action. The point is a critical one for game designers to consider and implement. Imagine if, in your own life, you were asked to step aside and watch as a critical event unfolded, and you were not actually able to participate during the course of this great action or event. For a player watching a cutscene, the effect can be similar. So, rather than read about an uprising among a militant group within the game or see the uprising happening through the cutscene, the player can be a *part* of or the cause of the uprising or a part of another group that is similarly affected by it.

What other ways do game designers allow players to participate?

RPGs provide perhaps the greatest example. Consider that the core of these games is character development. Through exploration and combat, players are continuously engaged with the core of the game. The story is often the impetus for progression in the game. In combat and in exploration, there are a multitude of player decisions, from how to attack, what to attack, where to attack, and so on. The story serves as the key, informing players about what is important and how to go about addressing it, which adds meaning to the decisions. Each of these many meaningful decisions leads players to their rewards—progression of their characters. Designers create a pattern of sorts—player control/designer control/player control/designer control. This pattern keeps meaningful choices front and center and makes story an integral component as well. The player makes choices about how the character develops, which is, itself, fueled by experience gained through quest completion or combat, yet another choice-driven system. The game supports the core of player development and that development happens within the confines of a story.

## SETTING AND CHARACTER

Two of the most important decisions designers make are the "who" and "where" of games (with story being the "what" of the "who, what, and where" equation). The roles the players take on and where these roles play out are of significant importance to the success of story-driven games. A used-software salesman in Vegas might seem an unlikely character and setting for a game, but the strength of *Leisure Suit Larry* and its many sequels suggests otherwise. An Italian plumber who began life looking for a princess is the biggest hero of them all. Anything is a potential topic for a video game, provided it is carried out well, supported by solid gameplay, and follows a story arc that draws the player in.

People play games because they provide an opportunity to explore a world that they would be unlikely to explore and play out an experience they would be unlikely to have in real life. People want to play cool characters. They want to explore exciting destinations. Sometimes, as in *The Sims*, they just want to experiment with everyday life and make their own stories.

## CHARACTER DESIGN

Characters are about much more than concept sketches. They come from somewhere and have strengths and key weaknesses. They have memories and histories and more. When creating a character for a video game, the designer knows that character inside and out, and if presented with a hypothetical situation, the designer knows how the character would respond and why. Two great game characters, Duke Nukem and Solid Snake, have survived the test of time and become classics based not so much on how they look or even the games that they're in but rather on the strength of *their character*—the personality beyond the looks. Within this character, games allow players to make decisions, and they invite the player to step into this role. In-game characters like NPCs can have similar depth.

Many designers actually "interview" their characters in an effort to evoke the character's personality and solidify the person in their head.

## ENVIRONMENT DESIGN

Great environments do more than "wow" people with expansive polygon-filled scenes. While those may be important, the thrill of great graphics wears off.

Environments are more about feel. Consider how one might feel in a strange building, in a bad part of town, alone and unarmed in the dark. In such a scenario, the fear is palpable, and it's *all* about the feel, not the graphics. Furthermore, consider two identical parking garages. We know one is secure. The other was the scene of a brutal crime the previous week. Identical scenes with totally different feels. Environments, mechanics, and narrative work together to determine how the player *feels*.

By thinking back to a certain time when they felt a certain way, designers use memories to recreate experiences for players. Shigeru Miyamoto, the creator of a great many successful games including the *Zelda* series and the *Mario* franchise, used childhood memories to influence the locations in several of his games. From the caves he explored as a child to a mountain lake he took to be an enormous body of water, Miyamoto remembers the sense of wonder he felt, and recreates that experience for his players.

For every game maxim, however, there seems to be multiple exceptions to the rule. For instance, Jason Rohrer's art game *Passage* lets the player play an everyman walking through a graphically unimpressive life. The game is, nonetheless, exceptionally engaging, and its minimalist graphics contribute to the aesthetic.

## WORKING BACKWARD

Once the story arc is decided upon, some game developers work backward to determine individual plot points, much like puzzle designers sometimes start with the solution and work back from that point.

For instance, consider a wizard locked up in a castle. A series of questions and answers can assist you in determining how the player might get the wizard out:

- Why can't I get into the castle to kill the wizard?
- *The door is locked.*
- Where's the key?
- *It's with his most trusted assistant.*
- Where is his trusted assistant?

Sometimes, the process of working backward helps designers brainstorm plot points or side quests they hadn't otherwise considered.

## CHOOSING MECHANICS TO MATCH THE STORY

Sometimes, the designer knows the story before he knows the treatment for it. This is particularly true of non-digital game design and designs made from IP. For instance, if you were to make a game about a favorite movie, you might have an idea of the story, but you would have to consider various options before deciding upon a game genre or the mechanics necessary to pull that genre off.

In almost all cases, stories directly map to one or more common digital genres or non-digital designs. For instance, consider a classic book like John Steinbeck's *The Grapes of Wrath*. In the book, Tom Joad and his family leave Oklahoma during the dust bowl and the Great Depression in search of riches in the fertile fields of California. True to Aristotle's arc, there is a dramatic reversal when they arrive, and they are left to overcome more than they'd originally planned. Without ruining the ending, the book is one of survival and exploration.

In assessing which mechanics to use to make this story, take a step back and first ask yourself which genre the story best fits. Theoretically, *The Grapes of Wrath* could be any one of these:

- Adventure game
- Action game
- RPG
- Educational game
- Tycoon game

Which one is the best? That depends on your treatment for the story. Do you want to focus on the main character and his struggles? It could be similar in style to a 1920s version of *Max Payne*. Do you want to focus on the plight of the migrant farmer? It could be a persuasive tycoon game where the rich farmers build off the backs of those they have effectively imprisoned. Do you want to build a game that educates people about the Great Depression? Each of these could be a viable game, but each one would have entirely different mechanics.

Apart from a game genre, one can also explore various core dynamics. Common dynamics that might work with *The Grapes of Wrath* include the following:

- Territorial acquisition
- Power struggle
- Exploration
- Race to the end/to the other side
- Building
- Character advancement
- Collection

The genre and dynamics that you choose will only assist you in choosing mechanics to match. There are literally hundreds of mechanics to choose from. The book *Patterns in Game Design* is an excellent resource for designers and will expand your horizons. Take territorial acquisition as an example. How many ways can you take over or control a person's land? How many different ways can you explore? How many different ways can you collect resources?

The single best way to choose mechanics to go with your story is to have a head already full of them.

## CHALLENGES

The challenges in this section allow you to explore the various components of story creation.

### CHALLENGE 1—WHO ARE YOU?

Memorable characters in video games—Link, Lara Croft, Master Chief, Duke Nukem, and Solid Snake—are sometimes bigger than the games in which they initially appeared. However, for every well known character, there are at least 100 characters that have faded blissfully (if regrettably) into obscurity.

For this challenge, your goal will be to create a character from the ground up. You need more than a visual, though. To complete this challenge, you need a fully rounded character with a time and a place, a past, and plans for the future. Your character may be fictional, but it must exist in the real world in the past or present.

#### Components Required

- Internet connection for research

#### Deliverable

- Concept sketch (optional)
- Character interview
- Biography including strengths, weaknesses, personal history, and two defining moments
- Story arc (optional)

**Suggested Process**

1. **Select a time period and a place for your character.**
   If your character is for a particular game that you have already been working on, then maybe you're already finished. Otherwise, select a time period or a place that you're interested in, but do not know a lot about. This natural curiosity will serve you well as you research your character's history. (If you don't care much about the history of Ireland in the year 800, then randomly selecting it for your character isn't going to make you care about it more.) If you are completely uncertain about what to research, type the formula into a cell in Microsoft Excel: =RAND()*2009. The formula will kick out a random year between 0 and 2009. You can set the cell to show you no decimals or just ignore them. Every time you press F9, you'll get a new year. If you prefer a non-digital method, roll three 10-sided dice to get the last three digits of the year, then roll a fourth die for the thousands digit and re-roll if it isn't 0, 1 or 2.

2. **Complete the interview.**
   For your character, pretend you are interviewing that person. Think about how he would answer these questions. Answer them for yourself, on your character's behalf.
   - What is your name? Gender? Race? Religion? Age?
   - Where were you born? What about your parents—where are they, and are they alive? When you were growing up, did you struggle, and if so, in what way?
   - What year is it now?
   - How would someone stereotype you at a glance?
   - Do you have a romantic partner? If so, whom?
   - Who is your best friend and what is he/she/it like? How would your friend describe you?
   - What is your economic situation? What have you done for work?
   - Would you steal? How do you feel about lying? Can you be trusted by your friends? Do you have any other vices?
   - What makes you happy? What makes you sad?
   - What is the one secret that no one must know about you?
   - Are you afraid to die?
   - Do you have any phobias?
   - Are you quick tempered or patient?

3. **Create deliverable.**

**Variants**

Instead of creating any old character, create a nemesis for yourself: someone who targets your weaknesses. Take this challenge seriously, and it usually produces insightful results.

Create a story arc for your character that involves a dramatic reversal. This arc need not be based on a real-life experience.

Trade the character created for this challenge with another team member, and ask him to create a right-hand man or woman that complements the character you have created.

### CHALLENGE 2—WHERE ARE YOU?

Think back to a time when you felt one or all of these things. Pause a moment on each to let your memories rise. The feelings are:

- Awe or wonder
- Fear or deep uncertainty (not an instance of being scared, however)
- A desire to explore

In this exercise, what comes to mind will the basis for a video-game setting. You need not translate the setting literally. For instance, if you felt fear when you took a wrong turn and got lost in an unfamiliar city. You don't have to literally turn that city into a setting. Rather, explore why you *perceived* the situation to be fearful. Perhaps you worried that you couldn't find your way out. Maybe the area was poorly lit and signs were few. Maybe there were people in the shadows. Perhaps you were already late for an event and that added to your anxiety. Maybe there was visible evidence that other cars left here had been parted out and their skeletons left to rot.

Create a list or a brief write-up of those perceptions (what made you feel the way you felt) and use each to create a video-game setting that evokes the same feeling.

#### Components Required

- None

#### Deliverable

- A paragraph or discussion that describes your memory
- A statement of the emotional response you want the player to feel
- A list of the perceived things that caused you to feel that way
- A description of the level or world you propose to design along with a detailing of how you plan to incorporate the elements of your inspiration

#### Suggested Process

1. **Write the paragraph first.**
   Let your imagination go back to the time when you felt some or all of the above feelings, and do your best to put yourself in the same state of mind. Think of the details that you remember: Did you notice a particular smell, sound, or sight? Did something seem wrong, strange, or out of place? Immerse yourself in the memory. Then write about it.

2. **Describe the emotions.**

   While the memory from above is still fresh in your head, continue to write about your feelings and emotions at that time. The paragraph you wrote earlier describes what happened; now describe your reaction to what happened.

3. **Define the mechanics.**

   If your life were a game, then your emotions at that time in your memory would be the aesthetics. What were the mechanics that caused them? Why do you think you felt that way? What aspects of your emotions were caused by you, your experiences, and your personality? What aspects of your environment and situation contributed to the emotional response? Brainstorm everything that you can think of on scrap paper. When you're satisfied, rewrite your notes as an organized list.

4. **Create deliverable .**

   The last thing to do is translate what you've already written into actual game mechanics. Consider the systems in the world around you that led to your emotions and how you can model them in a game in such a way as to create the same emotions for a player.

**Variant**

Design the actual level, on paper or digitally.

### CHALLENGE 3—WHAT'S THE POINT?

Exploring different story arcs allows designers to consider multiple possibilities for a single story concept. In this challenge, your goal is to develop an arc for a single story concept and suggest gameplay mechanics that might facilitate your story's progression. The concept for your story is up to you.

Select from the story arcs covered earlier in this chapter—the three-act story arc, the five-part hero's journey, and the 14-part arc from the Screen Writer's Master Chart. You may also use the character you developed in Challenge 1, if you like.

**Components Required**

■   Internet connection for research

**Deliverable**

■   Paragraph statement on your story's basic premise
■   Three-act story arc or
■   Five-part hero's journey arc or
■   14-part Screen Writer's Master Chart arc

**Suggested Process**

1. **Choose a premise.**
   If you have a story in your head, you're already part-way there. If not, there are a lot of places you can look for starting points. Choose a character, or a situation, or a goal, and build from there. Or look at the different acts in a typical story arc and ask yourself what you would want to see in each act. You can start at the beginning with an inciting moment, or you can start at the end and then work backward.
2. **Grow your story.**
   From your starting point, work your way forward and backward, adding detail until you have a complete story arc.
3. **Think of gameplay.**
   For your story, what kinds of mechanics and dynamics would fit well?
4. **Create deliverable.**

## CHALLENGE 4—THE COMMON UNCOMMON

Sometimes average people are called to extraordinary measures. It happens in movies, in books, and on television all the time. Innumerable action movies pit people against one another, and pushed past the point, the "common man" or "common woman" becomes quite uncommon. Erin Brockovich is a classic example of such a person.

For this challenge, your task is to select a common man or woman in a common job in a common world. There is nothing that might cause you to think twice about them. To test this, ask yourself, "Would I presently watch a movie that covered the last week in the life of this person?" If the answer is "yes," then odds are you don't find them all that common after all.

Think of a common, but not specific, person you meet in your everyday life: a doctor, nurse, grocery-store employee, construction worker, bus driver, or a cabbie. Any profession that's common will do.

Think of how you could build a game based around this character's everyday life when it suddenly takes a dramatic turn.

**Components Required**

- None

**Deliverable**

- Brief description of a common man or common woman character
- Details of a realistic, inciting moment that makes the character uncommon
- Non-digital game based on the character

**Suggested Process**

1. **Pick a common profession and a common man or woman.**
   If you can't decide, go out for a walk in your neighborhood. As you pass people on the street, see if you can guess their profession just by looking at them. Choose the person you see who most inspires you.
2. **Determine what the inciting moment will be.**
   It could be something as dramatic as the death of a loved one and the desire for re-venge (*Max Payne*) or as seemingly trivial as the race to fill seats and serve people in a restaurant (*Diner Dash*). One could say the inciting moment in the latter game is when the diners start to overwhelm Flo.
3. **Determine a type of game to build.**
   What kinds of core dynamics would suit the character well? Building? Exploration? Race to the end? Or something else? What kinds of mechanics fit those dynamics? Does a game board feel right, or are cards or tiles more suitable? What kinds of actions would the player(s) take in the game? Have you played any non-digital games that could be re-themed?
4. **Create deliverable.**

**Variant**

Turn an uncommon person common through a similar, but reverse, inciting moment and explore how that affects the character.

Develop a story arc based upon the character.

Instead of a board game, write a proposal for a video game featuring your character as the protagonist.

## IRON DESIGNER CHALLENGE 5—NARRATOLOGIST'S REVENGE (LIVE)

In game design, much attention is paid, and rightly so, to the game's mechanics. Sometimes, however, we forget the impact that story can have. Done well, story can actually give rise to mechanics, rather than play second fiddle to them.

For this challenge, your job is to host a live narrative exercise with 4–10 players, start-ing with the setup below and two rules:

1. Rules will be made up as the story evolves.
2. Once a rule is made up, it is applied throughout the game world from that point forward.

*The Setup:*

One player must serve as the narratologist. (The game will work more easily this way. However, if there is no one who wishes to play the narratologist, then set up the group to act as a collective narratologist. See the "Variants" section for more information on that.)

- Players 1–4 should be visiting or residents of a small town. They need not know each other and may be scattered across the town. What town? We'll get to that shortly.
- Players 5–7 should start with a problem of some sort. What that "inciting moment" or plain ol' problem might be is up to you.
- Player 8 has just arrived in town and is on the lam.
- Players 9–10 are working together on something.

The setup, as you certainly see, has some holes in it. Those holes will be filled by your players.

*Starting the game:*

- Sketch a very skeletal city on a whiteboard, blackboard, or piece of paper that all players can see. Your city shouldn't include much more than roads and maybe a couple key things, like the police station and maybe a park.
- Ask players to select a number between 1 and 10, and tell them who they are based on the number they have selected. For instance, a player who selected number 4 could be a resident in that small town.
- Ask the newly minted player where he or she wants to be located in the town. They are free to make up locations. Feel free to set some limits on the types of locations they can make up. Decide up front if you'll accept "spaceship landing site" or "dragon's lair." Whatever your player says, draw his or her number and the location on a map. Ask all other players to determine their starting position.
- Ask player 1 what he or she wants to do or allow the player to ask questions he or she might have. For instance, players can say, "I want to go to the restaurant," or ask, "Do I have a weapon?" When the player is finished performing his or her action, the turn goes to the next player.

*Q&A:*

How long is a turn? It's up to the narratologist. If the restaurant is half a city away, maybe they only get a quarter of the way there.

How do you handle questions? Invent rules to allow the player story to function. A good suggestion is to use a die to determine the answer. For the question above, you could say that rolling a 1–4 indicates you're not armed. A 5 or 6 means that you are armed.

How do you handle events? Again, invent rules to handle them. Let's say that player 1 ends up in a battle with a creature. You can solve the whole thing with a single die:

- Roll the die to see who hits first—the player or the monster. High die wins.
- Roll the die to see where the winner hits the other creature. Apply numbers 1 through 6 to various body parts.
- Roll the die to see how powerful the hit is. A 1 is slightly painful, and a 6 knocks its block off. You can also use dice to determine a hit point system. (For example, roll the die to see how many times to roll. Then, add up the numbers rolled during these subsequent rolls.)

How does the game end? Again, it's up to the narratologist.

This exercise requires a sharp mind and the ability to juggle lots of information. In effect, it's a freeform game mastering experience.

### Components Required

- Dice or another method to resolve issues as they arise
- Whiteboard, chalkboard, or other medium upon which to draw that the group can see

### Deliverable

- None

### Suggested Process

See above

### Variant

Instead of assigning one person to play the narratologist, allow the group to play the role of a collective narratologist instead. To do this, you will need to give each player an index card and a pencil. Also, have two six-sided dice on hand. When a player wishes to perform an action that seems uncommon or to create a new rule, each player must vote on how difficult an action they think this is.

- 12 is an action that is extremely difficult or a wild rule that is not currently in play
- 1 is an action or a rule that is trivial to perform, but not currently in play

Any player can declare that an action requires a vote at any time. So, if player Cindy says she wishes to summon aliens to her city, Bob can demand a vote on the likelihood of that succeeding.

Each player writes down a number between 1 and 12 on his or her index card and keeps it hidden until everyone is done. A 12 means that the likelihood of this happening is near impossible. A 1 means that you think the rule or action should happen.

All players flip their cards at the same time. You may decide the difficulty in one of several ways (decide on this ahead of time):

- The highest value shown
- An average of all the values shown
- By player discussion and mutual agreement

Once the difficulty of the action is decided, the player must roll to see if he or she succeeded. The player must roll above or equal to the difficulty number. So, in order to get an alien, Cindy needs to roll a 12. In order to own a car in the game world, Bob only needs to roll a 2 or better.

## NON-DIGITAL SHORTS

Stories were a part of games way before electricity arrived to bring us video games. These non-digital shorts allow you to practice that. Before designing these, you may want to explore the card game *Once Upon a Time* by Reiner Knizia.

1. Create a tile-based exploration game inspired by the story of a famous explorer.
2. Using a novel or a play in the public domain, create a board game that closely follows the arc of the story.
3. Create a card game that teaches the art of storytelling (not just a remake of *Once Upon a Time*).
4. Create a game in any medium about a dejected storyteller who becomes a great storyteller.
5. Think of someone you personally know who inspires you. Create a game in any medium that reflects that inspiration.
6. Design a strongly themed board game where each player plays a hero, and the goal is to follow a hero's journey story arc of your design.
7. Story arcs become more dramatic when they overlap with the intensity of player decision making. Take an existing non-digital game and add story elements to it. Try to make it so that the story's dramatic climax comes at key moments during play. Reiner Knizia's *Lord of the Rings* is a great reference for how to do this well.
8. Modify an abstract strategy game by adding a story. Do not modify any rules at all. Play it with friends and note the effect that the story had (or did not have) on the player experience.
9. Modify the game from the previous non-digital short by changing one or more rules to fit your story better. Play it again and see if the experience is improved.
10. Think of an existing non-digital game that has a lot of thematic elements but not very much gameplay (for example, *Candy Land*). Create a new game with the same theme but a completely different set of rules. Make the rules fit the theme as tightly as possible.

## REFERENCES

[1] "What Every Game Developer Needs to Know about Story" by John Sutherland. Available online at http://www.gamasutra.com/features/20050727/sutherland_01.shtml.

# Part IV | Additive and Subtractive Design

# 14 | Adding and Subtracting Mechanics

It usually starts like this: "Wouldn't it be great if…?" Next thing you know, someone wants you to add something to or take something out of a game.

We add or remove mechanics in games in order to make them more compelling all the time. Free parking in *Monopoly* is just one example. The original rules state that nothing at all happens when you land on it, but most people play with a house rule that gives some kind of bonus. Sometimes, we add or remove mechanics from games in order to make them easier to play, too. One of the authors of this book routinely modifies the rules of traditional pencil-and-paper role-playing games like *Dungeons & Dragons* in order to make them more palatable to players new to both *D&D* and gaming as a whole.

In the game industry, mechanics are added or removed for similar reasons. For the aspiring and practicing game designer, your ability to add and remove mechanics from a video game while maintaining the game's overall vision and enhancing its quality is a key skill.

## WHY ADD MECHANICS?

Game designers often need to add a feature to a game. Ideally, they know about the feature or mechanics *before* the game enters production, but since games are an interactive medium, sometimes there's just no way to know how good or bad something is without putting it into motion.

The following sections explore the reasons developers add features.

### PUBLISHER DEMAND

Developers in the mainstream game industry, and the console industry in particular, generally release games through a publisher. The publisher funds the production of the game in return for numerous things, including a hoped-for return on their investment. As the primary funder of the game, the publisher has more than a bit of influence in its production and may request changes from time to time.

Developers work with a producer or a senior-level designer on the publisher's side. It's their job or their team's job to play the various builds of the game, assess playability, and recommend course corrections or additions.

### CHANGES IN THE MARKETPLACE

The game industry is competitive, secretive, and constantly changing. As a result, it's not uncommon for a whole group of developers to be caught unawares when an amazing new piece of technology hits and alters the whole playing field. Games like *MYST*, *Doom*, and *Magic: The Gathering* certainly had this effect, as did the transition from 2D to 3D.

Many times, though, it's smaller and more subtle changes that get developers. If you were working on *Ravishing Radishes VI* (yet another terrible made-up IP you're free to steal), and your number one competition added an autosave feature, you might feel compelled to add one—particularly if fan and press reaction were favorable. Developers stay on top of the market, regularly playing games, networking with others in the industry, and following industry news to keep their product as competitive as it can be.

### THE GAME SUCKS

As has been mentioned several times, game design is an iterative process, and barring experience in the process, developers never really know for certain how something's going to turn out until they have a chance to play it. In comparison, imagine being a cook facing a counter full of ingredients and spices with only a general recipe in mind. Creating a game is similar, in some respects. Recipes are refined through an iterative process, too.

Sometimes, the game just doesn't turn out. People play it, and don't feel at all compelled to go back and play it again. The feature that a designer thought was going to make all the difference seems pointless. The testers can't figure out what the heck is going on, and though people want to be able to perform a certain action, the game doesn't let them do it. All of these instances might suggest additions.

Does this actually happen in real production games? Count on it.

### A SEQUEL

When developers work on a sequel to an existing franchise, new mechanics are almost always added. The industry moves ahead, players want more, and the blogs light up with cool suggestions, some of which you seriously consider. You may be starting with the old game's code base, and to it, you will add these new things.

### THE BRAINSTORM

You're playing the game when it hits you—something that would truly take your game from A to AAA or at least move it up a notch. Usually, when ideas like this hit, you can bet there won't be enough time in the schedule to do it. The time that you had scheduled for just such an eventuality was already eaten up by other problems you hadn't foreseen.

The whole team agrees with you that the idea is great, and they're willing to put in the *extra* overtime in order to make it happen. The byproduct of brainstorms, "feature creep," is a common problem in the industry. Sometimes, though, it's truly worth it.

## WHY CUT MECHANICS?

Removing a mechanic in a game—particularly a digital game—can have amazingly destabilizing and costly effects. Having spent design, programming, and possibly art time to realize its implementation, making the decision to remove a mechanic doesn't always come easily.

Why would developers possibly do such a thing? Not surprisingly, the first three items in the previous section also apply here. Publishers, market conditions, or bad gameplay might warrant killing a feature and its associated mechanics.

However, there are some unique reasons developers might put mechanics on the chopping block, too.

### RATINGS

Toward the end of a game's development, it is submitted to a ratings board for review and ultimately a rating. In the United States, that rating board is the ESRB. If the developers are hoping for a "Mature" rating and receive an "Adults Only" rating instead, the implications are huge. Most significantly, an "Adults Only" rating severely limits distribution of a title. Most retailers won't stock such games.

In the event a developer receives a rating higher than planned or acceptable, he will have to remove something before resubmitting again. That something may very well involve the cutting of gameplay mechanics.

### TO DELIVER ON TIME

… Or in *better* time than they otherwise would have. Toward the end of a game's production, features that people were willing to die for (figuratively, of course) suddenly don't seem so critical after all. So they get cut. When they get cut, mechanics go right along with them. Although many gamers may not realize it, there are whole levels to games out there that have never seen the light of day, and in shipped games, there are plenty of half-finished, still buggy features that have been commented out of the code but are still very much there.

## CORE CHECK

During the course of development, it's not uncommon for developers to review their existing feature list and check it against the core of the game—the one thing that game is about. Does that feature make the core stronger? Is it superfluous? Will you spend time and money on it, and not really make your game stronger? Could that same time be used to make a necessary feature better?

## AFTER THE TINKERING

The iterative process of game design works the same whether you're on the adding or the cutting end. Change it, play it, and evaluate. Repeat. Sometimes altering mechanics can have unintended side effects that are overpowering or underperforming. You never know until you play. Anyone who's had any experience in virtual worlds has likely experienced this process live as the world's designers tweak one thing or another. First, a profession in the game is too strong, then too weak, then too strong…and so on.

Stuff like this happens all the time whenever developers add anything to a game:

■ Add a new spell, weapon, or ability, and it is way too powerful or too weak.
■ Add a new profession to the game, and it's so good, no one selects anything else.

Those with experience developing games know that even the simplest change can have adverse, unintended side effects. The only way to uncover these is to play the game and evaluate how your present change affected other things in the game.

## CHALLENGES

Games often contain several interlocking systems, and one small change in the mechanics can have ripple effects that drastically alter the balance of the game in other systems. As you'll see with these challenges, you need to playtest the entire game and not just one small system whenever you make any nontrivial change to the mechanics.

### CHALLENGE 1—POKER AND DRAGONS

Many RPGs, for some reason, have gambling mini-games in the form of an in-game casino. Sometimes, these games are exact copies of real-world gambling games like *Poker*, *Blackjack*, and *Roulette*. However, in a fantasy world, it can help player immersion to give these games an exotic twist—something that has familiar elements, but is also unique and original. Such a game can be implemented in a video game, and can also be used in a tabletop RPG. ("Your party enters the inn to rest. You spot a group of friendly looking travelers playing some kind of card game over in the corner…")

For this challenge, start with *Poker*. There are dozens, if not hundreds, of poker variants (*Draw, Stud, Texas Hold 'Em, Hi-Lo*, etc.), and you can choose whatever version suits you or create your own if you want.

To this game, add some four-sided dice (any number of dice, but at least two). These dice must be part of the play of the game. Modify the rules of the game, as appropriate, to include these new components.

Remember, your game should be familiar enough to be instantly recognizable as a *Poker* variant, but different enough to feel otherwordly.

## Components Required

- A basic deck of cards
- A pile of four-sided dice

## Deliverable

- A complete set of written rules for your playable game

## Suggested Process

1. **Research.**
   If you are unfamiliar with many *Poker* variants, read the rules of at least three different kinds and play them in a group. You can find rules online or in books like *Hoyle's Rules of Games*, or you can find friends or colleagues who can teach you.
2. **Brainstorm.**
   Answer key questions about the game. What elements of *Poker* do you feel you need to keep, and what mechanics can be changed or discarded to give it a more fantastic feel? How can you integrate dice into the game? How do you determine who wins each hand? What are the different steps players go through during the play of each hand?
3. **Playtest and iterate.**
   Try playing the game in a group. Are your mechanics fun and interesting? Do the dice add something to the experience, or do they feel tacked on? Experiment with different rules variants until you find one that is sufficiently compelling.
4, **Create deliverable.**
   After writing the rules down, play a few hands to make sure that you didn't leave any details out of the rules.
   Your rules should include the following:
   - Setup. How does each hand begin?
   - Progression of play. What is the order that things happen in each hand?

- Betting. At what points do players wager money? What are the mechanisms for doing so?
- Determining winner(s). Who gets the money that is wagered? Under what conditions and when?

### Variant

Choose a different card game than *Poker*. Games like *Rummy*, *Euchre*, and *Pitch* are good candidates, but there are literally hundreds of card games that could be used.

### Variant

Instead of dice, choose a different component. Add a second deck of cards. Or add (or remove) the jokers. Or play with a deck from a different game instead of a standard *Poker* deck. Or add a single 20-sided die instead of several four-sided dice. You get the idea.

### Variant

Instead of adding components like dice, add a new rule. For example, all players are dealt three hands instead of one. Or players are dealt a different number of cards, and *Poker* hands are made from four or six cards instead of five. (This would require you to change what the winning hands are and what their relative ranks are.) Or there are two pots instead of one, and they have different functions during gameplay. Or something else—use your imagination.

### Variant

Add "instants" to the deck, allowing you to steal cards from other players, swap hands, or draw again.

### CHALLENGE 2—SOCIAL NETWORKING: THE GAME

In any social-networking site, there is a meta-game going on: Who has the most contacts? Who has the *better* contacts? Who has the *coolest* contact of all? For this challenge, design a game to be added to a social-networking site that takes advantage of these natural tendencies. At minimum, there needs to be some kind of challenge and at least one overall goal. Furthermore, since it's a social network, there must also be gameplay interaction between the players, and not merely a ranking system of sorts (for example, who has the most friends). The game must be about more than the high score.

The game need not affect the social network itself, but can take advantage of it, much like fantasy football takes advantage of real football players and stats without affecting the game itself.

### Components Required

- Internet connection and membership in a social network (such as Facebook, LinkedIn, or MySpace.com)

### Deliverable

- Game-design document
- Informal pitch listing the game's features and how it integrates into the larger social network as a whole

### Suggested Process

1. **Research the social network.**
   For the social network that you chose, list the attributes of an individual's profile (such as his or her friends list, photos, and e-mail address). Highlight those attributes that change when the individual engages in some kind of social activity, such as adding a new friend.
2. **Brainstorm mechanics.**
   Do any of these attributes, or especially the activities that change the attributes, suggest mechanics or dynamics for a game?
   In a group, discuss potential concepts. Allow two hours to agree on a single concept, and flesh out some basic details.
3. **Create deliverable.**

### CHALLENGE 3—STRONG ARM SCRABBLE

You have Q, U, and I tiles. If you only had a T—or if you could take one from somewhere—you could score big. Fortunately for you, and for the sake of this challenge, you are playing *Strong Arm Scrabble*, a home-modified version of the game that allows you to take letters when you need them. In order to do this, you must add one or more mechanics to the game. Where you take these letters from and the consequences for doing that (if any) are up to you, the designer.

### Components Required

- *Scrabble* board game or a suitable equivalent

### Deliverable

- Modified *Scrabble* game
- Written description of the modification(s) to the original game rules
- New complete set of rules (optional)

**Suggested Process**

1. **Consider your options.**

   Note that there can be multiple ways to take tiles, and possibly even a way to defend against it. You don't want people to say, "Hey, that's not fair…" or something similar and become irritated at the mechanic you add. Find ways of adding this mechanic that do not unbalance the game. Also, the mechanic that you add to the game shouldn't break the current state of play. If the player lifts a T off the board, it shouldn't leave words in a partial state of finish, unless you succeed in working that elegantly into the rules. Your game should be both playable and logical.

2. **Playtest and iterate.**

   After adding each mechanic, test the game immediately. Don't spend a whole lot of time debating the merits of one addition or another. A few turns of play can settle any arguments by making a modification's merits and flaws immediately obvious.

3. **Create deliverable.**

**Variant**

Using the same mechanics present in *Scrabble*, attempt to create another tile-based game that requires you to collect certain tile groups before laying them down. For instance, instead of letters, consider dungeon pieces or forest pathways. Anything that can be created by linking one tile to the next is a possibility.

**Variant**

Add a similar "stealing" mechanic to a different classic board or card game. Consider *Strong Arm Monopoly*, *Strong Arm Rummy*, *Strong Arm Candy Land*, and so on.

## CHALLENGE 4—EVERY CENT COUNTS

If you've been reading the chapters of this book in order, you probably have some board, card and dice game designs from Chapters 5–8 that you are quite proud of. Choose your favorite.

Now, suppose that a board-game publisher has offered you a contract to mass-produce your game. Congratulations! There's only one problem. In order to sell the game at the desired price point, they're going to need you to reduce the materials.

Without adding any new game materials, or swapping one material out for another, you must remove at least one of the following: all of the dice, all of the cards, all of the cardboard tiles, or the game board. You may alter the game rules as needed to deal with this change, as long as you don't add any new physical components.

Since the objective is to decrease costs, you can't "remove" a component that your game didn't originally use. Requiring players to supply their own dice is also out of the question. If you're going to remove the dice, you must remove them from the game mechanics, not just the box.

If it feels like you're extracting a kidney, then this exercise is giving you a realistic taste of what it's like when subtractive design is forced on you by outside influences. If this challenge seems trivial, choose another game.

**Components Required**

■ None

**Deliverable**

■ An updated deliverable of the previous challenge (for example, either a revised set of rules, or a new playable prototype, or both)

**Suggested Process**

1. **Figure out what's broken.**
   The removal of a vital component should immediately make the game unplayable by the existing rules. Before you do anything else (including panic), make a list of what rules *have* to be modified because they refer to parts of the game that no longer exist. You might find it easiest to just print out the rules and use a highlighter. This will give you a starting point.
2. **Repair the damage.**
   In some cases, you may find other ways to represent the old mechanics without adding new components (such as adding additional information to the board that used to be on the newly deleted cards). These are the easiest fixes, because they let you preserve the old mechanics with a minimum of fuss, so do those first to get them out of the way.
3. **Reshape the missing pieces.**
   For the remaining mechanics, start thinking about new mechanics to use in their place. Forget about what the game was originally trying to be, because it might no longer be possible to preserve it anymore. You may have to alter the very core of the game to get things to work well again. Instead of lamenting about how this change has ruined your game, think of it as an opportunity to make a *new* game. Preserve what you can, but don't be afraid to completely change what you must.
4. **Alter the prototype and playtest.**
   Create a new prototype with your new rules and try it out. Iterate as necessary.
5. **Create deliverable.**

### IRON DESIGNER CHALLENGE 5—PICK A MECHANIC, ANY MECHANIC (LIVE)

Making a game from a single mechanic is perhaps the ultimate additive exercise. When a random mechanic is foisted upon an unsuspecting board game, it becomes both an additive and a subtractive challenge, and that's what this challenge is all about.

For this challenge, you and another designer or team of designers will go head to head to create something exceptionally challenging. There are three stages to this challenge:

1. Select a game (preferably one that plays in a short period of time, 30 minutes or less, in order to allow for more iteration).
2. Select a mechanic or play dynamic from the BoardGameGeek.com mechanics list at http://www.boardgamegeek.com/browser.php?itemtype=game&sortby=mechanic.
3. Give it to another designer or team of designers to integrate into the game you've selected.

Since the other team has to deal with your choices, feel free to be creative or cruel. It's virtually certain that the exercise will require the other team to both add and subtract mechanics to make the game fun again.

#### Components Required

■ Internet connection
■ A selection of game components: dice, pawns, wooden markers, etc. (optional)
■ A copy of the chosen board game (or preferably, one copy per team)

#### Deliverable

■ Playable prototype of game in question and written rules that describe the play of the game or
■ Informal play demonstration of the new rules.

#### Suggested Process

1. **Research.**
   Consider the mechanic you're given. What other games have you seen it in? If the answer is none, search for games including that mechanic on BoardGameGeek.com and read some play descriptions to get an idea. Most mechanics have a wide range of uses within a larger game.
2. **Brainstorm.**
   Think of interesting ways to use that mechanic and possible ways to tie it into your game.

3. **Playtest and iterate.**

   When you think you've found an idea with potential, try it out. With your copy of the game, try playing a few turns with your new mechanic and see how the game responds. Make modifications as needed or go back to the drawing board if it just doesn't seem to be working.
4. **Create deliverable.**

## NON-DIGITAL SHORTS

Games often contain several interlocking systems, and one small change in the mechanics can have far-reaching effects on the entire play experience.

1. Choose a common board game you consider to be mediocre or terrible. Add or subtract one mechanic that improves the game.
2. Alternatively to #1, add as many mechanics as necessary to make the game genuinely fun. Try to do it with as few additions as possible.
3. Alternatively to #1-2, try doing it by subtracting mechanics. Try to succeed before the game disappears!
4. Choose a classic two-player board game (such as *Backgammon*) and redesign it to be playable by four players.
5. Choose a game you have created from a challenge or non-digital short from a different chapter in this book. Select one mechanic from it and redesign the game as if that mechanic had been cut due to publisher disapproval.
6. Choose a common children's game (such as *Go Fish*) that you can reasonably consider to have an "E" rating. Add one mechanic that will bump the rating to Teen. Continue as far as you are able—one mechanic per rating level.
7. Choose a game you have created from a challenge or non-digital short from a different chapter in this book. Find three people unfamiliar with the game to suggest a mechanic and then add these to your game without breaking it.
8. Think of a new mechanic that can be introduced into your favorite collectible card game. Create five original cards to showcase your new mechanic.
9. Design a means for combat to occur in a turn-based tabletop RPG. Now, simplify it by taking a mechanic out of it.
10. Select a tile-based building game like *Carcassonne*, re-theme it to make it your own, and add a new mechanic to it.

# 15 "But Make It Multiplayer"

In the early 1990s, marketing departments throughout the game industry could be heard to utter this line no matter the potential, possibility, or sensibility of the request in question. Games—traditionally a multiplayer medium—had enjoyed a short and historical blip in their otherwise spotless history in which they were not social uniters but social isolators. Players turned on their computers and disappeared into game worlds by themselves.

With the ready acceptance of modems and later broadband into the average home, however, multiplayer games began to reappear. At about the same time, network connectivity allowed whole offices or communities of geeks to network and play games together.

The result was that multiplayer games sold like hotcakes. While people at universities had long had access to games on mainframes, the machines were outside the reach of the average game player. Modems and networking changed that, however. For many, the first game to introduce them to the medium of multiplayer computer games was *Doom*. Going head-to-head against their friends in what John Romero coined "deathmatch" play, people in offices lost many hours of productivity.

Early entries in the RPG field also courted people from the single-player world. Blizzard's *Diablo*, an action RPG, let whole parties of individuals venture down into a dungeon in search of monsters and loot. Unlike the traditional "hard-core" RPGs of the time, *Diablo* was relatively easy for newcomers to pick up, and since the game offered excellent network play, players could be assured that virtually any question they had would not go unanswered for long. *Ultima Online*, an MMORPG from Origin, hosted hundreds of thousands players within its virtual walls. Within the game-development community, it is not at all inaccurate to say that weeks of work were lost due to the "research" invested in these games.

If multiplayer hit like mad in the 1990s, what's the point of discussing it today?

## LOOKING FORWARD

Although non-digital games, PCs, and consoles have facilitated multiplayer for quite some time, the industry has many more opportunities left to explore.

## BEING ALONE TOGETHER

In MMOs, for instance, while we can talk with one another and perform various missions with each other, players are really alone as individuals or as small groups within a much larger world. The game's "instances" force individuals or groups of individuals to queue through the same set of missions one after the other. Sure, you can opt to do mission C instead of mission B, but all in all, there is sometimes a sense that we are not truly experiencing the same world and hearing all the same things at the same time, particularly when we're waiting in line to address the same NPC as the five players ahead of us. Even creature population is done dynamically, so that there is always enough to encounter for player A and player B. We might think we're all encountering the world together, but very often, we are separated by an instanced narrative that has us on rails right next to another person also on rails. Apart from a chat system, we are, in essence, alone together. That said, however, the social landscape in these games is very much real and massive.

"Instances" were an innovation developed after multiplayer games had been around for a while. These instances specifically addressed the problem of having thousands of players in the same area simultaneously. That some players are presenting these instances as a problem is indeed ironic since instances were originally developed as a solution to an earlier problem.

Nonetheless, this issue of "alone together" has led some to question whether there isn't something more to be had from MMO design. Clearly, judging from player numbers, the design isn't a failure, but still, some wonder if there is something more.

## MULTIPLAYER, MULTIPLATFORM

Though the game industry has firmly embraced multiplayer play, *multiplatform* play is another beast entirely. Consider a virtual world that welcomes everyone simultaneously, no matter their device, and customizes the display and options to the device's abilities and optimum bandwidth output. The concept is prevalent for all kinds of Internet services, but not so well adopted in the game world where much of the content is visual and high priced, and therefore doesn't move medium to medium as well as one would like.

At present, most games are constrained to their platform. A player playing *Poker* on his cell phone cannot play that game with the person sitting directly across from him using his PDA. It may be tempting to say, "Well, no kidding," but it's more forward-looking to say, "Well, why not?" In this regard, digital games have taken a step back from their non-digital brothers and sisters. A board game is ready to go on any table, anywhere.

## MULTIPLAYER, MULTIPURPOSE

At present, most games that feature multiplayer or massively multiplayer play are entertainment games. However, just as play is more fulfilling in a group, so too is work. Multiplayer games are now in use and are being created which put many people in situations for training or education. *Second Life*, for instance, was one of the earliest and most successful MMO worlds to be used by academics looking to explore the virtual space with their students. Consider the possibilities for collaboration in all kinds of disciplines if virtual worlds were used to their fullest extent.

## SOCIAL NETWORKING

Elsewhere in this book, there is a full chapter on social networking (Chapter 21, "Social Networks and Games"). However, it clearly has a place here, too. Facebook and its ever burgeoning game community is mostly a multiplayer community at present, but it is only the smaller scale of people's social networks that keeps these networks from hitting the "massively" multiplayer milestone. In the years to come, these networks will eventually be harnessed for games housed outside of the social network but that draw upon it extensively for player socialization, recruitment, and play.

## TYPES OF MULTIPLAYER GAMES

When marketing departments asked for multiplayer games in the 1990s, they meant it in a general sense—let people play with their friends. They didn't particularly care how this happened, provided that it happened on some level. Since that time, technology and design have advanced (or, in some cases, repurposed old play styles), leading us to define multiplayer games in one or more ways.

### QUANTITY-BASED DISTINCTIONS

Multiplayer games are regularly separated depending on the number of players the game supports. For instance, multiplayer games support anywhere from two to hundreds of players. When we start speaking of thousands and millions of players, we call these games massively multiplayer games.

The design of a game must be approached differently depending on how many players are interacting with one another at a given time. A two-player game, for example, does not have to consider social dynamics such as trading and negotiation that come into play with more players. Once a game exceeds four to eight players, it becomes rarer to see free-for-all gameplay where everyone is out for himself; with larger numbers of players, it is more common to have them grouped into teams, which brings a host of team dynamics into the considerations of the game designer. With thousands or millions of players, the designer must answer questions like "How can a single player feel like he makes a difference," not to mention technical questions like "How can we support this many people simultaneously without the game server dying for lack of bandwidth?"

### PLAY-BASED DISTINCTIONS

Multiplayer games feature four types of play:

- Real time
- Turn based
- Competitive
- Cooperative

Usually, games are a mix of these.

Co-op games (also called player versus environment, or PvE) allow players to play together to solve a particular goal. Competitive games (player versus player, or PvP) pit player against player or group against group in pursuit of a goal. Most massively multiplayer games offer both, and let players choose the style they like.

### TIME-BASED DISTINCTIONS

Real-time games allow players to move simultaneously. They may be synchronous and force players to play together in order for a game to happen, or asynchronous and allow players to play whenever they want, whether together or alone. Turn-based games force players to take turns when moving or performing other actions. Some games are a mix of real-time and turn-based play styles. For example, some games feature real-time adventuring and turn based combat. A common non-digital example is the card game *Slap Jack*. The game is turn-based until a jack is flipped. Then it becomes a real-time blur as players fervently attempt to slap said jack first.

Turn-based games allow players time to consider their moves—for days if desired. Some games use timers to limit turns (*Chess* commonly does this), but many games just go on the "show up when you can" model. As play across social networks continues to broaden, these turn-based, social net, multiplayer games are likely to represent the first wave of a new paradigm in casual games.

Nowadays, turn-based games are largely the domain of PCs, but there are signs this may be changing. Good turn-based strategy games are appearing on consoles, and as consoles make inroads into the casual game market, this type of game play is sure to reassert itself.

### TECHNOLOGY-BASED DISTINCTIONS

Throughout the course of multiplayer games, they have been referred to as many things. Among them are the following:

- MUDs: Multiuser dungeons, multiplayer text-based worlds
- MMO: Massively multiplayer online games
- LAN game: Local area network games
- BBS door: Bulletin board system (BBS) game hosted client-side
- IP-specific: Services like Valve's, Steam, or Xbox Live

## ISSUES IN MULTIPLAYER GAME DESIGN

Apart from the many technical challenges imposed by a multiplayer game, the design of a multiplayer game presents development teams with unique issues they wouldn't face in a traditional single-player game. Bear in mind that this is but a brief overview. Whole books have and will continue to be written on this subject.

## DYNAMIC SCALABILITY

When multiplayer games don't have a fixed number of players, they must support dynamic scalability. Players may come and go as they please, but the game itself should remain playable.

Consider a day in the life of a typical MUD. Let's say the MUD just started, and there are presently two people online, both of whom work with the company in question. As the press releases run in the media, players show up by the tens and then by the hundreds. In advance of this, the designers need to find some way to have the world react to the number of players in it. So, usually, creatures are spawned in accordance with the number of people in a zone. For instance, if there are 300 players, the game may seed the zone with 600 creatures at any given time so that it feels properly competitive without it feeling too easy or like a slaughter in the works. Typically, massively multiplayer games scale items, gold, and the number of creatures in a particular area based on the number of players present.

For other kinds of multiplayer games such as FPSs or online versions of traditional card and board games, the designer must answer a different set of questions. What happens if a player drops out early—should an AI bot take over for the player who left, or can the game continue on seamlessly without interruption, or is the entire game ruined? Can a new player join a game already in progress, or must he wait until the current match is finished? Is there a limit to how many players can play in a single match at once (maximum or minimum)? Should players be able to rank each other's reputation as a means of creating a hoped-for optimal experience?

## GRIEFING

The process of attacking or otherwise negatively affecting other players for enjoyment is known as "griefing." Since the earliest days of gaming, people inside and outside of games have been griefing one another, whether by trash talking across tables, online flame wars, or player killing. So popular was player killing in the early days of MMOs that the griefers were regularly referred to as "PKers," as in "player killers." While griefing may be fun for the instigator, it is rarely enjoyable for the unfortunate players who are the targets of the griefer. It is, in fact, the ruination of other people's fun that is fun for the griefer.

To combat unwanted griefing, games employ several techniques, including player-versus-player (PvP) servers, reporting and recording abilities, and the ability to block communication and contact on a player-by-player and player-to-player basis.

Although modern-day gamers tend to think of "PKing" as something reserved for MMOs, many a person has lost his life over a game of *Poker, Rugby, Cricket, Soccer,* and many more games. These PKers date back hundreds of years.

## COMMUNITY FORMATION AND SUPPORT

While all games (or at least all good games) have a fan community, nowhere is it more integral than in multiplayer games, and particularly in massively multiplayer games. Here, community managers make sure that the forums and various means of networking within the community are up and running and that information is flowing freely from the developers to the guild to the individual player.

Designers should consider how the community can be supported, and if there are any means within the game to make player contact meaningful. This includes support for player-created groups (often called "guilds" or "clans"), the ability of players to keep lists of friends online, and special recognition within the game for player community leaders.

## Attract the Old or the New?

There are several kinds of players who must be considered with online games, especially massively multiplayer games. First, there are players who have never played an MMO before, so everything is new to them. Then there are players who are familiar with MMOs but are new to this game in particular. These players often move in migratory herds with their friends from one game to another. Sometimes, entire guilds transition from game to game. Lastly, there are players who have played the game for a while (perhaps since the beginning). With respect to the design of multiplayer games, some mechanics make a game more friendly for new players but less compelling to experienced ones (like level caps, where there is a limit to how powerful a character can become), or vice versa (like PvP environments, which favor the more experienced players).

## Interface Issues

In board games, nowhere is the issue of multiplayer interface more clear. Rather than one screen per player, the designer is now tasked with one player per side, on average. Exactly how would one put 20 people around a single board? What about 1,000? However, non-digital games with thousands and even hundreds of thousands of players do exist. Examples include ARGs (alternate reality games) and big urban games. These games take players away from their computers and into the real world.

## CHALLENGES

Like any type of game, the only way to get experience working on multiplayer games is to actually work on them. These challenges will give you an idea of some of the issues that designers grapple with when they consider multiplayer games.

## Challenge 1—Old Games, New Life

When multiplayer RPGs and MMOs took off, many makers of classic RPG series failed to make the transition. The single-player games featured the same basic combat as the MMOs, but their vast narratives found in these single player games would be challenging to pull off in a world where anyone can come in at any time. Do you run nine million instances of the same massive story where *unique* possession of items, alliances, and information matters? Theoretically, yes. In practice? Not so much. In MMOs, it's not really why people are there. As a result, a lot of these old series stopped publishing altogether.

For the sake of this challenge, let's say that a developer's agent approached you. She wants you to take a look at these old games and see if you can envision one as a modern day MMO. In their heyday, she tells you, each had an audience of over a million. You may select from the following old-school RPGs or their contemporaries:

- *Wizardry*
- *Might and Magic*
- *Bard's Tale*
- *Advanced Dungeons & Dragons: Eye of the Beholder*

The agent notes that she doesn't want you to merely recreate an existing MMO with a new narrative. Rather, the players of the original series need to recognize it as the new, multiplayer incarnation of their old RPG home.

### Components Required

- Internet for research

### Deliverable

- A list of features that captures the old series and what players would expect from its IP as applied to an MMO
- Concept doc for a new MMO
- Optional: Prototype of play in a digital MMO that gives players the ability to create their own content, such as *Metaplace* or *Second Life*

### Suggested Process

1. **Research the original game.**
   What mechanics made your chosen game stand out as being different from other single-player RPGs of its time? Where did the game innovate within the genre? You may want to research other RPGs and not just your chosen one, in order to draw these comparisons.
2. **Research similar transitions.**
   Look at other old-school RPGs that made the transition to MMO, such as the *Ultima* series becoming *Ultima Online*. What design changes did the developers make in the transition? Based on your own experience or from reading professional reviews, what aspects of the new design worked well, and what did not?
3. **Apply your research to your game.**
   From your description of the core of your chosen game and your list of what to do (and what *not* to do) when creating an MMO version of an older RPG, make a preliminary list of features for your new game.
4. **Create deliverable.**

### Variant

Take any casual game that is not presently multiplayer (such as *Tetris*, *Bejeweled*, or *Diner Dash*) and make it playable by more than one player. The addition of multiplayer must change some facet of the game's play, and can't merely be one player taking half of the turns. Consider adding a PvP mode.

### CHALLENGE 2—"BUT MAKE IT MULTIPLAYER!"

Adventure games were once a whole lot of fun for a whole lot of people… until those people wanted to start playing with other people, that is. Complicating this matter, adventure games aren't terribly replayable. Unless the game offers substantially different paths through the story with multiple endings and even multiple beginnings, its replayability is low.

Lately, however, your company's marketing department has been taking another look at these games. A multitude of new platforms like cell phones and the newer handhelds make these games a potentially lower risk than other types of games. And besides, the licenses to older games are cheap, comparatively speaking.

For this challenge, your marketing department wants you to take any older adventure game, such as any of the *King's Quest* or *Monkey Island* series, *Day of the Tentacle*, or *Grim Fandango*. The programmers can worry about porting the older game to cell phones and handhelds. Your job is to make the game multiplayer.

### Components Required

- Internet for research
- Successful adventure titles such as *The Shivah*, *Psychonauts*, *Indigo Prophecy*, or others.

### Deliverable

- Name of the old game that you plan to modify
- Description of multiplayer gameplay

### Suggested Process

1. **Research existing adventure games.**
   What are the common mechanics that define this genre? What similarities and differences are there between the games you've played? What parts of adventure games do you (or other people) find fun or entertaining? Obviously, you'll want to research the game you've chosen particular as well.
2. **Convert to multiplayer.**
   How do you take a genre that's almost exclusively single player and turn it into a multiplayer experience? Think of the means in which you plan to do this. Is it simultaneous multiplayer? Asynchronous, synchronous, or even turn based?

If you're having trouble thinking of ideas, research other genres that have already made this transition. For example, MUDs (and by extension, MMOs) are derivative of single-player text adventure games. FPSs are derived from older shooting and action games (going back all the way to *Asteroids* and *Space Invaders*), which were primarily one-player experiences.

3. **Create deliverable.**

### Variant

For added difficulty, create a playable version of your adventure game using note cards or a pencil-and-paper module format.

## CHALLENGE 3—MIGRATORY HERDS

It might be the biggest thing going right now, but in another year or two, the MMO of the month will likely be out of favor. While it may seem unlikely from today's perspective, consider that no one imagined anything would come along to top *Asheron's Call* or *Everquest* and, of course, both are no longer top of the MMO world.

As a designer on a new MMO, it's your job to take on a job called "community capture." The producer of your project wants you to study an existing MMO market and figure out what you need to do to capture it in your upcoming game. Consider features that would make their transition as easy as possible. How do they make their current "home" a home? How have previous companies done it? Why should they come to you and your game versus someone else's?

### Components Required

- Internet (for reference) and the games in question
- Previous experience playing an MMO is desirable

### Deliverable

- Analysis of a particular game and its largest guild
- List of features that would be critical and useful for a "community capture"

### Suggested Process

1. **Identify an MMO and its most popular guild.**
   You may choose any MMO you wish. Once you choose one, finding a popular player group within the game is simply a matter of research. If you are unfamiliar with the game and don't know this off the top of your head, try finding and browsing public message boards or fan Web sites (often these are linked to from the game's or developer's main Web site).

2. **Study existing features of the guild.**

   Most popular guilds have their own player-created Web site. Look around and try to discover what makes this one particular guild so popular within the game. If you have a player account in the game, log in and interview other players about it.

3. **Research the process whereby other companies capture migrating populations.**

4. **Develop a list of features.**

   What features does the game have that its most experienced players (especially within the identified guild) really like? What aspects of the game make it different from other MMOs? Do you see any persistent complaints on player message boards of annoying gameplay or desired features that the developer has not yet addressed? Use this information, along with all of your other research, to develop a list of features that would be particularly compelling to this specific player group.

5. **Create deliverable.**

## CHALLENGE 4—STEALTH EDUCATIONAL MMO

You've been brought in by one of the largest educational outfits in your country and have been asked to create a "stealth learning" MMO. (That is, a game where the players are learning educational material without realizing that they are learning.) This project can be for any level of history, provided the project is realistic and suitable for school-aged children. The administrator cautions you that this might not be the right time for a game on a war, but certainly all other kinds of virtual worlds are possible. The MMO needs to teach the following:

- The physical climate and geography
- The social environment
- The socio-political environment
- The economic environment

While teaching these concepts, the game should not be preachy or layer it on too thick. Remember, this is supposed to be a game, and students are supposed to learn while having fun, not by being banged over the head with the topic.

The administrator needs to see a basic design from you that she can then turn around and pitch on the national level.

### Components Required

- Internet for research

### Deliverable

- Concept doc that includes the items listed previously, as well as a list of gameplay features

**Suggested Process**

1. **Choose a topic to cover.**
   Consider a list of time periods and locations that are covered in a history class. (You may want to look at a world history book, available at the local public library if you do not own one, and flip through the table of contents.) Of these potential topics, which ones stand out as having many interesting decisions for individuals to make—that is, which historical topics suggest good gameplay?
2. **Research that topic.**
   If you are unfamiliar with your chosen topic, learn about it, at least as much as would be required at the grade level where you want to teach it.
3. **Create deliverable.**

## IRON DESIGNER CHALLENGE 5—*SOCIALTAIRE*

In keeping with the spirit of this chapter, this challenge works best if you have enough people to divide into teams.

Each team chooses a *Solitaire* game that uses a standard deck of playing cards. There are hundreds of such games; the one that most people call "*Solitaire*" is more properly referred to as *Klondike*. You can find rules online, or in a book such as *Hoyle's Book of Games*. Randomly assign each game to a different team. (If you are doing this challenge alone, choose a game randomly.)

Take the game you are assigned and modify the rules so that it is a competitive two-player or multiplayer game.

**Components Required**

■ One deck of playing cards per team

**Deliverable**

■ Complete set of written rules for your game

**Suggested Process**

1. **Learn the rules.**
   If you are unfamiliar with your *Solitaire* game, read the rules and play it a few times to familiarize yourself with the mechanics and dynamics of the game. Try to get a feel for which aspects of the game need to be preserved and what can be safely modified or removed without destroying the core of the game.

2. **Identify potential sources of conflict.**

   In a single-player game, the only challenge or conflict is between the player and the game itself. Which aspects of this play could be transferred from the deck of cards or the rules themselves to another player? There are two ways to approach this, and you are encouraged to explore both. You could make the players symmetric: preserve most of the rules, so that both players are competing with each other but also with the game's systems. Or you could have the players be asymmetric, where one player partially or completely replaces the game rules (by perhaps stacking or re-ordering the deck) and the other player follows the normal rules of the game. Realize that most *Solitaire* games are difficult to win, so you may want to redefine the object of the game to make it fair, especially if you create an asymmetric game.

3. **Build your rules.**

   Try playing some games, inventing the rules as you go. Most *Solitaire* games don't take very long to play, so you should be able to playtest and modify a lot within a short period of time.

4. **Create deliverable.**

## NON-DIGITAL SHORTS

Adjusting the number of players in a game or using a system at a single time is a common designer issue. These exercises give you a chance to explore these possibilities.

1. Take a standard deck of playing cards and create a turn-based game in which teams of two players compete against one another to complete a series of card runs (for example, three cards in a series, four cards of a suit, and so on). The individual members of the teams should work together in support of the team while working to defeat the other team.

2. Using the same series as in Challenge 1, create a board or tile-based game that up to 20 players can play. Players should be able to come and go as they please and solve missions and function independently of other players or with them, provided they are playing the game simultaneously. As a designer, your biggest challenge will be to determine how the game ends or if it ends at all. How will you provide your players continuing entertainment? What's to stop them from racing through in a single play?

3. Non-digital games tend to build up a following as large as—or even larger than—digital games. *Settlers of Catan*, for instance, has sold more copies than *GTA 3*. *Magic: The Gathering* sold its way into record books pack after pack. Their shelf lives are far longer, they don't require specialized hardware, and almost anyone can play them. But do they have migratory herds, as discussed in Challenge 3? Absolutely. Right now, there are herds of *Magic: The Gathering* or *Pokémon* players who would enjoy at least trying something similar. Players of Eurogames often look for something similar to play next. For this task, your goal is to create a non-digital game that is designed to capture players of another popular game.

4. Design a game to be played in a well-known public setting, such as a museum or a shopping mall.
5. Design a board game to be played on two distinct boards in two separate locations. Assume the players at each board cannot meet each other face to face or exchange real-time communication.
6. Choose a common competitive board game (such as *Risk*) and redesign it to be co-operative.
7. Choose a game you have created from a challenge or non-digital short from a different chapter in this book. Redesign the game to accommodate twice the number of players for which you originally designed.
8. Choose a common turn-based board game (such as *Parcheesi*) and redesign it to include real-time play.
9. Create a four-to-ten player party game where people are rewarded for coming up with the best stories. The game must include multiple mechanics to create the stories and a means for determining who the winner is.
10. Create a turn-based, tile-based adventure game for two to four players where the story unfolds as the game is played. Optionally, you may give players the ability to change the course of the story.

# Part

# V Special Topics

# 16 Creating a User Interface

User interface (often abbreviated UI) is a rather geeky term from the early days of computer programming, and it is used here to describe the way the player and the game communicate with each other. In a video game, the UI consists of two distinct parts: how the players communicate their chosen actions to the game (the" input," usually referred to as the controls), and how the game displays the results of those actions to the player (the "output," such as the screen display and controller vibration). These two are interlinked in many ways, which is why we talk of UIs as individual entities even though they are composed of smaller parts.

Every game needs a UI, and at some point in every game developer's career he or she designs or implements at least part of one. With that in mind, this chapter allows you to practice your UI design skills. Keep in mind that UI design is a huge topic; many books (of varying quality) have been written on the subject, and you are encouraged to continue your study of this vast topic if it interests you. A list of recommended reading appears at the end of this chapter.

## GOALS OF THE UI

Occasionally, there are situations where the game is designed with the UI as a starting point (in the form of a special controller or control scheme), and mechanics are then layered on top. But more often, the control scheme is one of the last parts of a game that is designed. While developers may know the controller upon which they're designing, in the early days of design, they may not know enough about the game itself to determine how they will map its controls on to the controller. So the mechanics are created first, and then a suitable UI must be created to allow the player to invoke those mechanics. In these cases, start with known mechanics and answer the question, "How does the player take each possible action?"

To answer this question, you must first ask a more basic question: What is the purpose of the UI in the first place? Usually, the UI represents a (potentially frustrating) barrier between the player and the game. The player wants to take an action in the game and must translate that desire into a physical action, such as a series of button presses. The goal of the UI designer is to create a set of controls that is as transparent and easy to use as possible, so that the player can concentrate on actually *playing the game* rather than mastering the controls. While more complex controls can be taught to players in the form of tutorial levels, it is better to make the controls as simple as possible to reduce the need for such tutorials in the first place.

There is a major tool in a designer's toolbox that can be used to simplify controls: the use of affordances.

## AFFORDANCES: RIGHT = EASY, WRONG = HARD

Donald Norman, in his book *The Design of Everyday Things*, first used the term "affordance" in the context of UI. An affordance is an obvious, readily apparent action that can be performed on an object. For example, a controller button can be pressed; anyone who has ever seen a small, circular button before is familiar with this action and this behavior, so we say that the button "affords" pressing. Buttons do not afford sliding, or throwing, or chewing, or any other action that we do not normally associate with them.

To make use of affordances, there is one main principle: each control should do only what it affords. Said another way, it should be easy for the player to use each control in the correct way, and difficult for the player to use the wrong control at the wrong time. Doing things right is easy; doing things wrong is hard.

It's important to note that affordances are dependent not just on the object, but also the person trying to use that object (and that person's past experiences, culture, and physical abilities). Dual analog sticks easily afford a left stick = move, right stick = fire control scheme for an overhead shooter, but only for people who have played similar games like *Robotron 2084* and *Smash TV*; for people unfamiliar with video games in general, this control scheme may not be immediately obvious.

This suggests that, as mentioned many times in this book, developers must be aware of their target audience. For the PlayStation 2, for instance, the vast majority of games use the X button to accept a menu selection and the O button to cancel. This is an easy affordance for numerous reasons. First, it draws on players' former experience with other games on the console. Second, Sony requires that button setup. In fact, developers would have to make a compelling argument to Sony to change this convention in your game. Being consistent with other games is one of the easiest affordances to take advantage of.

Ironically, the use of X to select and O to cancel is actually not that great an affordance for American players who have never used a PlayStation controller before. In American culture, "X" denotes "no" or "not," so the X symbol suggests a cancel action (and likewise, "O" denotes acceptance when placed next to an "X"), so this reversal of established roles between X and O confused many American gamers when they first encountered this convention.

With computers, the mouse/keyboard control comes with a whole host of affordances—not just from other computer games, but from non-game applications. You can expect players (even those who have never played a game before) to understand the relationship between the physical movement of the mouse and the movement of an on-screen cursor. Computer users can be expected to recognize push buttons and know that left-clicking on a button activates it. To enhance this affordance, developers make buttons 3D instead of flat, so that they *look* like they can be pushed. They also highlight buttons or make them glow when the mouse is hovering above them to make it really obvious that the mouse is in a position to press the button. These are ways of enhancing the natural affordances of the button, making it *really* easy to use.

The Nintendo Wii controller also comes with many affordances, but these come from the real world rather than computer experience. Many of the early games made for this console involved holding the remote and making physical motions that mimicked what you wanted to do on the screen—swinging a golf club or rolling a bowling ball, for example.

These last two examples suggest that even when creating a completely original game that requires inventing a never-before-seen control scheme, it's good to rely on affordances from outside of the world of games. If you want to broaden your market, you probably should.

## A NOTE ABOUT ACCESSIBILITY

Some people are deaf, or blind, or colorblind. Some are quadriplegic. Others have arthritis. Some are very young or very old, and lack extreme motor coordination. Many of these people would like to play and enjoy games, if only developers let them.

It turns out that making a game accessible makes it more playable for all gamers. If the game has separate meters for health and mana, differentiating them not only by color but also by shape and icon makes it possible for a colorblind player to interpret them. It also makes it easier for everyone else. In general, the more ways that a developer conveys information across various senses, the more accessible the game is and the more obvious that information is to everyone.

Here are some points to consider when defining your inputs:

- Avoid requiring the player to press multiple buttons simultaneously. Some people lack the coordination, especially if both buttons must be pressed with the same hand. As an alternative, consider mapping several similar controls to a single button and making it context-sensitive.

- Allow the player to redefine the controls. Some players are used to certain button functions in certain places, and they may not match the default control scheme. This is especially true on computers, where some people prefer to use the WASD keys for movement and others prefer the arrow keys.

- Consider ways to reduce the number of controls… even down to a single up/down switch or button if you can. The fewer the buttons, the less intimidating the game is to inexperienced gamers. Reduce the controls sufficiently, even if it's limited to a special game mode, and the game is playable by everyone, including those who may have lost the use of their limbs.

- Support multiple difficulty levels. Even if the game is targeted mainly at the "hard-core" player, nothing is lost by adding an "easy" mode that lets newer players enjoy the experience, too.

- Use simple, clear, and concise language. Many otherwise excellent games could be thoroughly enjoyed by young children, if not for the fact that their dialogue was apparently written by someone with a Ph.D. in literature from Harvard.

- Do not differentiate screen elements by color alone. Use different shapes, sounds, and textures. For the majority of gamers, this makes those elements of the game far easier to tell apart, and the UI feels more responsive. For the colorblind, the game is no longer completely unplayable.

- Where there is text, make it large (or allow manual resizing). Some players don't have 20/20 vision. Some players have crystal-clear vision and an old, fuzzy TV. If the text is too small, players can't read it. Including an audio track adds another way to get the message across—a critical one for gamers who are partially illiterate.

- Allow contrast adjustment. Again, this has to do more with the variation in display devices. If the game is too dark or too bright, it is unplayable even for someone with perfect vision.

For an amusing example of what happens when your UI is not accessible, download and play *Game Over!*, billed by its developers as "the world's first (and hopefully only) universally inaccessible game." You can read about and download it from http://www.ics.forth.gr/hci/ua-games/game-over/.

## FEEDBACK

So far, we have talked mostly about player input. Games also must give the player information on the current state of the game in the form of visual, auditory, and sometimes tactile (physical sensation) feedback. These, too, can be made much clearer through the use of affordances. Common conventions in UI include life meters (drawn in a red color), mini-map of the immediate surrounding area (centered on the player), and the use of icons instead of full-text descriptions.

Developers can also make information easier to access by grouping. If several pieces of information relate to each other, place them in close proximity on the screen. If the player's hit points and mana points are equally important and affect each other (for example, if mana is used primarily to heal hit points), placing their respective meters on opposite sides of the screen just makes the game harder to play. Making them adjacent lets the player get all the information he needs at a single glance.

Aside from persistent information like the player's health and location, also consider events that happen in the game that the player needs to know about. If a player gets hit and takes damage, he needs to know either through the screen flashing red, a sound playing, the controller vibrating, or a combination of all three.

## THE PROCESS OF UI DESIGN

UI design follows some fairly straightforward steps. First, designers list all of the elements that are needed in a UI. Then, they prioritize them based on how often the player uses each one. Make note of any natural affordances the game's UI can take advantage of. Then, prototype, playtest, and repeat. Throughout the process, look for ways to simplify the controls, and make sure the player receives immediate, understandable feedback in response to his or her actions.

### WHAT ARE THE INPUTS/OUTPUTS?

List all of the actions that the player performs in the game. List all of the game-state information that the player needs to know.

### PRIORITIZE

Note next to each input and output whether the player uses it constantly or only occasionally. The ease of accessing each item should be proportional to how often it must be accessed. For example, critical information should not be buried in a subscreen, or else the player constantly moves back and forth between the main game and that subscreen. Meanwhile, information that is only useful once every hour should not be displayed constantly on the main screen, or it simply clutters things and draws attention away from the more important information there.

### FIND THE AFFORDANCES

For each player action, consider what control best affords that action. If there are several actions that naturally map to the same control, perhaps use both actions, if possible, and make it context-dependent.

If the best input is unclear, ask others their opinions. "If you wanted to fire your torpedoes, and you hadn't read the manual, what would you try first?" After asking a few people, a strong consensus will likely develop. Although it may not be clear *why* people assume the right shoulder button should perform a certain action, they *do*, and that gives a UI designer an excellent starting point. For best results, of course, ask people who are part of the target market.

For outputs, there are several considerations. First, there is the question of whether to display the information at all. If it is unimportant, or if part of the game involves keeping some information intentionally hidden from the player to increase tension or uncertainty, developers may not want to show it at all. They only show some of the information, such as a fuzzy progress bar, rather than a specific number.

Second, if information must be displayed to the player, the next question is where. Consider where the player's eyes are normally looking on the screen. Critical information should be placed nearby, so that the player does not have to glance around at all corners of the screen. This is part of the reason why in many modern FPS games, the ammo remaining is actually printed on the gun the player carries. Aside from being aesthetically pleasing and immersive, it also puts the information close to the center of the screen where the action is.

### GIVE IMMEDIATE FEEDBACK FOR YOUR INPUTS

When a player tries to take an action and nothing happens, it can be very frustrating. Even worse is when something *does* happen, but the player is not aware of it, so he takes the same action again and again, only to find out later he has unintentionally done too much.

The best way to avoid this is to give the player feedback whenever he does something. Again, this can be visual, auditory, tactile, or some combination of all three. It makes the game feel satisfying and responsive—assuming that the feedback is obviously responding to the input and not something else (again, we see the use of affordances).

### REDUCE EVERYTHING

With over 100 keys on a typical PC keyboard, and over 10 analog controls on some console controllers, there is the temptation to make use of everything. For a realistic flight simulator that is *supposed* to be complicated, having dozens of different controls can add to the experience. For a typical FPS, it just makes the UI frustrating to use. Think of ways to reduce and collapse the controls so that they use a minimum of joystick and button movement.

Likewise, make every game screen, menu, and subscreen fight for its life. If the player has to go three levels deep into a menu system to do something as simple as using a healing potion, rethink the UI. Most game actions—especially those that are used frequently—should be no more than a single button press away at all times.

### PROTOTYPE

If there's one place where rapid prototyping can really benefit a game, it's the UI. By definition, the user interface is active and happens in real time. A passive, unmoving design document cannot begin to show the level of UI quality. Likewise, a written document runs the risk of miscommunicating to the programmer, if someone other than you is implementing the UI design. A working prototype with moving parts is much better at communicating the idea.

How does one make a UI prototype? Start with paper: draw a screen mockup on a whiteboard or posterboard, for example, and use index cards to show screen elements. This has the advantage of making changes painless: it's as easy as moving index cards around! Use a finger as the mouse cursor, if the game works with a mouse.

Eventually, consider developing a digital prototype. A game's UI consists of moving parts, and evaluating its quality requires setting it in motion and interacting with it (much like game dynamics). The game logic doesn't need to be implemented (fake data can be used), but make sure that all of the moving parts actually *do* something. Adobe Flash can be useful for this, as it is easy to make screen mockups and respond to mouse clicks with a minimum of fuss. In cases where the UI involves simple behavior from mouse clicks, a prototype can be as simple as a series of screen mockups linked together in HTML. UI designers with no technical experience at all often team up with a programmer who then implements the digital prototype.

### PLAYTEST!

The importance of playtesting UI cannot be overstated. During focus tests or play sessions, developers watch people who have never played the game try to use the UI. Often, players press the wrong buttons accidentally or complain that the game is too hard because they lack critical information (or simply did not notice it). Instead of chastising playtesters for missing "obvious" things, the wise developer takes this as a strong signal that the UI is not intuitive enough and makes things easier for the player to understand by changing the controls around or adding new feedback to the screen to make critical events more obvious.

With every change, there's also another round of testing with a new batch of testers. It's important to use new testers continuously. Once a playtester has learned the UI and become familiar with it, he no longer notices if things are unintuitive any more than the developer would notice it.

### INTENTIONALLY "BAD" UI

So far, we have discussed how to make UI as easy to use, intuitive, and seamless as possible. Every developer's objective is to make the UI get out of the player's way and become transparent so that the player thinks of what to do and the game responds exactly as the player thought it would. In the vast majority of games, this is, in fact, the ultimate goal. Players want to experience the *gameplay* after all, and any attention that must be paid to the UI is attention taken away from the game itself.

Is it ever useful to make a UI that is intentionally frustrating, difficult to use, or opaque? Would developers ever make things *less* usable in order to make a better game? The answer is yes—but to do so, one still has to know what the rules of *good* UI are before breaking them.

An example of such a UI would be Persuasive Games' *Disaffected!*. This game is designed to make the player feel the frustration and stress of being a FedEx Kinko's employee. The controls are slow and unresponsive, the avatars of co-workers are constantly getting in the player's way, and the goals are unintuitive. The UI comes together to make the player feel, well, disaffected—which is the design intent of the game.

To make a bad UI, the designer must first understand *why* a "good" UI is good. For controls that are common conventions, what originally made them so? Why do most life meters have a dark-reddish color? Why does the Esc key in a PC game bring up the menu that allows players to exit from the game? Understand how these conventions came to be, and one understands the effect on the game experience when these conventions are changed.

## CHALLENGES

Think of UI as the seats in a movie theater. If it's uncomfortable, no one's going to stay for the show. These exercises are designed to take you through the process of creating, crafting, and refining UI.

### CHALLENGE 1—THE SPORTS UI

Designing the UI for sports games (especially team sports) is difficult. In most games, the player only has a single avatar. In team sports, there are many avatars that must be controlled simultaneously.

For this challenge, take a team sport that you are familiar with and create the UI for a video game based on it.

#### Components Required

■ At least one modern game of the sport you chose and a machine to play it on; or, if unavailable, an Internet connection to research the UI

#### Deliverable

■ Screen mockups of all major screens during the play of a two-player game, showing the information displayed on each screen and the approximate location of each element
■ For each screen, a list of all controls on that screen, using any modern console controller

#### Suggested Process

1. **Make a list of states.**
   What are the different play states (for example, for baseball, states would include "before a pitch," and "immediately after the pitch but before the swing")? What decisions are players making during each state? Each state needs its own separate set of controls and deserves its own screen mockup.
2. **Make an action list.**
   For each state, list what actions each player can take and what information about the game is important to each player. This gives you a good idea of what controls and screen elements are necessary; once you have that list, the next steps guide you toward turning these into the deliverables.
3. **Research conventions.**
   Look at other sports games, and answer the following questions:
   ■ For sports that involve choosing different plays secretly (like American football), how do you do this in a way that lets you know what you've selected without giving that same information to your opponent?

- What camera angles are available for viewing the game and how are they controlled?
- In two-player games, is it better to have a single camera view or a split screen (horizontal or vertical)? What are the advantages and disadvantages of each?
- What kinds of information should be displayed on the screen at all times during play (and at breaks in the action, if any)?
- What is the best way to control all of the people on your team at once? Do you control one player at a time and have some intuitive way to switch between players, or can you direct the entire team concurrently?
- Did you find any controls or actions in the professional video game that did not appear on your lists from your state list and action list that you created earlier? Add them.

If you do not own a game to do this research, look at screenshots included in professional game reviews. However, ownership of the game itself is heavily recommended.

4. **Explain the conventions.**

   For conventional UI, what parts take advantage of affordances? Make sure that you keep those (more or less) as they are. Are there any controls or feedback that seem unintuitive to you? If so, you have to decide between conforming to conventions that are familiar to the target audience versus improving the UI in ways that might force players to learn a new set of conventions.

5. **Create deliverable.**

   Your screen mockups can be crude hand drawings with stick figures, boxes, and text if you prefer not to use your artistic ability (or if crude hand drawings are your artistic ability). Make sure you show all relevant screen elements. You need only include screens that are found during the play of a two-player game. Saving/loading screens, the main menu, etc. do not need to be included. For each screen mockup, include a diagram of a controller on the modern console and show what controls map to which in-game actions.

### Variant

If you've completed the "Sports Games" challenge (Chapter 8, Challenge 1), create the UI for that game instead.

## CHALLENGE 2–TWISTER 360

Suppose Milton Bradley and Microsoft just announced a new partnership to make the classic party game *Twister* available on Xbox Live Arcade. Through your incredible luck (either good or bad, depending on your viewpoint), you are the lead designer on the project.

It is made clear to you that the play experience of the original game should be left as intact as possible. Multiple players on a single console are obviously preferred, but the game should support online play as well.

You are encouraged to make use of a controller that already exists (either the default 360 controller, or perhaps a dance pad or something similar). However, you may also propose a new controller design for use with this game, but you must be prepared to justify its necessity since a specially manufactured controller adds significant costs and risk to the project. If you really feel it adds to the gameplay experience, they are open to discussion.

### Components Required

■ A copy of the physical board game *Twister* with rules, or suitable substitute

### Deliverable

■ Game-design document, including a complete description of the UI, or
■ One-page formal business e-mail (printed) that describes the need for a special controller, if you cannot take advantage of a controller already in use with other games. A description of the controller itself and its use with the game should be contained in the game design document

### Suggested Process

1. **Twist.**
   Most people played *Twister* as a child. If you have access to the game, play it. If not, try to remember the experience. Often, adults are reluctant to play the game due to the potentially embarrassing situations it can put one in. That, of course, is half the fun. Write down what the *Twister* experience was for you. This is the experience you are attempting to simulate in the game. Why did you enjoy playing it? Why did you enjoy watching others play it?

2. **Brainstorm.**
   In groups of two or three people, brainstorm possible UIs for this game. Don't automatically think of a *Twister*-sized mat on the floor. Start with the controls you know and your publisher wants—a console controller, the Wii remote, a DDR mat, or even a PC camera. How can you recreate the experience you identified in the previous step?

3. **Develop a list of possible control schemes.**
   Narrow your possible input devices down to two. Next, attempt to define the control scheme for each:
   ■ How does the player see herself on the screen?
   ■ How does the player select movements in the game?

- How does the player determine if the movement will cause her character to bend impossibly or comfortably?
- How do you recreate the experiences you have identified?
- For many designers, it helps to hold the controller in your hand (if applicable), close your eyes, and pretend that you are actually playing the game.

4. **Mock up controls.**
   Map all possible actions to the input device of your choice.

5. **Create deliverable.**

## CHALLENGE 3—ACTION RPG SUBSCREEN

In many cases, you won't be designing the entire UI all at once, but rather a single piece at a time. This happens more often in projects where the mechanics are designed before the controls. For this challenge, you'll be designing a single component of a much larger game.

The game in question is a simple action-RPG for the PC. Better known games in this genre include *Diablo, Baldur's Gate: Dark Alliance*, and *Titan Quest*. If you are unfamiliar with the genre, you need to research it in order to proceed.

The mechanics for this game are simple, compared to other games in the genre:

- The player controls a single character.
- The character has hit points and mana. Hit points decrease when damage is taken and increase by finding healing shrines in the dungeon. Mana decreases when casting spells, and it increases by finding magic shrines in the dungeon. Both are completely restored by returning to town. Neither can be restored through use of items.
- The character has two stats: strength and magic. Each extra point of strength adds +1 hit point and adds +1 damage to all of your physical attacks. Each extra point of magic adds +1 mana and adds +1 damage to all of your spell attacks.
- The character gains experience points. At certain thresholds, the character gains a level, which allows the player to increase his strength by +2, or magic by +2, or strength and magic by +1 each.
- The character can carry up to six items. There is no concept of item size or weight, and items cannot stack. You can drop an item to remove it from inventory. There are no consumable items in the game. There are three kinds of items: gems, weapons, and spellbooks. Gems are not useful in any way; they take up inventory slots, and they can be sold for a lot of money in town, but they provide no benefit while being carried. Weapons increase the damage from physical attacks when equipped, and do nothing when merely carried
- You can equip up to one weapon at a time, and equipping a new weapon unequips the previously equipped one (if any). You can equip up to three spellbooks at a time; each spellbook enables you to cast a spell while equipped. Spells do damage to enemies (within a range of possible values) when cast.
- The character has a certain amount of money. This money is found in the dungeon and by selling items in town, and can be used to purchase new items in town. Money does not count as an item and does not take up any room in inventory.

For this game, design the UI for the subscreen (or series of subscreens) that allows the player to view and manipulate their inventory.

Since this is a PC game, assume a minimum screen resolution of 800 × 600. Make your prototype that size.

## Components Required

■ Graph paper

## Deliverable

■ Screen mockup of all subscreens, along with a text description of all controls on that screen.

## Suggested Process

1. **Consider your options.**
   You have a lot of information to display. Think of how the information should be laid out so that it's easy to find. Think about how and when you should draw the player's attention to certain critical information, such as whether they can level up. Is there any information that you can keep hidden from the player, or that only needs to show up at certain times? Should you display the effects of equipped spellbooks all the time on the subscreen or only at certain times (for example, when they're highlighted, or when the mouse is hovering over them)? Lastly, consider the tradeoff between having one screen with all of the information (it may be a bit dense and cluttered if you're not extremely careful) versus spreading things out onto several subscreens and including a way to navigate between them (which then requires the additional question of which information goes on which screen).

2. **Create deliverable.**
   It's much easier to implement this in digital form if you have something to start from. Take a sheet of graph paper and draw a large, to-scale rectangle on it, and start drawing the screen elements in. Use a pencil and experiment with different placements. Think about the tasks a player wants to perform, like leveling up or looking up character stats. How does the player accomplish these tasks: clicking, double-clicking, clicking-and-dragging, hovering the mouse, or using the keyboard (or some combination of these)? Are the most common tasks easy to do, without requiring many mouse clicks and heavy movement of eyeballs around the screen? Do the controls follow genre convention, where appropriate?

3. **Implement a digital prototype (optional).**

   To improve your design, implement it on a computer. Use whatever development tools you have available and are familiar with (popular choices include Microsoft Visual Basic and Adobe Flash). First, take care of the noninteractive components, such as the display of current stats that don't change. (You can use made-up numbers.) Then create the interactive parts that can be manipulated: the ability to level up, drop items, and equip/unequip weapons and spellbooks. Lastly, add graphical polish that is meaningful to the UI: make things glow or sparkle to attract the player's attention, for example.

4. **Playtest and iterate (optional).**

   Try out your digital prototype and perform all of the tasks that you designed. Are they as easy as you thought they'd be? If not, go back and alter your prototype. If there are bugs that cause the prototype to crash or otherwise not function properly, this can be acceptable, as long as your design intent can be observed. Find some friends or colleagues who are familiar with the genre and watch them play with your prototype. Ask them to accomplish certain tasks and see what they do. Do they ever try something unexpected? Are they unable to accomplish the task you set them because they don't understand the controls? Make a note of it and redo your prototype to compensate.

### CHALLENGE 4—THE CONSOLE RTS

Since the invention of the genre, real-time strategy games have been developed almost exclusively for PC, because the genre lends itself well to mouse/keyboard control. When an RTS game is developed for console, it's usually a direct port from a PC title, and it's usually terrible. Why? The control scheme changes so radically that it also causes an unintentional change in the game mechanics, thus rendering the game something other than what it used to be.

For this challenge, you are on a design team working for Sony, tasked with porting a modern RTS game on PC to the PlayStation 3. You may choose the game and expect that Sony is able to procure the license. The only restriction is that you may not choose a game that has previously been ported to this console.

You are expected to use the default Sixaxis controller (for example, no fair requiring a USB mouse/keyboard to play the game). On the bright side, you have been given free license to change the game mechanics, as long as you keep the general storyline and feel of the original game. Also, you do not have to worry about multiplayer on a single console. Assume either single player against AI opponents or multiplayer online.

You must solve the problem of porting the UI from one platform to another. Since this is a port, you don't have to worry about the rest of the game's design for the purposes of this challenge.

### Components Required

■   Internet connection for research
■   Original PC game (optional)

### Deliverable

■ Screen mockup of the main gameplay screen (and subscreens, if any)
■ A list of all gameplay controls for each screen. Use a diagram of the controller and show the effects of each button.

### Suggested Process

1. **Research the original game.**
   Familiarize yourself with the game, including:
   ■ Storyline and overall look and feel
   ■ Actions that the player can take during the game
   ■ Core mechanics
   Play the game, or read professional reviews and look at screenshots. Decide what aspects of the game must be preserved, and which (if any) can be changed without ruining the experience.
2. **Find affordances.**
   As of the time of this writing, there have been few, if any, successful RTS games on console, so you do not have the benefit of existing conventions to draw on in this genre. Instead, consider the affordances that would make the most sense, and consider other kinds of games and other non-game experience that your players have.
3. **Decide—change the mechanics or change the UI?**
   For each UI element in the game, find the most natural mapping on console. Some elements, you might choose to preserve as is; others, you might change to make the game easier or more natural to play on the new platform.
4. **Create deliverable.**

### IRON DESIGNER CHALLENGE 5—INVISIBLE INTERFACE (LIVE)

Think of your favorite action movie. Got it? Good. Consider this—if it's your favorite movie, odds are you feel completely immersed in its world and are able to feel suspense, anxiety, sense danger, and so on all without the aid of a HUD. Roller coasters and other theme park rides are also noticeably HUD free. Some designers are beginning to ask, "Why do we need HUDs in video games?"

In the early days of computer and video games, there were no colors and no graphics to convey how well someone was feeling. So game developers listed health numerically. You want to know Zynaryx the Mage's health? It's 38/50. Gradually, graphics took over text to *show* us instead of *tell* us. Some games are going so far as to abandon the HUD entirely. One of the earliest games to do this was *Fight Night Round 3*. The game conveyed information in a number of ways including these:

- As fighters tire, they move more slowly, and their arms drop lower in their stance.
- The player sees just how hurt the character is in flesh and blood.
- The crowd shows its excitement by standing, sitting, and cheering.
- The ringside announcer provides ongoing gameplay commentary.

If movies don't need HUDs, why do we?

For this challenge, divide into groups of two to four people. Choose any RPG, RTS, or FPS and give that game to another group. Your goal is clear, but challenging: figure out a way to remove the HUD of the game you're saddled with, but provide the player everything he needs to know.

### Components Required

- Internet connection, to view screenshots of your game

### Deliverable

- Hand-drawn mockup of the main screen of the original game, with HUD, or a printed screenshot (for comparison)
- Hand-drawn mockup of the main screen for your now HUD-less game
- Text description of how the information in the old HUD is now conveyed to the player, in cases where it is not obvious from your screen mockup

### Suggested Process

1. **Start with a screenshot.**
   Look at the HUD of the original game and make a list of all screen elements that you must remove. You can tackle these one at a time, independently.
2. **Brainstorm.**
   For each element of the HUD, come up with as many ways as you can think of to represent that same information.
3. **Collision checking.**
   Make sure that you don't map two HUD elements to the same thing. For example, if you change a character's color when it is running low on health and also when it is under the influence of a Haste spell, things could get confusing if both happen at the same time. Try to keep your representations distinct from one another, *especially* for two bits of information that have nothing to do with each other.
4. **Optimize.**
   The HUD isn't the only unrealistic aspect of modern UI. Icons and names don't float over people's heads in the real world, nor does text appear out of thin air when you perform an action. Make things as realistic as possible to improve player immersion.
5. **Create deliverable.**

## RECOMMENDED READING

If you would like to gain a deeper understanding of UI, the following books are helpful:

- *The Design of Everyday Things*, by Donald Norman. This book explores the UI of everyday devices such as doors, kitchen stoves, and radio alarm clocks. Norman goes into great detail on the use of affordances and usability. Once you realize how something as simple as a door can be difficult to use, you will never look at a game's HUD in the same way.

- *Visual Explanations: Images and Quantities, Evidence and Narrative*, by Edward Tufte. For all the adherence to genre conventions, one might think that there are only one or two ways to display a life meter or ammo count. Tufte shatters this illusion, showing many different ways to display important information, and the benefits and drawbacks of each.

- *User Interface Design for Programmers*, by Joel Spolsky. The only reason this book is "for programmers" is that it explains things in terms that overly logical programmers can understand. There is little to no actual programming in this book. Rather, this book explains in plain English what good software UI design is, why it is important, and how anyone (even a programmer with no human empathy whatsoever) can create software that feels responsive. If a good UI for a word processor can make people happy, imagine what can happen when you apply these lessons to an entertainment game!

# 17 Games as Art

When one of the authors of this book decided to create a text adventure game in 2007, it clearly wasn't for commercial reasons. In fact, it wasn't for professional reasons or with any particular person or client in mind. Rather, she created the game because she believed that there was a certain beauty in video games of long ago, when the player could talk directly with the designer, and the designer could talk back.

That game is what one might refer to as an "art game," a game created to make an artistic statement or with artistic intent. To some degree, all games can be considered art games since games themselves are a form of interactive art. In contrast to traditional games, though, games classified as art games tend to feature designs that *purposefully* don't fit neatly within any particular genre or within the conventions we expect from a particular genre.

Unfortunately, the definition of "art" is even more contentious than the definition for "game." So when you put the two together, it's a definition minefield. For the sake of this chapter, we will evade the issue entirely by stealing a pseudo-definition from another space—you know an art game when you see it.

Just as people have created songs, paintings, movies, documentaries, books, poems, and spoken-word performances, so, too, are designers embracing digital games to make a point, a statement, and an exploration of a particular idea or ideal.

## BEYOND THE VISUAL

In games, the art is not always visual. This may seem like an odd statement to make. Indeed, many games do have amazing graphics with environments and characters that are breathtaking. As processing power increases, there is no doubt that the modelers, animators, texture artists, level designers, riggers, and environmental artists *are* indeed creating *art*. Many would agree that there is beauty in 8-bit art, too, and many are still working in that medium today.

However, there is art in the *game*, too, and a game need not have graphics at all to be a game. As we explored in Chapter 2, "Game Design Atoms," a game is a collection of components—mechanics, systems, players, goals, and more. So, when considering a game as art, it is important to look beyond that which can be seen.

It is a temptation—a form of learned response—for people to judge games first by their graphics. Some dismiss a game based on this impression alone. This is an unfortunate thing.

Oddly enough, there are many who chase great graphics in games, only to be disappointed by lackluster gameplay. That experience is rarely remembered when the next polygonal powerhouse comes along.

If one considers the game as a set of interacting systems that are governed by a set of rules, games can actually be more expressive than other artistic media in the right circumstances. Consider the emotion of childlike wonder and imagination invoked by lying on a hill and gazing up at the clouds on a bright, sunny day. A book can describe the feeling in great detail. A movie can show an individual child's external reactions. A song can attempt to stir those same emotions in the listener. But a game can actually let the player experience this emotion firsthand, in a way that is impossible with noninteractive media. This is, in fact, what the game *Cloud* does. This feeling comes not from the graphics or music, but directly from the gameplay.

When exploring a game as art, it is important to look beyond the graphics to the underlying experience. *Passage*, reviewed below, is a perfect example of an experience one might have.

Some games mingle the visuals with the mechanics to create art. *Lost in the Static* is one such game. It features black-and-white static on a screen. The game takes place within that static by creating multiple static fields and using the differences in those fields to give necessary information to the player.

Board games like *Fluxx* and, before it, *Cosmic Encounter* and *Nomic*, play with the concept of fixed, binding, and unchanging rules that is sometimes used as a defining concept of a game. However, the rules of both of these games challenge that concept, and in that challenge, there is something one could call art, too.

## BEYOND FUN

For most people, sitting down to play a game is an escape, a form of entertainment, and a whole lot of fun. It's *rarely* about deep thoughts or artistic explorations of a concept. It's almost never about feeling something we'd rather not feel or even think about. That's not to say that games don't have all of these themes and more, but rarely are these themes the point of the game. With the advent of "art games," though, this is changing.

Games are an expressive medium, and a new breed of interactive artist has begun to explore this medium for its artistic potential. At present, artists and developers are only scratching the surface of the tremendous potential that lies underneath. Furthermore, games need not entertain to be considered "a game." They don't even need to be especially fun. Games can say whatever the artist wants them to say.

In the following sections, we'll explore two such games, as well as a deeper exploration of games as art. Unlike previous chapters, we have sidestepped the traditional "how to" exploration. Rather, we'll provide an exploration of the concepts, the games, and the argument through the words of others.

## *PASSAGE*: A GAME THAT ALMOST MADE ME CRY
## PATRICK DUGAN, GAME DESIGNER

*The following review was authored by Patrick Dugan on December 6, 2007 and appeared on Play This Thing (http://playthisthing.com/passage), a site that reviews indie games. It is reprinted here with permission.*

*On his site, Passage's creator, Jason Rohrer, includes a creator's statement, but he hopes you play the game before reading it. You can find that statement on his site at: http://hcsoftware.source-forge.net/passage/.*

*The production of such games is Rohrer's full-time job. He gives away his games and software for free. He is supported through donations on his site.*

*Passage* is a special kind of game made by an unusual kind of game developer. Jason Rohrer lives with his wife and child in a cabin in upstate New York. This cabin is specially insulated to maintain heat during the winter; it has a means of collecting rainwater and a fully implemented garden in the back yard. As a result, Jason and his family live on around $800 a month. He has an MS in Computer Science and experience doing network applications, but he doesn't play the Corporate America game. Instead, he's free, and he's free to make beautiful art games that, like his house, are technically and experientially tight to the point of self-sufficiency.

*Passage* is about the literal passage through a maze, but it is also about the passage of time. You begin as a young man; you have a wall foregrounded directly to your north, and can move to the right or explore the maze to the south. Early on you encounter a woman; if you bump into her, you will fall in love and become her companion. Together, you walk through life, illustrated as a variation in wallpaper; you age together, you explore together.

Exploring downward involves an algorithmically generated smattering of pillars and walls that you navigate in order to find treasure chests (representing money or success or something) or maybe just to see if there's an ultimate limit to how far down you can go (this limit is an inevitable byproduct of the algorithm, which increases the frequency of walls the further you go). Being with the woman limits how much you can explore, and yet, this is where the game's genius shone through for me; I was more than happy to give up the utility of easier exploration for the benefit of not being alone. I'm talking about eight-color pixel sprites making me feel something that *Final Fantasy* could only pull off noninteractively with cheap (read: extremely expensive) parlor tricks of CG and professional voice acting.

Balancing the exploration vs. progress mechanic is the limitation of the screen view; you're only able to see a single row at a time, which effectively gives a sense that you aren't exploring a maze but a lifetime. Further fleshing out this metaphor is the pixel-stacking effect. At the beginning, you can make out the pixel patterns of distant phases, but they're only single columns of pixels, and as you progress they become elongated layer by layer. Once you pass mid-life, the emphasis shifts: now most of the stacked pixels are behind you, and you find yourself centered closer and closer to the right-most edge of the screen. This is both an interesting visual effect and the best illustration of the concept of Phi that I have ever seen.

Whether you try to explore a lot or you go for the boring mediocrity of a long, stable, repetitive life, you will become old and gray, and eventually your wife will die. And when you see this happen, so abruptly, you may feel something more dramatic and real than when

Aireth was impaled. You may feel a genuine sense of loss, blow-back from a five-minute emotional investment, and then you too will collapse to dust while the title passes over again.

## COLUMBINE, VIDEOGAMES AS EXPRESSION, AND INEFFABILITY
## IAN BOGOST, PERSUASIVE GAMES

*The following article was authored by Dr. Ian Bogost on May 21, 2006 and published on Water Cooler Games (http://www.watercoolergames.org/archives/000558.shtml). It is reprinted here with permission.*

*Super Columbine Massacre RPG is a game designed and created by Danny Ledonne. It is an exploration of the disturbing events that took place at Columbine High School. It is available online at http://www.columbinegame.com. The artist statement for* Super Columbine Massacre RPG *can be found at http://www.columbinegame.com/statement.htm.*

*Super Columbine Massacre RPG* puts the player in the shoes of Eric Harris and Dylan Klebold and attempts to paint a picture of their motivations, plans, and actions on that terrible day. It's a controversial topic to be sure, but exactly the kind of subject we should be taking on in videogames: hard problems for which there are no easy answers.

I knew that public reaction to the game would be largely negative. I've received plenty of hate mail just for talking about the game. But I don't think I was fully prepared for the widespread ignorance that has accompanied reception to the game. I think those of us deeply mired in the fields of Serious Games or Games for Change or Videogames with an Agenda or even just videogame development underestimate just how long a road we still have to tread for videogames to be treated as a medium of expression commensurate with film, literature, and art.

After my coverage, Kotaku's Brian Crecente interviewed a Columbine survivor about the game, a terrific, careful, and enlightening piece of coverage. He then wrote an article for the Rocky Mountain News with the careful headline "Game reopens Columbine wounds." The article was balanced, including interviews with victims' families, with survivors, and with the game's then-still-anonymous creator. Brian then also posted the full interview with the creator on Kotaku. All of this coverage was very good, both as journalism generally and as videogame coverage of an unusual specimen.

Then the AP wire got their hands on it.

Wire services are dangerous. They pull the "best" news from local sources, cut it down into sound-bites, and then send it out all over the world for reprinting. Brian's fantastic coverage was cut down to a fraction of the size and detail. But more interestingly, the story got retitled, and retitled again everywhere. The careful ambiguity of "reopening old wounds" was contorted into wholesale disapproval and censure. *USA Today* ran it as "Columbine video game draws relatives' ire." A local Denver TV news program ran it as "Columbine Video Game Sparks Protest, Disgust." You can find others at Google News.

The widespread attention the AP wire story brought only begat more press coverage, the most important of which is yesterday's *Washington Post* story by frequent game writer Jose Antonio Vargas. Vargas explained that the creator had been "outed" after a friend of one of the Columbine victims managed to discern his identity and post it to the game's discussion boards. Danny Ledonne has now gone on the record as the game's creator.

But for me, the most interesting feature of the *Washington Post* story is how Vargas characterizes the role of videogames as cultural commentary. Take a look at this:

> ...it's no surprise that the game, based on the 1999 shootings at Columbine High School in Littleton, Colo., now is generating controversy.
>
> For it's one thing to have a documentary ("Bowling for Columbine"), a movie ("Elephant"), and several books ("No Easy Answers," "Day of Reckoning") about that dark day, but it's quite another to have a game.

Vargas does not expand or support this claim in any way. Why is it "quite another thing" to have a game about Columbine? Is it because video games do not have the power to address such issues? Is it because they do, but the public does not understand them? Vargas does not offer his opinion, but instead uses an appeal to emotion to explain it away. This paragraph follows the one cited above:

> "There's a video game?" asked a shocked Linda Sanders, widow of William "Dave" Sanders, a teacher slain that day. "On what happened?"
>
> She was too distraught to keep talking.

Of course, our hearts go out to Ms. Sanders and everyone who lost friends and loved ones that day. Would she have had the same reaction to an interview about "Bowling for Columbine?" Or about "Day of Reckoning?" It's hard to say. But the notion that an artifact in a medium about a subject is a priori hurtful, damaging, immoral, corrupt, or otherwise objectionable should send up a huge red flag for those of us interested in video-game expression. Despite the widespread press coverage, the news stories are not about the game's representation of Columbine. They are about the fact that a game that represents Columbine in some way exists. Clearly most of the authors, interviewees, and readers of these stories have not played the game (which has logged 30,000 downloads since these stories broke earlier this month, a relatively small number given the massive exposure). Many of the journalists who have called me about the game have admitted that they haven't played it, claiming technical problems with their office computers or trouble downloading when I press them.

If he had played it, perhaps Brian Dwyer of News 10 in Syracuse, New York wouldn't have argued that "games like this prove just how important anti-violence programs are," since the violence in the game is deeply disturbing and meant to force the player to consider the dire and tragic state of affairs that made these boys take the fateful actions they did.

Perhaps Stefanie Cohen of the *New York Post* might not have called the game's creator "twisted" and "sick" in her article, and she may have understood that the game's "amateurish scenes" and "clumsy 2-D graphics" invoke the fatal amateurism of Harris and Klebold.

Readers, we have our work cut out for us. We must remind ourselves that public opinion and the popular press gets more mileage out of sound bites for shock value than for careful, researched journalism. Despite the relative renown and value of game journalists like Brian Crecente, their work caters to those of us who already have deep video-game literacy. Once these stories get out into the broader press, we can expect naïveté, ignorance, and journalistic laziness. Don't look for support from the Electronic Software Association (ESA) either; while they are the predominant supporters of video games as speech, they are also funded as lobbyists by the major publishers, and thus support those corporate interests alone.

Finally, I want to say something about ineffability, a disturbing trend in American politics and culture that goes beyond the medium of video games. One of the common objections to this game is that it offends, or might offend, victims of the tragedy and their families. Embedded in this sentiment is the notion that any representation about a difficult topic or event is simply off-limits. Recently, we saw some debate along these lines about the film *United 93*, which tells the story of the hijacked plane that crashed in Pennsylvania on 9/11. But even coverage of that film argued for its value, largely because the journalists and reviewers actually went and saw the movie before they felt qualified to write about it. Even in the second- and third-tier press, writers asked "how can we not see this film" and argued that "it's never too soon for an important movie." Not so for *Super Columbine Massacre RPG*. Consider this snippet of an editorial from the *San Antonio Express-News*.

> [The game's creator] refused to identify himself, but in an e-mail interview with the *Rocky Mountain News*, he said he wanted to "promote a real dialogue on the subject of school shootings."
>
> ...
>
> If his intentions were as pure as he claims, the producer could have sparked a dialogue without assaulting the feelings of those already hurt enough—the loved ones left behind.

Danny Ledonne rightly offered that the victims, despite their egregious suffering, do not own the public response to an event like Columbine. Another counter-argument comes from Richard Castaldo, who is paralyzed from the waist down from his Columbine injuries. Said Castaldo of the game, "It's weird for me to say this, I guess, but there's something about it that I appreciated, seeing the game from the killers' perspective." Of course, this is the power of the video game, both the medium in general and this game in particular. It's not easy, and it shouldn't be. It shouldn't be easy to try to understand the perspective of the killers. But if we are really interested in avoiding these tragedies in the future, we must admit that such empathy might be productive. In his fantastic book *Killing Monsters*, Gerard Jones argues that a complex array of influences create school shooters, perhaps the most important being a support network, including parental support. Playing from the vantage point of these fatally troubled kids might help spark a greater interest in interrogating the complex scenarios that produce tragedy.

Most of all, I am deeply worried by this culture of ineffability, a culture that would rather not talk about anything at all for fear that it might make someone uncomfortable. This trend descends from Theodor Adorno's argument that the holocaust becomes "transformed, with something of the horror removed" when represented in art, thus his famous statement that to write poetry after Auschwitz would be barbaric. These events are considered "ineffable"—unspeakable, unrepresentable. It is a tired sentiment that we must move beyond. Of course, topics like 9/11 should make us uncomfortable. Of course, Columbine should make us uncomfortable. But that is no excuse to put these issues away in a drawer, waiting for some miraculous solution to spring forth and resolve them for us. If we do so, history is much more likely to forget them. I don't care if we make video games, films, novels, poems, sidewalk art, cupcakes, or pelts as a way to interrogate our world. But we must not fear that world.

## ON AUTHORSHIP IN GAMES
## CLINT HOCKING, DESIGN DIRECTOR, UBISOFT

*The following article was authored by Clint Hocking on August 10, 2007 and published on Click Nothing (http://clicknothing.typepad.com). It is reprinted here with permission.*

*In the article, Hocking takes issue with movie critic Roger Ebert's assertion that video games are not art. Ebert's original writing that sparked the responses can be found in his Answer Man column from November 27, 2005 (third answer from the top): http://rogerebert.suntimes.com/ apps/pbcs.dll/section?category=ANSWERMAN&date=20051127.*

*Barker's reaction was given live at his keynote address to the Hollywood and Games Summit in 2007. Some of his quotes are reprinted here: http://www.gamesindustry.biz/ content_page. php?aid=26131. Ebert's response to Barker is at: http://rogerebert.suntimes. com/apps/pbcs.dll/ article?AID=/ 20070721/COMMENTARY/70721001.*

*Hocking's article (reprinted here) is at http://clicknothing.typepad.com/click_nothing/2007/08/on-authorship-i.html.*

Not that long ago, famed film critic Roger Ebert stated that games are not, and indeed, cannot be, art.

Recently, following up on a response made by author/game convergence guy Clive Barker at the Hollywood and Games Summit, Ebert clarified his claims.

Ebert's basic argument is that art requires authorship, and that games abdicate authorship to the player, and therefore cannot be art. This is certainly a compelling and useful argument, as it strikes at the nature of our medium, not at the content we so frequently produce. Ebert is clever not to bother arguing whether or not another boring old rehash of the game where you use 24 different weapons to kill six different types of aliens in 18 unique levels and save mankind from annihilation is art or is not. He is going for the kill, and good for him.

As a student of the "school" of design that often loudly and passionately advocates abdication of as much authorship as possible to the player, I guess I need to step up and help Ebert understand what he's trying to say and what it means.

Ebert claims that because games—or indeed, any interactive medium, abdicate authorship to some degree to the player, that this at least diminishes, and potentially destroys the capacity of an interactive work (or at least a game) to be art. He also tugs gently at the idea that it is potentially in the interaction with the work that the artistry lies, and thus any artfulness in a game or other interactive work is not innate but rather, if it exists at all, is imbued by the audience.

Ebert is wrong for two important reasons.

First, there is authorship in games, no matter how much we abdicate. The form of the authorship is different, and hard to understand, but no matter how much we try to abdicate it, it will always remain. It is undeniably there, and it is inextricable from the act of creating a game.

Second, interacting with a work does not shape the work, it only reveals it. Therefore, while there can be an art of expression in the way someone reveals the art, this does not necessarily diminish the art in the design of the work itself.

As both Ebert and Barker acknowledge, we could debate endlessly what is and is not art, or what is and is not a valid definition of art. For the sake of argument, I will accept Ebert's roughly stated thesis that art requires authorship. In fact, I actually agree with him. I think he just does not understand where authorship lies in games.

Here is how it works:

- I am able to express my ideas, thoughts, and feelings through the design of interactive systems.
- Because a game is a complete formal system, the entire possible range of outputs from those systems is determined by me.
- People interact with those designed systems and receive the outputs I have determined.
- People literate in the medium can reconstruct my ideas, thoughts, and feelings by experiencing these outputs.
- Therefore, by definition, there is an unbreakable chain between my ideas, thoughts, and feelings and the player's experience—I author mechanics that yield deterministic outputs in the game dynamics that lead the player to experience the aesthetic I want them to experience (within a given tolerance).

Now—by way of clarifying this explanation as well as pre-empting some of the counter arguments, I'll try to lay out the best and most valid ones.

### The Epistemological Argument

First, there is the epistemological argument—which counters by saying "How do you know you are able to express your thoughts and feelings in the design of interactive systems." Believe it or not, this is the best argument, because the best rebuttal is simply to say "I just know it." You could ask "How do you know the sentence you are speaking is not nonsense?" I know because I understand it. What I am expressing makes sense to me both intellectually and emotionally. If others do not understand it, it is not really a question of whether I am expressing myself, but rather one of whether I am expressing myself clearly.

Beyond the subjective epistemological edge of this argument, there is a requirement that the audience be literate. Hieroglyphics can't express anything to me, but clearly the people who wrote them had the capacity to express themselves, and they knew it. In the end, while this is a compelling argument, it degenerates quickly to a purely epistemological one, and arguing on that front is not going to enhance anybody's understanding of the issue of authorship in games. I'd like to think even Ebert is not interested in pursuing this argument any further.

### The Argument to the Incompleteness of Authorship

The next argument is whether or not it is, in fact, true that the entire possible range of outputs from a game's systems are really determined by me. Well, honestly, no—they are not. Games are extraordinarily complex, and there are many outputs which are not literally determined precisely by me.

If we were to conduct a sort of inverse Turing test and put me in a room and have me attempt to return the exact same outputs (ignoring ridiculous factors such as speed and precision of calculation) to a player playing *Splinter Cell: Chaos Theory* as he or she would receive from an Xbox… well, I would fail to pass myself off as an Xbox running *SC:CT*. I did not write every line of code in the game, nor do I have a complete comprehension of that code. Therefore, the argument could be made that my authorship of the game is only approximate, or incomplete.

The rebuttal to this argument lies in a comparison to film or to music or to any other collaborative artistic creation. Is every single note of a symphony perfectly determined by the composer? Is every single photon of light that enters the retina of every single viewer of a film determined by a director. No. There is noise in these systems too—some of it comes from the collaboration of others, and some of it comes from random noise. We do not deny "Ode to Joy" its status as art because it is playfully manipulated by a conductor, nor because the third clarinet breaks a reed. It is the same with games. The outputs are broadly determined by me and heavily formalized by a large crew of people working with me to deliver on a promised aesthetic. Sometimes we make mistakes, and there are bugs. Even mediocre art can tolerate this approximate or incomplete authorship, so I am forced to assert that games can too.

**The Arguments from Noise and Nonsense**

The next argument would be that audiences cannot reconstruct the meaning I intend them to by way of interacting with systems. At very least there is a legitimate challenge here in saying "Maybe they could reconstruct it, but they can also construct so many random meanings or contrary meanings, or generally just bring so much noise into the experience as to dilute the meaning to the point where it is not legible."

This is an interesting point, but again, this is not unlike other works of art. People can watch *Citizen Kane* and fast-forward the "boring parts." They can watch it in 10 sittings or fall asleep during parts of it and forget what it's about. This does not strip the film of its status. So, yes, I would concede that because (some) games offer the player so many ways to play, players might well "miss" the meaning, but I don't think the likeliness of missing the meaning should determine the artfulness of the work. There are some paintings hanging in far away back rooms of the Louvre that would likely take four hours of walking full speed non-stop to get to—this does not diminish their artfulness. If the audience does not participate with the work, they may never perceive the art, but that does not mean it is not there.

And what about those nonsensical interactions? The argument here is similar to the one above, and suggests that people can interact with games in all kinds of silly ways that don't support or develop the meaning the creator intends them to experience. That's true. I can play *GTA 3* purely as a racing game, without ever doing any of the non-racing missions. How does that support the game's central meaning (which I take to be about freedom and consequence)? Well, the answer is, it doesn't. But hold on… I can also use *War and Peace* to prop up the broken leg of my couch, or view Warhol's Campbell's Soup Cans in a pitch-black room and then say I don't get the message. The point is that the audience must always interact with a work on some level (in games, this is very literalized), but their ability to interact with a work in nonsensical ways does not diminish or destroy the art.

You could say that in the Tolstoy example, the book is not being read, and in the Warhol example, the painting is not being viewed—but in my *GTA* example, the game is being played… and that's the difference. I would actually simply say that is inaccurate.

When you're only playing one tiny part of *GTA*, you're not really playing it at all, any more than you are reading Bram Stoker's *Dracula* if you are only reading the sexy bits.

### The Argument from Legitimacy

Another argument against the existence of real authorship in games is the argument about the legitimacy of the kind of authorship I am talking about. In his responses to Barker, Ebert says:

> "If you can go through 'every emotional journey available,' doesn't that devalue each and every one of them? Art seeks to lead you to an inevitable conclusion, not a smorgasbord of choices."

In other words, he is questioning the nature of an authorship focused on providing a single perspective, versus an authorship that affords the player a range of perspectives.

I agree with Ebert that there is a difference in these two kinds of authorship. *Romeo and Juliet* is one love story. The play gives us a specific and authored understanding of what Shakespeare wants us to think about love in this specific case, between these two specific characters, in this specific set of circumstances. But Ebert is wrong to suggest that games—in affording a different kind of authorship—somehow do not lead to inevitable conclusions, or that they offer a simple "smorgasbord" wherein "every emotional journey" is somehow possible.

In a sense, the kind of authorship in a movie or a play requires an inductive approach to understanding the meaning. If I start with the specific love of two star-cross'd teenagers in Renaissance Verona whose families despise one another, and then try to generalize what love means, I am likely to end up with a lot of useless conclusions. It's an inductive and error-prone process to move from the specific to the general. With all of the inductive errors possible, what can I truly understand about love in general from *Romeo and Juliet* alone? I could reasonably induce that real love can only exist in the convoluted set of circumstances of the play where one lover drinks a sleeping potion, and the other—distraught at seeing their love "dead"—suicides with poison, so that the first can then prove their love equal and true by also drinking poison on awakening.

Certainly that would be an absurd notion of love, and that problem with induction is fundamentally why we continue to write love stories at a breathtaking rate… because when you are providing singular examples of love, and trying to facilitate the audience feeling love, you will always have room for more examples. You can write unique and powerful love stories forever and never exhaust the infinite scope of the material "love." Examples piled on examples forever will never pile up to infinity. Regardless—and for good reasons—this "inductive" form of artistic expression is the kind of authorship that we see in most media (and it is wondrous).

In games, it is different. The artist does not only create the specific case of the convicted criminal suddenly set free when his prison transfer bus is ambushed… it does not only tell the story of one criminal learning about the importance of liberty and the consequences of unchecked freedom. The artist is also capable of creating an entire expressive system space that explores a potential infinity of different notions of freedom and liberty. Where most other media require the audience to induce their meaning, games afford the audience at least the possibility of deducing their meaning.

In other media, "supporting material" that is coherent with the central themes of the work is pushed to the side in a B-plot… in games, this supporting material affords the artist ways to illuminate the meaning from many, many possible directions, allowing the player to explore the meaning the artist is trying to provide. Potentially, because the game designer is able to express himself in systems rather than in examples, infinities can be examined.

Now, I guess this is kind of hard to wrap your head around, but surely this is a concept Ebert can understand. Many filmmakers, from Taratino to Inarritu to Haggis and dozens more have been increasingly attempting to explore stories from multiple angles in an attempt to mimic—in a medium severely limited for this purpose—what games can do innately. If Haggis' Best Picture winning *Crash* was 100 hours long, and contained 100 different interconnected plots all echoing the same themes of racial tension from different perspectives, would it suddenly lose its status as art? It probably wouldn't be a very good movie, because 100 hours of movie is painful. In any case, no matter how long you make *Crash*, you will never fully explore the domain of the themes of racial tension in modern America. One hundred hours is just $50\times$ what the movie already offers, and is no closer to the infinite depth of the theme than is the existing two-hour film.

*GTA: San Andreas* on the other hand—which I played for a good 100 hours or so—gave me such a world transforming view of racial tension and inequity in early 1990s California, that I have been shaken to the core, and have been forced to re-examine a huge part of my world view.

In a response to a reader letter dated November 27, 2005 Ebert said:

"To my knowledge, no one in or out of the field has ever been able to cite a game worthy of comparison with the great dramatists, poets, filmmakers, novelists and composers."

Well, here you go. Let me state it clearly and for the record:

Taken as a whole, *GTA: San Andreas* is a more compelling, meaningful, and important work of art than *Crash*.

Admittedly, not everyone will agree, and admittedly, I have a high level of literacy in reading systems. The point here is not to enter a subjective debate about what is a superior work of art, rather the point is to say that—yes—if a game is offering a smorgasbord of unrelated mechanics that are neither supporting each other nor driving toward a coherent theme, if they are not providing the player with a broad range of perspectives on a specific meaning that the creator is trying to express, then Ebert is right.

But if a game creator does have something specific he is trying to communicate, and he designs his game well, and the mechanics and dynamics are coherently supporting that aesthetic, and providing the player—more or less whatever he does (assuming it is not willfully nonsensical)—with insight into that meaning, then yeah… it's art.

**The Argument to Migrated Authorship**

The final argument that I see remaining is the one that asks "Who is the artist here anyway?" Ebert says:

"I believe art is created by an artist. If you change it, you become the artist."

This is a much easier point to tackle simply because there is a fallacy in Ebert's argument. He is implying that interacting with a work is the same as changing it. But this is not true. My "paint" is not "what the player does." My paint is "the rules that govern what the player can do." The way the player expresses himself is a form of artistic expression (or a least it can be), but it is impossible for him to change the rules or even to express himself outside the domain of the rules that I have created. And it is not simply a case of saying "People who make paint are necessarily artists, while painters can be artists." I do more than "make paint." If all I did was "make paint," I would concede the point in Ebert's response to his reader where he states games cannot move "beyond craftsmanship to the stature of art."

If I created "magic paints" that could only be used to paint flowers that appeared highly vaginal, would I be less an artist than Georgia O'Keefe? While some painters using my paints could make crappy paintings of vaginal flowers that were not artful, and others could create beautiful masterpieces—I think it would remain clear that I was an artist for having created "paints that constrained the set of possible paintings achievable to those that dealt with a set of themes I had chosen." There is a statement there—a statement about flowers and vaginas (and paint) and it is as important as any statement in any of O'Keefe's works. It may even be as important as all of the statements made in all of O'Keefe's works combined... but we don't need to get ahead of ourselves here.

The best analogy here, again, is that of a symphony. There is an art in the composing of the symphony itself—the creation of the song and the recording of the instructions for reproducing that song using a symphony orchestra. Yet, because of the comparative fuzziness of the transcription, there is often a high degree of malleability in interpretation of those instructions, and the ability to interpret those instructions well and to facilitate an orchestra to actually play the symphony is an artistic task. There are ways to do it non-artistically. Technically, a metronome and sheet music could do the job of conducting an orchestra, but we make a lot of room for conductors because in their art, they can add a tremendous amount of beauty to what is already a beautiful work.

Ebert's fallacy extends to suggest that "Ode to Joy" is not a work of art once a composer conducts it, and that the conductor's art is not art for long anyway, because as soon as a musician plays it, he or she becomes the artist. The reality is, they can all be artists, and when an artfully composed work is conducted by an artful conductor, and played by artful musicians, the full perspective of the work is truly appreciable.

It is the same with a game and a player. Technically, a game could be played by a computer—many games are played by computers. While the beauty of the particular play experience might be diminished or even destroyed by doing it that way, it does not diminish or destroy the artfulness inherent to the game itself.

Such is the relationship between the designer and the player as I see it. The designer is the composer, the player is the conductor. The orchestra is the hardware and the sheet music is the software.

### Conclusion

I think that about sums up my rebuttal to Mr. Ebert. When he made his first statements months ago, I was mostly just upset and insulted, but with his latest clarification of those original statements, he has not only looked more carefully at the real and relevant question, but he has opened the door to have the real nature of authorship in games described.

I hope—should he happen past here and read this—he'll finally understand the scope of the issue and admit that he's wrong.

## CHALLENGES

The challenges in this section ask you to reflect upon the works above and to consider games as an art form. Unlike other chapters in this book, not all challenges require you to create games or designs for games. However, by standing back and appreciating a game as something other than a fun and entertaining experience, we increase our appreciation of the medium as a whole and push our own horizons.

### CHALLENGE 1—WHAT DO THEY SEE?

By this point, you may have read Patrick Dugan's review of *Passage* that appeared earlier in this chapter. If you flipped through the chapter to get to the challenges, don't go back and read it now. In this case, it's not a bad thing.

For this challenge, it's your thinking and not your design skills that are going to be pushed. Your goal is to play *Passage* and determine why so many high-profile, established game designers think it is a work of art. In your analysis, consider your reactions to the game as you play it, and consider how you play.

#### Components Required

- Internet connection to download *Passage* (available from http://hcsoftware.source-forge.net/passage/)

#### Deliverable

- Discussion and personal reflections on *Passage*

#### Suggested Process

1. **Download and play *Passage.***
   Without reading the artist's statement of purpose or other thoughts on the game, download *Passage* and play the game several times. Keep a pencil and paper with you to record thoughts that you have on the game.
2. **What is art?**
   Think about your own preconceptions and definitions of what makes an original work "art" (or not). Consider also other views of what "art" is, such as those discussed earlier in this chapter.

3. **Interpret the intent.**

Consider the reactions you had while playing *Passage*. What did you feel? What were you thinking of? Consider the author. What do you think Jason Rohrer was trying to say with this game, if anything? Was he making a statement about some aspects of the human experience? Were there particular emotions that you think he wanted the player to feel?

4. **Apply your definition.**

Is *Passage* a work of art in your opinion? Would you consider it "fine art" or "high art"? Why or why not? If your answer is no, go back and read Patrick Dugan's review and search the Web for other similar reactions (if you have not already done so). You do not have to agree with them, but at least try to understand why the matter is open to debate, and do your best to understand the other side.

5. **Create deliverable.**

### Variant

Explore another art game and your reactions to the same. The following games are recommended:

- *flOw*, playable for free online at http://intihuatani.usc.edu/cloud/flowing/
- *Cloud*, downloadable for free at http://intihuatani.usc.edu/cloud/
- *Knytt*, downloadable for free at http://nifflas.ni2.se/index.php?main=03Knytt
- *Samarost*, playable for free online at http://www.amanita-design.net/samorost-1/ or its sequel, *Samarost 2* at http://amanita-design.net/samorost-2/
- *game game game game and again game*, playable for free online at http://www.secret-technology.com/gamegame/agame.html

### CHALLENGE 2—GAMES AS ART... OR NOT

For this challenge, you are tasked with either a) rebutting or b) supporting Hocking's thesis that games are, in fact, art. Defend your own arguments by assessing each of Hocking's points against a contemporary game, and explore in detail why you believe what you believe. As Hocking's piece discussed games in a general sense, your analysis should be specific, detailing the game's various aspects as necessary to support your point.

#### Components Required

- Internet connection (for research)
- Hocking's article, which appears earlier in this chapter
- Any game

**Deliverable**

- A presentation or discussion detailing your position, or
- A paper detailing your position, or
- Prepared notes for discussion

**Suggested Process**

1. **Form an opinion.**
   Since you're reading this book, you probably already have an opinion on whether games are art. Choose the basic core ideas that you'd like to express in your argument.
2. **Choose a game.**
   From your experience, find the best example you can to support your opinion. If you do not own the game, find some reviews, screenshots, and other materials online. If you plan to use these in your deliverable, be sure to credit your sources.
3. **Research.**
   Read Hocking's piece earlier in this chapter. You may also wish to seek out additional commentary online, either on the "Are games art?" discussion in general or your game in particular.
4. **Create deliverable.**

**Variant**

Explore other reactions to Roger Ebert's assertion that games are not art, and his follow-up reaction that games cannot become high art (http://rogerebert.suntimes.com/apps/pbcs.dll/article?AID=/20070721/COMMENTARY/70721001). Consider how these reactions contrast with or support Hocking's stance.

## CHALLENGE 3—MONA LISA

Her smile has captivated millions. It's the subtlety, the lack of motivational certainty that makes us wonder, "What does her smile say? What is she thinking?" In her smile, DaVinci seemed to capture something that we've not yet been able to decipher, but it draws us still.

For this challenge, you are tasked with exploring two different questions:

- Do games have a Mona Lisa moment, something so deep and enduring?
- If you were tasked to create a game about the experience of Mona Lisa's smile, what would the design of that game be?

**Components Required**

- None

**Deliverable**

■ A written list of "Mona Lisa moments" in games, with each moment you can think of supported by a paragraph explaining why it qualifies
■ A game concept for a game based on the experience of Mona Lisa's smile

**Suggested Process**

1. **Research.**
   Read what at least three art critics have written about the *Mona Lisa*. These reviews may be contemporary or centuries old, and may be found online or in physical books. This helps you put words to what you (and especially others) feel when looking at this painting.
2. **Consider parallels in games.**
   Once you can put the feeling of the *Mona Lisa* into words, think of the closest feelings you've had when playing games. If you are having trouble thinking of any, consider games that have made you feel any emotion at all—other than adrenaline rush and power fantasy.
3. **Brainstorm game concepts.**
   Alone or in a group, think of ways to express the emotions stirred by the *Mona Lisa* in a game. Consider other games that express emotions, like *Cloud* or *flOw*, as a starting point.
4. **Create deliverable.**

### CHALLENGE 4—CREATE AN ART GAME

As *Passage, Cloud,* and other art games show us, games can explore a variety of different concepts—life, aging, environmental issues, and more. Other games explore issues in non-conventional ways. Consider artists like Warhol who explored topics like Campbell's Soup cans, or O'Keefe who captured natural beauty in new, dramatic ways.

Select something similar—a concept, a process, something from the everyday, and create a game design from it.

For this challenge, your game concept may be for a digital or non-digital game.

**Components Required**

■ None

**Deliverable**

■ Two- to three-page written game concept

**Suggested Process**

1. **Research.**
   Explore other art games to see what's already been done. Then, turn your exploration to look at both conventional and nonconventional modern artists. Interactive artists may prove an excellent source of inspiration.
2. **Choose a topic.**
   What would you like to explore artistically in a game? Remember that games contain systems, so you play to the strengths of the medium by expressing something that has several parts that interact with each other when set in motion.
3. **Create deliverable.**

## IRON DESIGNER CHALLENGE 5—WORLD OF PAIN

How can a game world facilitate our exploration of a difficult topic and force us to consider a subject from another perspective? Games like *Darfur is Dying* and *September 12* force us to walk a path we'd never choose for ourselves. They seek to open our eyes by using the only medium that truly provides an active versus a passive experience.

For this challenge, your goal is to explore a difficult topic in the form of a non-digital game. Break into groups of two to four people, grab a box of prototyping materials, and get started.

### Components Required

- Internet or books (for research)
- Prototyping materials

### Deliverable

- Playable prototype of a board game or card game

### Suggested Process

1. **Research.**
   Select an event or a difficult topic. If you are unfamiliar with the topic, learn fast. Pay particular attention to those elements that can be expressed clearly in games: systems, tradeoffs, and cause-and-effect relationships.
2. **Brainstorm.**
   Come up with ideas. Do you attempt a literal conversion of the topic or something more abstract?
3. **Create mechanics.**

Work backward. What do you want your players to experience during play? Choose dynamics that can create that play experience. Then choose mechanics that can create those dynamics.

4. **Create deliverable.**

### Variant

Explore a different difficult topic of your choice. The topic need not be as controversial as Ledonne's *Super Columbine Massacre RPG*, of course. In fact, exploring a similar subject in a similar way would mean little more than a modification of Ledonne's original work. Push your own boundaries in this challenge to create something original.

### Variant

Instead of a physical game prototype, create a concept for a digital game.

## Non-Digital Shorts

Non-digital shorts allow you to explore various concepts quickly. Sometimes, because of the tactile nature of the medium, non-digital games may be more suited for such topics.

1. Design a game that introduces children to the concept of grief.
2. Design a game that introduces people to a religion of your choice.
3. Redesign *Risk* to advocate world peace.
4. Redesign *Monopoly* to illustrate the effects of the Great Depression.
5. Choose a common game token, such as dice or tiles, and create a game that uses these materials in a non-standard way.
6. Alternatively to #5, design a game that uses a non-standard turn structure or pacing.
7. Create a card game whose win condition constantly changes or is impossible to understand.
8. Create a card game based on an "impossible choice" (or a series of them)—a dilemma where both choices mean certain failure.
9. Design a game that is intentionally incomplete, requiring player authorship at runtime to be playable.
10. Choose a digital game that you consider to be art and create a non-digital version of it. How does the difference in medium affect the message?

## Resources

http://experimental-gameplay.org
http://www.playthisthing.com

# 18 Games as a Teaching Tool

Seriously? Absolutely.

There's something magical going on with games that educators can appreciate. Many might lament the hours spent in front of games, but others pose a formidable question: "What does that game have that my courses don't?" The answer is *more* than "entertainment," because courses can be entertaining, too. We see children with ADD tune out after 10 minutes of a lecture, yet these same students stay engaged in a game for hours at a time. What's going on?

Fortunately, many individuals are studying this exact thing. Others, like the writers of this book who are both industry veterans and educators, have already integrated games into their classroom with much success.

## WHAT ABOUT THOSE CRAZY STORIES I HEAR?

There certainly are many crazy stories out there about video games, just like there were about rock music 20 years ago, pencil and paper games 30 years ago, and comics 50 years ago. This relatively new medium, like the new mediums before it, is a concern for some.

Studies have shown that violent media, regardless of its source, has the potential to increase the likelihood of violence in some individuals. Fortunately, M-rated games and R-rated movies are not used in the grade-school classroom. As of the year of this writing, in fact, only eight percent of the video games submitted to the ESRB were rated M, a fact that may be reassuring. M-rated games, like R-rated movies, are intended for individuals 17 and older.

There are lots of good stories about games, too. Consider this one: surgeons who play video games at least three hours per week and perform laparoscopic surgery complete the surgery 27 percent quicker with 37 percent fewer errors.[1] Other studies show video games protect our brains from aging.[2] Games are even being used to treat soldiers who suffer from post traumatic stress disorder.[3] Good news about games even prompted the BBC News to title an article, "Video games 'good for you.'"[4] These studies are just the tip of the iceberg. Games are being used for all kinds of good purposes. Learning is just one of them.

## Using Games as a Catalyst for Learning

In 2007, one of the authors of this book held a game-design workshop with a group of at-risk teens. For these students, their current classroom was the last educational stop on the block. They'd been removed from one classroom after another due to their disruptive behaviors. Some had already been to jail. At the same time, some of the kids had also expressed a desire to be game designers when they grew up.

The game-design workshop turned out to be magic for both the students and the workshop leader. Few students were disrespectful. In fact, the students were all very excited about the prospect of learning how to make games. When they were told that English, math, science, and history were critical subjects for game designers, they saw new purpose in those studies. When students were asked to apply a concept from history and use it in a way that would make a game, they did. The students had lots of fun, as did the workshop leader. They learned, too. However, the learning was secondary to them. If learning is what it takes to make games, so be it.

To get into the next game-design workshop, these at-risk kids are voluntarily competing by getting *good* grades and writing *optional* papers about the game they want to design.

There is a message here: games have a unique power to draw people into an interactive world as a player or as a designer. It is up to us as players, as parents, and as educators to harness this medium for its strengths.

How do you integrate games?

## Designing and Modifying Games for Students

In kindergarten, a teacher sent home a matching game. Students were asked to pair up words and then use them in a sentence. It worked well for a while. After a short time, however, the children became bored with it. Eventually, many parents abandoned the game, too. One parent, however, happened to be a professional game designer. She modified the game to offer a reward structure. She added a high score and bonus cards that introduced some unpredictability into the game. As a result, her daughter stayed interested much longer. The modifications were minor, but lasting and learning power of the game was increased.

When creating a game that must be educational as a *design* goal, one may wonder: Aren't "fun" and "educational" mutually exclusive? After all, many so-called "edutainment" games are not particularly fun, and children who have played enough of them are rightfully skeptical when any adult brings in a "fun game" that is supposed to teach something. By simply layering a game on top of inherently boring content, well-meaning educators create games that are derisively referred to as "chocolate-covered broccoli." We can and must do better.

There are several approaches teachers can take.

### Find the Fun

In the case of designing an original educational game, start with the fun—not in game mechanics, but in content. Every subject has aspects that are interesting, exciting, or so obviously useful that students want to learn them. If the designer can find the fun in the educational content, designing a game around it is not as difficult as it may seem: all one has to do is not remove the fun and find a way to let people play with it. Westward expansion can become a game filled with adventure, terrifying encounters, and occasional settlements. A relatively new board game, *1960: The Making of a President,* continues to receive rave reviews, and it's about the 1960 Presidential election. Not only did its designers find the fun, they knocked it out of the park.

Keep in mind using the term "fun" doesn't strictly mean games that are entertaining in a sitcom-type of way. Think of documentaries, art exhibits, great speakers, thought-provoking books, or lectures. Each of these is fun and entertaining, too, even if it encourages us to explore a challenging, painful, or emotionally charged topic. In finding the fun, feel free to make games that simulate these difficult moments. At first glance, it may seem that making a game of a difficult topic trivializes it. However, nothing could be further from the truth. Rather, consider it an abstracted simulation that provides players with an ability to understand an event in a way that no other medium possibly can. By making something interactive, the dynamics naturally result in an effective hands-on learning experience. Games are an extremely powerful medium to promote this understanding.

## START WITH SYSTEMS

Remember that games, at their heart, are systems. By way of metaphor, the systems in a game are similar to an engine in a car. Systems are under the hood in digital games, and it is those very systems that make the whole game roll.

The simple atomic parts of the games (the players, mechanics, decisions made, and so on) interact with one another to form complex behaviors and results. Because of this, games are a natural fit for teaching content that is based on these same kinds of systems. For example, students in physical science learn about the relationships between mass, velocity, and force. A physics game that shows these things in motion is an excellent demonstration of these concepts, making abstract math equations more understandable and intuitive. Systems can also be found in biology, mathematics, economics—more subjects than not, in fact. If it fails to stay constant over time, there's a system that can be turned into a game.

Most games are driven primarily by player decisions. As discussed in earlier chapters, decisions become more interesting when there is a tradeoff or comparison. Pay 50 dollars to get out of jail or roll the dice? Attack your enemy now or wait until next turn? Run over open ground without cover to get the rocket launcher or hide in a bunker with a sniper rifle? These decisions all require weighing actions and consequences or placing relative values on two very different commodities. Tradeoffs such as these do not just happen in games; they are found throughout life. As such, any topic that involves understanding tradeoffs or comparisons is an excellent basis for a game. For example, the field of economics is based entirely on weighing the relative value of several commodities. It is no surprise, then, that many games include an in-game economy. The applied sciences also involve tradeoffs, especially when designing an experiment and considering the costs, risks, and benefits. Business classes often involve cost-benefit analysis, which is essentially what players are doing in games on a constant basis.

As a consequence of games being driven by player decisions, they show the relationships between cause and effect quite clearly. When two people play a strategy game, it is often clear to both players why one lost and the other won. Consider cause-and-effect relationships in classes. In chemistry, combining chemicals or adding heat can cause a physical change. In history, important events emerge from a series of identifiable causes. In computer programming, the machine does exactly what the programmer tells it, so there is a direct link between the programmer's actions and the computer's results.

When most teachers think of using games as teaching tools, they think of using games as rote memorization aids, hence the popularity of quiz-show mechanics and flash cards in the class. But content to be memorized is static, while the concepts and systems in classes—the interesting and important stuff—is dynamic, just like games. To take advantage of games as a medium, look beyond the content and locate those topics that are inherently game-like themselves.

## USE GAMES THEY PLAY

Take the games kids *already* play and modify those to your advantage by adding an educational component directly from your teaching. Better yet, ask students to do the integrating. If students have no particular suggestions, visit BoardGameGeek.com to get a list of potential games along with a player-based quality rating. *RISK*, for instance, could be modified to play on the map of North America, the United States, the Canadian Provinces, or any other location for that matter.

At the kindergarten level, games like *Pretty Pretty Princess* work great. Visit sites like PBSKids.org to see what types of games are made for children at that particular level. Even these games can be modified with new themes to educate students. Allowing the students to do the actual modification reinforces the material and allows them to enjoy the process of design as well.

In high school, *Monopoly*, *Carcassonne* or *Risk* are appropriate for modification. Accelerated classes may find luck with games like *Puerto Rico* or *Settlers of Catan*. Every one of these games can be modified to fit a particular subject. In fact, Mayfair Games even offers detailed information for teachers on integrating *Settlers of Catan* into the classroom.[5]

## ASSIGN GAME DESIGN

Another option is to challenge students to create new games focused on the subject matter at hand. While it may seem unlikely that students could pull off such a feat, teachers may be surprised. Today, students have a great amount of knowledge about games, and the mere thought of actually making one gets them excited.

For instance, let's say that students are trying to learn the individual states of the United States. As an assignment, task your students with creating a board game that promotes retention of the individual state names and locations. You can even provide an array of existing board games to inspire them. What happens? In the process of creating the game, the students:

- Learn the information you wanted them to learn
- Express creativity through artistic board design
- Practice spatial reasoning
- Practice teamwork skills
- Practice mathematical skills (since all games, at their root, are mathematical patterns)
- Have fun

Time and time again, we have seen success in doing so. So, in order to capture students' attention, use the games *they* know, and take advantage of pre-existing game designs. Taken in this context, *everyone* is a game designer.

## CHALLENGES

The exercises in this chapter offer a unique double challenge:

For educators, these challenges provide an opportunity to create games for use in the classroom to reinforce or deliver the desired educational content. The games are created outside of the classroom or in conjunction with other educators or the students themselves.

For students, the challenges provide an excellent opportunity to research an assigned topic and apply it to an existing game (likely their favorite) or create a brand new game from an assigned topic.

Naturally, the level of detail in each game, as well as the amount of strategy required, will need to be altered to suit the students' abilities.

### CHALLENGE 1—OLD GAME, NEW LIFE

Board games are extremely adaptable creatures. Consider *Monopoly*. There are presently over 1,200 different versions of Monopoly, each with a different theme. *Irishopoly, Dogopoly, Catopoly*—you name it, and it's been done. For this challenge, you must use any standard board game and give it an historical setting. For students creating games, the goal of this challenge should be topic mastery.

#### Components Required

- Internet connection or books for research

#### Deliverable

- A modified version of the board game, including new board
- A modified set of rules (optional)
- A modified set of game tokens (optional)

### Suggested Process

1. **Choose a game to modify.**
   All games are adaptable to different themes. The degree of difficulty comes only in understanding the directions of the *original* game. Be sure to pick something easily explained, understood, and played in a classroom in the time period you've allocated. A simple game of *Twilight Imperium*, for instance, is unlikely to be had, as the playing time is about four hours, not including the time necessary to explain the rules.
2. **Choose a topic.**
   The more specific the topic, the better. However, this is only a rule of thumb and not a rigid rule. Topics that are currently being studied are natural targets.
3. **Research your topic.**
   Once the topic is selected, research your topic using the Internet or other resources provided.
4. **Modify the theme.**
   Make a list of all the game bits and determine how you will replace these to fit the new theme. For instance, if you use *Clue* as a game, perhaps you could use equally famous historical settings and characters. Researching characters, sets, and the like is often a very fun process for game designers, and it is part of the reward of game creation.
5. **Make a prototype.**
   Once a topic has been selected, make a prototype of the game in question. Remember that board-game prototypes don't need to be pretty. Your goal here is to see if the game itself is playable and interesting. If you opt to add a gameplay mechanic, testing this prototype becomes more important than ever.
6. **Create deliverable.**

### Variants

There are numerous variants you can explore with this challenge.

Add a mechanic to the game that fits the chosen theme. You may have to modify several other mechanics to balance the new one.

Create a brand-new game from a topic. This is a very challenging exercise, particularly if students have no constraints. Consider giving them some direction, such as creating a game based around territorial acquisition or the race to the end paradigm common in games like *Candy Land*.

### CHALLENGE 2—EDUCATIONAL ENTERTAINMENT

"History time, kids!"

It might not be the rallying cry educators wish it were. Through games, however, perhaps it can be. Numerous games have been created that teach under the cover of entertainment. The history genre is probably the most commonly used. Games like *The Oregon Trail* and the *Civilization* series immediately come to mind, and there are dozens of others. The Canadian government even commissioned a Canadian history game that used the *Civilization IV* engine developed by Canadian company Bitcasters.

Other topics have been broached via games as well. Consider *Dimenxion*—an FPS that teaches algebra!

For this challenge, your goal is to create a concept for a PC game that teaches any middle grade school subject in a way that is entertaining without being didactic.

### Components Required

■  None

### Deliverable

■  A concept presentation for a game that explains how the game will teach a particular subject and why this might be entertaining

### Suggested Process

1. **Choose a subject.**
   As mentioned earlier in this chapter, subjects that are easiest to model in games are those with interacting systems, comparisons, tradeoffs, and cause-and-effect situations. Stay away from games that merely teach content through repetition and memorization. *Jeopardy!* has already been done before. More importantly, if you focus too much on content rather than concepts, you ignore the greatest strength of the medium: the ability to model systems and show what happens when they are set in motion. You do not have to teach a complete subject over the course of a full year. You can focus on one aspect of a subject that lends itself particularly well to games. The scale and complexity of your game should be proportional to how much course material it covers.

2. **Create a game model.**
   Find aspects of your subject that are inherently game-like. Think of ways to model the systems in the context of a game, based on the mechanics that drive the systems in the real world. If you feel stuck, a browse through BoardGameGeek.com should help. As you look over the descriptions of the games, think of how you could insert your subject into its design. You may encounter some content that needs to be preserved exactly in the game mechanics. Other content can be simplified so that the game isn't needlessly complex. The tradeoff between gameplay and reality is difficult in educational games, and as both educator and game designer, you need to consider both. From your choices, a set of core mechanics should emerge.

3. **Create deliverable.**

Note that for this challenge you only need a core idea, not a fully playable prototype. Of course, you can take your idea further if you desire.

## Variant

Instead of creating your own idea, critique someone else's. Find an existing video game that teaches any grade-school subject. Prepare an oral or written presentation that includes the following:

- The game's approach to teaching its chosen subject
- Whether the game succeeds at teaching the content, and why or why not
- Whether the game is fun, and why or why not
- Suggested improvements to the game

## CHALLENGE 3—HISTORICAL BATTLES

The details of historical battles can be lost on students, particularly because there are so many of them. How can we make historical battles come to life? The same way that millions of players have—by turning them into board games. In fact, there's a whole genre of games called "war games" that allow people to replay battles.

For this exercise, select a historical battle and create a game that incorporates key features of the battle into it. One way to do this is to modify an existing war game, such as *RISK*, *Axis & Allies*, or *Memoir '44*. Another way is to create your own game from scratch, which may be necessary if the battle you choose takes place under unique conditions that aren't easily covered by another game.

The purpose of your war game is to teach the choices that were faced by the leaders of each side. Therefore, the players should be making these kinds of strategic choices and not just rolling lots of dice.

## Components Required

- Copy of an existing war game (optional)
- Materials to create prototype

## Deliverable

- Playable board-game prototype

**Suggested Process**

1. **Choose a battle.**

   Most of the really famous historical battles already have several games based on them. If you are a history buff, choose a battle that is obscure enough that it might not have been done before, but interesting enough (from a game player's perspective) that it's worth doing. If you choose a well-known battle, do not seek out or play any other games based on it until you are done with this challenge. Do not allow your creativity to be constrained by what has come before. After your prototype is complete, comparing it to existing commercial games provides an excellent way to critique your own work. Either way, choose a battle where both sides had a real chance of winning. If one player always wins, it's not much of a game!

2. **Research and more research.**

   Games based on history require more research than your average game. Consider the following questions that you need to answer:

   - What is the historical context of this battle? Why was it being fought that made it important in the first place?
   - Who was in command of each side? What forces did they have at their disposal? What were the relative capabilities of these forces? (What terrain could they cross, were any forces stronger than others, did any of them have special equipment or abilities or training that made them different from each other?)
   - What was the goal of each side (such as routing the enemy or taking control of a strategic location)?
   - What terrain was the battle being fought on? Did this terrain favor or hinder either side? Did it have any effects on the way the battle was fought?
   - What aspects of this battle are interesting from a military-history perspective? For example, did a smaller force beat a much larger one, or did the leaders come up with some brilliant and innovative strategy or tactics?

3. **Create the core.**

   Consider all of the information you have about this battle. Highlight the information that is absolutely critical to gaining a deep understanding of the battle. Make sure that this is preserved in your gameplay. In fact, the most important aspects of the battle should be the basis for your core mechanics.

4. **Create the mechanics.**

   Making an exact simulation based on all of your data is easy, but not particularly fun. (The players will spend more time calculating shot trajectories and rolling dice than they do making the important and interesting decisions.) Instead, spend your time thinking of ways to simplify the historical data so that the general idea is preserved while still being as easy to learn and fun to play as possible.

5. **Create deliverable.**

### CHALLENGE 4—ELEMENTARY, MY DEAR LEVEL DESIGNER

Everyone has a home—from princesses to wicked warriors. For this exercise, you'll be creating another "home" of sorts: a level that contains the solution of a particularly baffling mystery.

Your mystery may be real or imagined, solved or unsolved, but should reflect themes found in actual historical mystery. Sample mysteries include the following:

- Earhart's plane
- Jack the Ripper
- The Moai of Easter Island
- The Bermuda Triangle

Your level must contain at least the following:

- Player entry point
- One physical puzzle
- One item puzzle
- One riddle
- Solution

Throughout this challenge and others like it, you can encourage students to explore not only topics but the mysteries behind them as well.

#### Components Required

- Internet for research
- Graph paper (optional)

#### Deliverable

- Rough sketch of the level, or
- Graph paper level design, and
- System of game rules that allows the level to be played

#### Suggested Process

1. **Choose your mystery.**
   Keep this challenge in mind. Since you are designing a level, mysteries that involve travel between several nearby locations are the easiest to work with. You must provide puzzles of several kinds, so make sure your mystery has those elements (or is structured so that you can add them).

2. **Work backward.**

   When writing a detective story or designing a puzzle, authors often begin with the solution. What is the final "answer" that the player or main character discovers? From there, ask yourself *how* the solution is discovered. What are the clues that can be pieced together, and where are those clues found? Step farther back. Why would the player visit the locations where the clues are found? What earlier clues lead to the later ones? Continue working backward like this until you reach a beginning. What events set the mystery in motion? How is the player involved?

3. **Sketch out the level.**

   Make your initial sketches very rough just to give you an idea of how the player might move through the level. At this point, you don't want to nail down all the little details. Rather, think "big picture."

4. **Design the level.**

   Add the clues and puzzles that the player needs to find. Set up the start conditions: player entry point, starting locations of all items and NPCs, and any other elements of the initial game state. Define the victory condition. What must happen for the level to be solved? What is the final challenge that the player must face (a puzzle or a hostile encounter, for example)? What happens when the player wins?

5. **Sanity check.**

   Walk through the level step by step. First, make sure it is possible to solve, and that you don't have (for example) two puzzles that each require the other to be completed first. Next, make sure that the player has access to all of the clues he or she needs to finish each puzzle. Preferably, allow each puzzle to have multiple solutions or multiple sets of clues so that a player who misses some small hidden detail will not be permanently stuck.

6. **Design the rules system (optional).**

   How does the player move around in this level? What actions can the player take? Are there additional considerations, like NPC movement or time limits? Is there a conversation system, and if so, how does the player choose what to say (and how does the game know how to respond)?

7. **Create deliverable.**

## IRON DESIGNER CHALLENGE 5—LIVING HISTORY

Games don't need to be played sitting around a table. In fact, they can be played live. Such events are often referred to as "LARPs" or "live-action role-playing games." For this challenge, create a LARP that represents a particular historical event. The LARP should be playable in a high-school or college class of 20 to 30 students, within a single class period (one or two hours).

You need to choose an event in which everyone can play a role. The event need not transpire exactly the way it did historically. In fact, it probably won't, and that's part of the fun. After playing, the students should understand that the event was complicated, and that many different parties had conflicting goals. When told how the event *actually* transpired, the students should understand how the result emerged from the initial situation.

## Components Required

- None

## Deliverable

- Set of printed rules for each student
- Character sheet for each student
- Teacher notes
- Formal lesson plan (optional)

## Suggested Process

1. **Choose an event.**
   The easiest events for this challenge are those where a number of parties, each with their own agenda, met in some kind of negotiation or conflict. Examples include the Constitutional Convention, the Kyoto Protocol, or World War I.

2. **Choose the players.**
   It's unlikely that your event will have *exactly* 20 to 30 participants. For events with fewer people, consider ways to assign several students to the same "team." For events with too many actual participants, choose the most important or influential ones.

3. **Create the goals.**
   For each player or team, ask yourself what their goals were, historically. Did they want to advance an agenda? Did they want money? Freedom? Power? Several of these things? Write them all down, organized by participant. More than likely, the participants had conflicting goals—otherwise, there wouldn't be much history in the event! If participants have several goals (or a single goal with several degrees of success or failure), assign numeric values to each possible outcome to determine a final score. All participants should have the same maximum possible score.

4. **Create the rules.**
   Do the participants ever need to engage in any kind of direct conflict? If so, you must provide a way to resolve it. Since the players will be constantly wandering around and talking to each other, conflict resolution must be kept simple and fast. Some LARPs use systems such as a single die roll or a round of *Rock-Paper-Scissors*. If participants have differing capabilities (such as military strength), make a note of this. You may need to add numeric stats or special abilities to each player's character sheet to be used in conflict resolution. Also make note of any other constraints: time limits, limitations on who can talk to or interact with whom, amount of team communication allowed, and so on.

5. **Create deliverable.**

   At this point, you should have all the information you need to formally write up the rules, and the player- or team-specific stats and goals and background (which is written up as a "character sheet"). You can also compile these into a series of compact charts and footnotes for the teacher. Optionally, you can also create a formal lesson plan. To the above deliverables, add some historical background notes that can serve as a short introductory lecture given before the LARP begins. Also add debriefing notes at the end, detailing what happened in the actual event, and a list of talking points and discussion questions about the actual event and the LARP outcome.

### Variant

Create a mini role-playing game. Similar to the LARP, create or select characters from a particular event in history and actually play it out. You must determine the basic skills and statistics of those characters, as well as what they will need to do to succeed. An RPG is normally played sitting down around a table (rather than standing around and interacting in a freeform way as with a LARP), so design for groups of four to six students and a single GM to referee the event. Larger classes would be expected to split into several groups, each playing its own version of the same RPG. In this case, a student would be the GM in each game (with the teacher overseeing everything), so in addition to the teacher's notes you would need a similar set of notes for the GM.

## NON-DIGITAL SHORTS

These challenges encourage you to use games within the context of education in a variety of ways.

1. Design a turn-based strategy game to be administered by a teacher in which students complete turns as homework outside of the classroom.
2. Design a game that prepares students for a rote memorization exam, such as art history or geography.
3. Design a game that illustrates the concepts of introductory algebra.
4. Design a game featuring systems based on the principles of genetic replication and inheritance.
5. Design a game that teaches players how to organize non-violent protests.
6. Design a game for your local transportation authority that teaches people how to get around by bus.
7. Redesign *Candy Land* to teach children about the spectrum and the physics of light and color.
8. Redesign *Go Fish* to teach children about geology. You do not need to use standard playing cards.

9. Redesign *The Game of Life* to illustrate life in 18th-century England.
10. Create a card game that teaches the interactions between different groups of elements from the Periodic Table.

## REFERENCES

[1] http://www.rosseramti.com/amti/topgun4kids/main.html

[2] http://www.theglobeandmail.com/servlet/Page/document/v5/content/subscribe?
user_URL=http://www.theglobeandmail.com%2Fservlet%2Fstory%2FRTGAM.2006020
9.wxbrains09%2FBNStory%2FScience%2Fhome&ord=111952&brand=theglobeand-
mail&force_login=true

[3] http://www.npr.org/templates/story/story.php?storyId=4806921

[4] http://news.bbc.co.uk/2/hi/technology/2943280.stm

[5] http://www.mayfairgames.com/ —click on "Teacher Zone"

# 19 Serious Games

Like any other form of art, games are good for more than just pure entertainment. For a moment, think of books. They convey information, educate, persuade, and provide a call to action among other things. Games whose primary purpose goes beyond entertainment are called "serious games," a term the game industry and even serious game makers use with something less than enthusiasm.

Why "serious games" then? For starters, to some, the term "games" implies that the topic has a degree of triviality. Games, they think, are fun and something we do purely to entertain ourselves. Unless preceded by the term "war," people rarely think of games as useful for any particular purpose. When attempting to sell games as a persuasive medium, those in the business early on found it useful to refer to this class of games as "serious games."

Since the early days of serious games, the genre has grown to become a multimillion dollar industry. A SIG within the International Game Developers Association devotes itself to the topic, and it has become the focus of multiple conferences around the world.

This chapter is designed to give you a brief overview of this type of game. Complete books have been written on the subject, and those interested are encouraged to research further.

## TYPES OF SERIOUS GAMES

The array of serious games is nearly dizzying. A quick trip to the site of WaterCoolerGames.com reveals no fewer than 20 different classifications of these games, and more are being added from time to time. In general, rather than class games by mechanic, dynamic, perspective, or play pattern as the traditional game industry does (for example, "first person shooter" or "platformer"), serious games tend to be grouped by purpose instead of play.

Some of the more popular types of games are covered below. As with many things about this emerging field, however, these names are neither hard andfast nor an exhaustive listing. Rather, they are meant to provide you with an idea of the possibilities within the space.

### TRAINING GAMES

Training games are designed to put a person through a specific scenario and allow him or her to gain comfort and perhaps even mastery over it before attempting to do the real thing. The most well-known type of training games are military flight simulators. Pilots spend untold hours in these machines before heading off in a plane of their own.

Corporate clients are also getting on board, however. Cold Stone Creamery, an ice-cream retailer, commissioned a training game expressly for their employees to teach them the proper technique and measurements for the company's products. Other retailers use simulations to allow salesmen to practice their trade on various customers while gauging the relative success or failure of their approach.

One of the more recent entries into the training field is disaster preparedness. Games such as *HazMat: HotZone* put players into a doomsday scenario to seen how they handle emergency service deployment, population management, and more.

For the most part, however, training games are smaller budget and with very specific purposes that target specific audiences. Games have been made for every purpose, from teaching younger children to avoid Internet predators to water conservation.

Interestingly enough, in looking at games as training games, we are actually looking back to the roots of games and of play. Play itself was a practice run for a real-life encounter, and game-play provided a chance to test strategies and tactics without fear of consequence. From the instinctual play of predatory animals to the war games that later evolved, games have always had a serious purpose.

## HEALTH GAMES

Health games represent both games that train people to perform health-related tasks and games that make people healthier. *GlucoBoy* and *Re-Mission* are two excellent examples of games in this genre. The popular *Wii Fit* is another. Games like *Wii Fit* are also often called "exercise games," or "exergames" for short.

Like precision military simulations, health games provide practitioners with an opportunity to train in a forgiving and instructional environment. Exercise games may end up being the larger market, however. As the console generation gets older, the desire for an all-around machine like the Nintendo Wii makes the "game machine" and the "exercise machine" potentially one and the same.

Although games like *Dance Dance Revolution* are often billed as "health games," strictly speaking, they're not. *DDR* and games like it certainly do a great job of getting players into shape, but that was clearly not the prime intent of the game.

## SOCIAL-COMMENTARY GAMES

Just as previous generations held sit-ins, rallies, and protests, this generation forms Facebook groups, starts blogs, and makes games (and sometimes does those other things, too). Games are an incredibly powerful means to get a point across and to spread that point via the Internet throughout the world. One example is *Airport Insecurity* by Persuasive Games, a biting commentary on the excessive restrictions on air travel in a post-9/11 United States.

Another form of social-commentary games are political games. Around election time every four years or so, a political party in one state or another releases a small game designed to show its party's policies in one form or another or show the fallacy of their opponent's policies.

Sometimes, social-commentary games are classified as art games since their primary purpose is a political as well as an artistic statement. In releasing *Super Columbine Massacre, RPG* designer Danny LeDonne offered both political and artistic reasons for his game, and ultimately released an artist's statement, which is available online. For more information on art games, refer to Chapter 17, "Games as Art."

## ADVERGAMES AND ANTI-ADVERGAMES

Some games are created for the primary purpose of advertising a brand. The Burger King games like *Big Bumpin* and *Sneak King* are recent high-profile examples. Many companies with lower budgets have at least a small Flash game on their Web site or a trivia game for fans of, say, a television series. These games are affectionately called "advergames." For more information on creating these kinds of games (and others that deal with licenses or IP), refer to Chapter 9, "What Is Intellectual Property?"

Other games are created with the purpose of actively damaging a corporation's reputation, and have thus earned the term "anti-advergames." One such game, *The McDonald's Game* by Molleindustria, created quite a stir when it was first released in 2006. Not in any way affiliated with McDonald's, the game gave players such choices as bulldozing native villages in order to grow soybeans or raising cattle for the chain's hamburger production. The game even featured a simulated boardroom where the "powers that be" made sly commentary on the perceived state of the corporation in the eyes of Molleindustria. Naturally, McDonald's was none too happy with the game's release, but being a form of social commentary, the fast-food company was unsuccessful in stopping its publication and ultimate distribution.

## EDUCATIONAL GAMES

Akin to training games, educational games usually target school-age children. From subject-specific games like *Math Blaster* or the *JumpStart* series to the more mainstream *The Oregon Trail* and *Where in the World is Carmen Sandiego?*, educational games use the game's natural ability to teach in order to present material in a way that promotes active learning. For those interested in the subject, Raph Koster's book *A Theory of Fun for Game Design* provides an excellent analysis on why games are excellent learning tools. Another book, *What Video Games Have to Teach Us About Learning and Literacy* by James Paul Gee, provides one of the best analyses of games as powerful learning tools yet written. Also refer to Chapter 18, "Games as a Teaching Tool." in this book for additional information on games in the classroom.

## SOCIAL-AWARENESS GAMES

When *Dying for Darfur* was released, no one particularly enjoyed playing the game. Its primary goal is horrible: you need to run to avoid getting hurt, raped, or worse. The game was created in order to draw attention to the plight of the people of Darfur. In spite of (or perhaps because of) making players uncomfortable instead of just trying to make a fun game, *Dying for Darfur* won several awards. Social-awareness games are particularly good at putting players in an incredibly uncomfortable situation—even if they merely *contemplate* playing the game.

## THE PURPOSE IS THE CORE

Every game has a core—the one thing that the game is about, whether it's blasting enemies away or bouncing from platform to platform or performing in a rock band. Serious games are no different. However, their core is precisely their purpose—the one reason that the game is being made.

Earlier, a game that protects children from online predators was mentioned. With its clear purpose, every feature in the game must be measured against how effectively it actually helps the game achieve that purpose. And unlike traditional games, often the means of getting to that purpose are a bit different than in traditional games.

## THE FOCUS TEST

Many serious games come with some serious funding, and those that provide the funds may want to see how well the game actually teaches what it was intended to teach. To do this, focus groups are set up. The process of setting up a focus group and monitoring the process of play, as well as the outcomes of play, is specific to each project. For instance, one of the authors of this book worked on a project whose focus test consisted of four separate groups of varying ethnic backgrounds whose knowledge of the subject matter was tested before the game, after playing the game, and yet again one month after playing the game. The results of these tests were important to the doctors and the government agency behind the game's design.

## WHY SERIOUS GAMES?

As people prepare to enter the game industry with high poly models in their eyes, the thought of making serious games seldom registers on their radar. Why would someone want to make serious games? Here are some reasons:

- To get a job in a much less competitive field, as compared to the AAA game industry
- To educate
- To persuade
- To present a personal belief in the digital realm
- To make a real difference in the world
- To avoid the big consumerism of the mainstream game industry

People come to serious games for many reasons. Designers working in the field often talk about how fulfilling it is that their product is being used to show kids why they should take life-saving medicine, for example.

## CHALLENGES

In this challenge section, you are tasked with creating games that inspire, educate, target, and inflame. If done in a group setting, the challenge leader may want to set limits of acceptable content, if necessary.

### CHALLENGE 1—KATRINA

When Hurricane Katrina blew New Orleans to smithereens in the early part of this century, the world watched and waited for help to arrive. As of the printing of this book, many are still watching and still waiting. For this challenge, your goal is to create a game inspired by Katrina. Your treatment of this—whether a simulation of a hurricane or an "art game"—is entirely up to you. Will you educate, provide social commentary, or do something else entirely?

#### Components Required

■ Internet for research

#### Deliverable

■ Concept doc for a digital game based on Katrina or
■ Non-digital game based on Katrina

#### Suggested Process

1. **Research the event.**
   Look at what happened. Read news stories and eyewitness reports. What aspects of the situation involved interactive systems that could be modeled in a game? What aspects of the event really touched you or upset you? Even something as simple as a person standing in the water angry as hell could be made into a game in the right designer's hands.
2. **Find the core.**
   Choose one aspect of this disaster to form the basis for your game. Define the key decisions players make and create the mechanics that drive those decisions.
3. **Create deliverable.**

#### Variant

Take any tragedy that personally moved you and consider how you would make a serious game about it. Games can be made to cover any material, so don't fear that using a game to cover something trivializes it. Only the treatment within the game can do that. However, as its designer, it is up to you to determine how that treatment is handled and portrayed.

### CHALLENGE 2—FESTIVAL OF ACRONYMS

"Coming back from GDC, I was talking with Jason from the IGDA. He said they were setting up some new SIGs. Eventually, I'd like to get involved with QoL or WiG. I'll probably see him again at MIGS or AGDC, and I'll mention it to him then."

The game industry is a festival of acronyms, and when people are hoping to make that transition from wanna-be to industry dev, they quickly become aware that there are a whole lot of acronyms that they do not know.

For this challenge, your goal is to make a game that teaches your fellow players about these industry acronyms. Of course, you don't need to be obviously educational in your approach. In fact, try not to be. While a trivia game might be the most obvious route to test knowledge, there are other ways for people to learn.

#### Components Required

- Internet for research
- Materials for a board game or card game

#### Deliverable

- A card game or a board game that teaches a minimum of 20 game industry acronyms
- A rule set

#### Suggested Process

1. **Research industry acronyms.**
   Find at least 20 acronyms. You might encounter them by reading gamasutra.com or gamecareerguide.com and looking up any acronyms you find, or you could try searching through Wikipedia.org. You can also take this list: IGDA, SIG, EMA, ESA, TRC, TCR, AP, EP, QA, OOD, QOL, ZBC, ECA, ESRB, SIGGRAPH, ROI, TDD, DD, AAA, and PMP.

2. **Brainstorm game ideas.**
   The goal of this game is to have players learn information, which makes it no different from any other educational game that requires rote memorization. You could simply start there, coming up with mechanics that facilitate learning. Think of games you've played that have done this successfully. There are probably not many of them.

   Another approach is to consider the specific kinds of information here: acronyms. Can you think of any mechanics that are specific to groups of letters, as opposed to generic information?

3. **Build and iterate.**
   Create a prototype of your game and play it with some friends (preferably friends who don't know all of the acronyms). What aspects of the game are enjoyable and what parts are boring or frustrating? Does the game accomplish its learning goals? Go back and revise the game based on your playtesting. Continue to do this as many times as is practical.
4. **Create deliverable.**

### CHALLENGE 3—INSPIRATIONAL GAME

For this challenge, your goal is rather simple sounding: inspire someone through a multi-player non-digital game. Pulling that off, however, isn't as easy as it seems. In order for people to be inspired, they often have to feel affected by what they see or are experiencing and, furthermore, feel that whatever has been stirred in them can actually be achieved. For instance, a painting might inspire someone with its beauty. What would they then be inspired to do? Where will that inspiration go?

### Components Required

■   Internet (for reference)

### Deliverable

■   A non-digital game that inspires
■   A rule set
■   A summary of your hoped-for inspiration, as well as a brief discussion on the mechanics you feel would assist in this process.

### Suggested Process

1. **Explore "inspiration."**
   There are many ways that you can inspire through games. Think of things players can do in a game that would lead them to think they can do things in the real world. One starting place, in fact, might be to think of this challenge in reverse. What things would you like to inspire someone to do? Help the homeless? Volunteer? How would you bring this about through play? You could also start by making a list of things you find inspiring.
2. **Settle on an inspiration.**
   Choose an inspiration and make a list of ways that one could create this inspiration and some rewards the inspiration could provide.

3. **Determine a medium.**
   What is the best way to inspire in the particular way that you chose? A card game, board game, or digital game? Or maybe not a game at all—perhaps a pamphlet or Web site would be more effective (in which case, choose a new inspiration).
4. **Create deliverable.**

## CHALLENGE 4—A STRONG STATEMENT

There is something you feel passionate about, whether it's for or against—a politician, a cause, those in support of another cause, or even another person. Or maybe it's something as simple and heartwarming as a game about your love for your grandmother. Whatever it is, this game should reflect your feelings about that topic in a mature, realized, non-digital design. Remember that in this design, you are also trying to persuade others to feel as you do. It is easy to merely create a game that flings bombs at something you don't particularly like. However, in doing so, you make a statement, but you likely fail to persuade. Consider what makes you feel the way you do, and see if you can instill that same feeling in your players.

### Components Required

- Materials for prototype

### Deliverable

- Playable board- or card-game prototype
- Set of written rules
- Brief creator statement declaring what your goal was and why you made the design choices you did.

### Suggested Process

1. **Choose a topic to cover.**
   Most people have strong opinions about *something*. What about you?
2. **Research that topic.**
   Depending on your topic, you may need to find some facts to support your work. For example, if your game is in support of stem-cell research, you might need to know how much money is spent on this kind of research, what the results have been so far, or what specific pieces of legislation are relevant.
3. **Create deliverable.**

### Variant

As an alternative and advanced option, consider making your feelings on the topic unknown at the time the game begins. See if you can persuade your players through play only and not through an obvious reference in the game narrative, name, or otherwise.

## Iron Designer Challenge 5—Seriously?

For this challenge, you will need at least one other designer, but preferably you can work in two or more groups with three to five members each.

Each group needs to make a list of six potential topics about which a serious game could potentially be made. The topics can be wild, so long as they are plausible. If you think someone would give you funding to make it, it just might be plausible (but those in the business know that this means nothing may be plausible).

Once the list is made, each team should roll a d6 to determine which topic they get from an opposing team's list. Using that topic, the team will then be tasked with coming up with a design for the selected topic.

### Components Required

- Internet for research

### Deliverable

- Concept doc for design or
- Non-digital prototype

### Suggested Process

1. **Research.**
   If you're unfamiliar with your topic, learn the basics.
2. **Brainstorm.**
   Who or what would the players represent? What is the object of the game? Are there any mechanics that immediately spring to mind when you think of the topic?
3. **Create deliverable.**

### Variant

Instead of creating a concept doc, create a non-digital prototype of the serious game. This requires you to have some components for the prototype on hand.

## NON-DIGITAL SHORTS

The benefit of non-digital games in the serious games arena is that they can be widely distributed where there are no computers or consoles handy. This makes them exceptionally versatile.

1. Design a game that trains people on how to stay safe while hiking or camping.
2. Design a game that helps people become better drivers.
3. Imagine you are hiring someone to clean your house or office once a week. Create a board game that would train this person to complete the task.
4. Design a game that helps diabetic children understand and use their blood sugar–testing device.
5. Design a game about exercise playable in first-grade classrooms.
6. Design an advertising game to advocate your favorite grocery store.
7. Alternatively to #6, design an anti-advergame for a store or company you dislike.
8. Design a game that comments on the war against drugs in the United States. You may choose to express either a favorable or an unfavorable perspective, but your game must have a clear, identifiable message.
9. Choose a topic or an issue in world politics and design a game that forces players into an uncomfortable situation based on that issue.
10. Choose any social issue that could be solved solely through awareness, rather than requiring action. Create a game that raises awareness of the issue in the players.

# 20 Casual Games

Fifteen minutes here. Ten minutes there. All over the world, people are playing casual games. From *Solitaire* to *Diner Dash* to *Bejeweled* to *Zuma*, casual games are a booming market, and generally speaking, they are amazingly popular with people who ignore other games entirely: the 30+ female crowd. It's a lucrative and growing market, too.

What is a casual game? It's not an easy question to answer. The IGDA's Casual Games SIG defines casual games as "games that generally involve less complicated game controls and overall complexity in terms of gameplay or investment required to get through the game".[1] The Casual Game Association defines casual games as those "developed for the general public and families" and that are "fun and easy to learn and play".[2]

It seems that there is an exception to every rule or description of what casual games are or should be.

- Casual games tend to be slower-paced and not as frantic as the more hard-core action games, but *Diner Dash* and even *Tetris* eventually end by overwhelming and overloading the player with too many tasks that happen too quickly.
- Casual games tend to have simple rules, but *Virtual Villagers* is quite complicated.
- Casual games don't require a large time commitment, but *Yohoho Puzzle Pirates!* and *Puzzle Quest* certainly give players incentive to play for many hours to advance their characters.
- Casual games tend to have a low difficulty level and be forgiving, but some of the puzzles in *Eets* and *Professor Fizzwizzle* are enough to make experienced gamers pull their hair out in frustration.

All of these games are not only classified as casual games, but successful ones.

What's the easiest way to understand what a casual game is? Play one, two, three, or four of them, and you'll understand. In fact, if you were a part of the arcade generation that was raised on *Pac Man*, *Centipede*, and the like, you already have a pretty good idea what casual games are like.

## Why Casual?

Casual games fit the lifestyles of many individuals. Where once hard-core gamers devoted hours at a clip to develop the nuances of their RPG parties, they now play a little here and there, amid family and job responsibilities. Meanwhile, others have discovered games through casual gaming, first with *Solitaire* on the PC and later with games like *Scrabulous* available on Facebook.

These games share numerous features.

### Easy to Learn

Most casual games have very limited instructions and take advantage of assumed knowledge, about the same amount of knowledge one would need to run a computer in the first place. Drag, drop, click. Games like *Diner Dash* and *Chuzzle* can be played with only these actions, as can the great majority of casual games.

Casual games begin with a two- or three-sentence description of play followed by actual play itself. The mechanics of play are almost always obvious just by looking at the game. In fact, most casual games offer excellent feedback that guides the player as she plays.

Contrast this with something like an FPS. For the average person, stepping into a play session in an FPS can be overwhelming. What weapon should you use? How do you fire? How do you change weapons? How do you even move? Many of these are things that gamers take for granted.

### Reduced Complexity

The rule sets in many of these games are rather simple. Consider the gameplay in the previously mentioned *Diner Dash*. The pattern goes like this:

- Seat the customer.
- Take her order.
- Place her order at the counter.
- Get the meal from the counter.
- Serve the meal.
- Pick up the check.
- Clear the table.

By casual game standards, it's a long line of tasks. However, it's a pattern we already know from just being a part of the world. This known pattern repeats itself again and again and again as tables fill and customers continue to come, and this play pattern holds players. The player can even earn certain upgrades through good performance, allowing the restaurant to operate more smoothly.

Games like *Chuzzle* and *Bejeweled* ask players to move things into sets of three. That's it. The game throws some roadblocks in your way, and it's up to the player to navigate around them. The simplicity of the groupings and the easy interface allow for a relaxed play experience that doesn't stress the player.

By contrast, compare the level of tasks one must complete to enjoy a typical RTS or RPG, and the list is simple by comparison. That's just what casual game players want—a break, not a commitment.

## CASUAL CONFLICTS

Because casual games are meant to be, well, casual, the conflicts present in the game must follow suit. A life-or-death, adrenaline-fueled situation in which the player gets blown away isn't particularly conducive to the casual mindset, nor is a four-hour, 40-player raid versus a boss in an MMO.

Generally, the conflicts in casual games take one or more of these forms:

- **Player versus game:** The pattern in the game gets progressively more difficult, either through speed or moderate shifts or blocks to the pattern's execution (for example, locks on movement in *Chuzzle*), until the player either beats the game (for example, *Solitaire*) or is overwhelmed (for example, *Tetris*).
- **Player versus score:** The player is trying to beat his or her last score, or the score of another player.
- **Player versus time:** The player is trying to do a task within a set period of time.

## SHORT PLAY TIME

Casual games generally have a short play time that is measured in minutes versus hours. Some games, however, have incorporated endless or Zen modes that let players play as long as they would like.

## LACK OF COMMITMENT

One of the beauties of many casual games is that they're willing to wait for players (or the opponent if it's a multiplayer game). If the player gets up, talks on the phone, answers the door, and comes back to the game, nothing's changed and nothing's lost. Days can pass, in fact. This ability to come and go, this lack of commitment, is one of the key features that draws people to these games.

## FAMILY FRIENDLY

For a game to be considered a casual game, it is, by default, family friendly and contains no objectionable content. If it did, the game would instead be classed in another category of games covered elsewhere in other books.

## CHALLENGES

Before doing the challenges below, it's recommended that you play a few casual games to the point where you'd rather be playing them for *fun* instead of education. At first, and particularly if you are a hard-core gamer, the games may seem trivial to you. After a while, though, you'll discover that their simplicity is also their great strength.

Digital versions of the challenges you succeed in also make excellent one-person projects.

### Challenge 1—Mismatch 3

Many casual games require players to match three similar objects by gathering them in such a way that they touch one another. Your employer is more than aware of this trend and wants you to come up with something similar… but different. He doesn't want you to just re-skin a game like *Bejeweled* with something other than jewels, though. He wants you to innovate the "Match 3" game style in some way, whether through level design, level blocks, or something else entirely.

#### Components Required

- Internet connection (for research)
- The free version of *Chuzzle*, as an example of how several new mechanics can be added to *Bejeweled*

#### Deliverable

- Card-game prototype of a digital game

#### Suggested Process

1.  **Research.**
    If you are unfamiliar with Match 3 games, play several of them (at least *Bejeweled*, *Zuma*, and *Chuzzle* to give you an idea of the genre conventions).
2.  **Brainstorm.**
    Think of the gameplay in a typical Match 3 game. Does it suggest any mechanics that haven't been exploited yet? Consider other casual games you are familiar with that are *not* Match 3 games. Can you think of any interesting mechanics that could be adapted to a different genre?
3.  **Create deliverable.**
4.  **Create digital prototype (optional).**
    Match three games are popular with developers who are just beginning to enter the casual space, mainly because they are easier to program than other types of games. If you have enough programming skills to make a *Tetris* clone, you should be able to implement your game idea in a fairly short period of time.

### Challenge 2—Click, Click, Click, Click…

The "click management" style of casual game, exemplified by *Diner Dash*, involves using a pattern that players already know (in this case, the pattern of seating and waiting on customers). The pattern is repeated, so that the player must keep track of several versions of it going at once. As levels progress, the pattern becomes faster, or more complex, or both.

Recognizing that many casual games use patterns we already know, your boss has asked you to identify one such pattern, other than waiting tables. Design a game based on that pattern, and then create a few pieces of concept art or a non-digital prototype that will convey the basic design.

## Components Required

- Internet connection (for research)
- The free version of *Diner Dash* for research on how patterns can get faster and faster and layer upon themselves
- Paper for concept drawings or components for prototype

## Deliverable

- Three separate concept drawings of potential game interface or
- Non-digital prototype
- List of steps in the pattern, either noted on the concept art itself or on a separate sheet of paper

## Suggested Process

1. **Choose a pattern.**
   Think back to *Diner Dash*. Flo, the star of the game, is repeating the pattern of taking orders, serving customers, and clearing tables again and again and again. Think of another pattern that we repeat over and over and over. Stretch your imagination by considering hobbies, weird things people do, and things with multiple steps to them. Highlight those that appeal to you.
2. **Detail the pattern.**
   For your pattern, write all the steps required to close the loop. What exactly does the character and player have to do to complete one loop of the pattern? Can the pattern be repeated in a round? The pattern should not be alien to the players. Remember, casual games are casual for a reason. The pattern should be familiar.
3. **Consider the feedback.**
   Click management is effectively your core mechanic of the game. The player's ability to move from point A to point B to point C (as well as points in between, if necessary) is the key to success. How will you signal what the player needs to do? How will you signal when a point is ready for interaction? How will you score the player's progress? How do you lose?
4. **Create deliverable.**

### CHALLENGE 3—IT'S OBVIOUS

In an effort to capitalize on the success of casual games on computers, you have been contracted to create a card, dice, board, or tile-based game that is truly as easy to play as a casual game. Your client hopes that by bringing a casual game away from the computer, people will be more inclined to play it with their families. A key factor in determining the success of your design is this: your players should be able to sit down and understand the game simply from the way it looks and the existing knowledge they have. You are free to use an existing IP if you like.

**Components Required**

■  Poster board and other components as necessary to create a board game

**Deliverable**

■  Playable game prototype

**Suggested Process**

1. **Find your core mechanics.**
   Many casual games take advantage of interface standards, like clicking, dragging, and dropping. What are some board-game mechanics that your players will already know? What mechanics already exist in the real world that you can translate to board games in a way that make their function obvious?

2. **Brainstorm.**
   Build a game from some set of mechanics you identified. Whenever you add a new rule, ask yourself whether the rule is obvious without having to be written down or told to players. In cases where it's not, you must find a way to make it so, or abandon the rule and try again.

3. **Create deliverable.**
   For this challenge, you only need to create the game components and not a set of written rules. Remember, you must have a game where the rules are so obvious that you don't *need* written rules!

### CHALLENGE 4—BREAKING THE RULES

In this chapter, we've explored the following shared qualities of casual games:

■  Easy to learn
■  Low complexity
■  Short play time
■  Indirect conflict

- Low commitment
- Family friendly

Choose one of these qualities and negate it (for example, hard to learn or direct conflict), while keeping the rest intact. Design a game that fits all of these qualities (including the negated one), but that is still a casual game.

### Components Required

- None

### Deliverable

- Three-page design document that lists the basic mechanics. Include at least one screen mock-up for clarity.

### Suggested Process

1. **Research your rule.**
   Consider the aspect of casual games that you've chosen to intentionally ignore. Why is it part of most casual games in the first place? What does it accomplish? What is its purpose?
2. **Break the rule.**
   Once you understand the rules, think about reasons why you might break them. Under what conditions is your rule no longer valid? Are you familiar with any examples of successful casual games that break your rule?
3. **Create deliverable.**

### Variant

Roll a die to choose one of the qualities to negate, rather than choosing one yourself.

## Iron Designer Challenge 5—Knit 1, Purl 2 (Live)

The door to your office bursts open, and your marketing guy rushes in. He's holding knitting needles. You hope he won't say it, but he does. "I've got it! Knitting! A knitting game!"

According to him, it's a perfect fit. It's better than *Deer Hunter*! It's better than *America's Army*! Knitting is now an incredibly popular hobby with the same audience that's into casual games (it's true, actually).

If you think you know casual games, it's time to put that to the test. Split into teams of two to four individuals. Have each team name a hobby that's popular with 30+ year old females. Each team is assigned a hobby by another team. You must create a concept pitch for a casual game, featuring the given hobby as its main theme. You have two hours.

If you're having trouble coming up with hobbies, use this list:

- Knitting
- Cooking
- Antiques
- Quilting
- Bird watching
- Jewelry making
- Gardening
- Walking
- Scrapbooking

### Components Required

- Internet connection (for research)

### Deliverable

- Informal concept pitch

### Suggested Process

1. **Research.**
   If no one on your team is intimately familiar with your assigned hobby, research the basics online. What makes the hobby fun (at least, according to its devotees)? What are the core elements of the hobby?
2. **Brainstorm.**
   What aspects of the hobby translate well to games? Think of a core mechanic that captures the essence of the hobby and then build on it to create the concept for a full game.
3. **Create deliverable.**

## Non-Digital Shorts

Practice your casual game design by exploring any of these topics in thought, paper prototype, or digital form.

1. Choose three of the attributes listed in Challenge 4: "Breaking the Rules" and design a tile game using these as the core.

2. Choose a lengthy but simple board game (such as *The Game of Life* or *Monopoly*) and redesign it to be playable in 10 minutes.
3. Most casual games are single-player. Redesign *Checkers* to be a solo game.
4. *Rummy* is a classic card game that fits many of the characteristics of a casual game. Redesign the game to follow the "player versus time" model.
5. Alternatively to #4, redesign *Rummy* to follow the "player versus score" model.
6. Choose a complex board game (anything more complicated than *Monopoly* will do) and redesign it to be learnable and playable by children ages six to eight. *Risk* is ideal for this exercise.
7. Create a casual game that also works as a "mixer." Mixer games allow individuals to meet and greet one another at large parties.
8. Impressed by the number of employees who are playing casual games, you are approached by a manager of a local retail outlet who would like you to create one such game for the company's training retreat.
9. Create a casual game that simultaneously teaches about sound environmental practices.
10. Create a casual game that mothers can use to teach their pre-reading children the alphabet. Do not use the "flip over and match" mechanic.

[1] http://www.igda.org/wiki/Casual_Games_SIG/Whitepaper

[2] http://www.casualgamesassociation.org/faq.php#casualgames

# 21 ▪ Social Networks and Games

Since the earliest days of computing, the industry has been heading progressively toward a convergence of social networks and games. Games have always been a social experience, and as game designer Greg Costikyan noted in his 1994 article, "I Have No Words and I Must Design," solo player games are a temporary aberration in the historical norm.[1] Once technology reached a certain point, people would be gaming together again. Today's MMOs and burgeoning social networks attest to that.

In speaking of social networks and games, there are really two kinds to consider: those outside of a game and those that are a part of the game. Leader-boards, chat rooms, and guild forums are all external to a game, no matter how closely the community may be tied to that game, and while a great deal of strategizing might take place there, there is no actual gameplay to be had. Conversely, games on social networks like Facebook not only use the social network to propagate the game player to player, but some also fully incorporate the social network, making it a dynamic of play. *Parking Wars* is one such game. The more friends you have playing, the more spots you have available to park your car. Sometimes, there is a blur between the two worlds, such as auction houses that are external to the game, but whose outcomes affect gameplay overall.

In this chapter, we'll explore games that fully incorporate the social network as a part of the game.

From a game-development perspective, there are three important considerations for both the developer and publisher.

■ Social networks own a built-in *free* distribution network.
■ Some social networks serve an audience of tens of millions of members, in effect, their own MMO.
■ Social network games have low asset requirements. They are exceptionally low cost compared to traditional game development.

## CATEGORIZING SOCIAL-NETWORK GAMES

While the games available on social networks tend to resemble casual games (for example, they are usually quick and easy to play), a level of difficulty is added for the designer.

Understanding the various categories of social-network games is important for those hoping to design in this space.

## MACRO-CATEGORY

At the highest level, games on social networks fit into one of three categories:

- **Network dependent:** These games cannot exist outside of a social network and rely upon the network for play dynamics. While these games can be altered to be independent of the network, the play mechanics of the game are so tied to the network that such a modification would cause the game to lose all its flavor. When the player adds the application, he immediately begins playing with all of his friends who also have the application. *Parking Wars* is one such game. Without friends' streets to park your cars on, there's no game to speak of.
- **Network integrated:** These games can exist outside the network, but their design makes them ideally suited for the turn-based gameplay that social networks support well. They use the social network to support multiplayer games. *Scrabulous* (a *Scrabble* clone) and other knockoffs of board games usually fit in this category.
- **Network independent:** These games don't take advantage of the social network, or if they do, they take advantage of it in a very limited way, such as posting information in your friend's newsfeed (or similar reporting structure). In many cases, they are single-player games where there is no form of direct conflict between the players. *Jetman*, a single-player arcade game where a man with a jetpack tries to fly through an obstacle course, is an example of this type of game.

## PLAY DEPTH
## SCOTT JON SIEGEL, GAME DESIGNER

In an article on his blog, game designer Scott Jon Siegel broke Facebook games down into three distinct categories based on their depth of play: flat, shallow, and deep. The following text is reprinted with his permission.[2]

- Flat games exist on Facebook, but they might as well exist anywhere else. They're almost always single-player, and do not involve the available social network through the gameplay. (I want to stress "through the gameplay," as many of these apps do take advantage of the network to create leaderboards and share high scores, but this does affect how the core game operates.) Examples are popular apps like *Jetman*, *Tower Bloxx*, and the copious arcade compilation apps that let users play classics like *Snake* and *Tetris*. Sometimes, these apps are simply Flash applications ported to Facebook.
- Shallow games do utilize the social network in gameplay, but usually to a fairly limited degree. Examples of this include *Texas Hold-'Em Poker* and the ever-so-excellent *Scrabulous* application, both of which use your friends list to organize potential opponents. *Scrabulous* was the first app I encountered that made smart use of Facebook, turning *Scrabble* into a divine play-by-mail-esque experience. Still, the gameplay is largely unaffected by the network.

■ Finally, deep games take more direct advantage of Facebook's features, building core mechanics around social networks and using additional methods to incorporate the whole of Facebook into the gameplay. The best example of this is the *Werewolves/Vampires/Zombies* application(s), which took the gameplay onto Facebook's walls and PMs, as players lured unsuspecting friends in order to increase their power. A more recent addition to the deep end is area/code's *Parking Wars*, which has users leaving cars on the streets of their friends in a strange parking-oriented version of "chicken." Both games re-imagined the social network as something else (be it food or free parking), and built gameplay around this fiction.

## CASE STUDY: AREA/CODE'S *PARKING WARS*

*Parking Wars* is a simple game. Players start with a street named after them and two cars. A player's goal is to find a parking place for those cars on someone else's street. The other streets are owned by people in the player's social network who are also playing the game. Green cars must park in open spots or spots that read "Green Cars Only" or risk being ticketed by the street's owner. The longer the car sits in one spot, the more money it earns. Sit in a single spot long enough, and the car tops off at $5,560.

Most parking spaces have constraints on them: red cars only, blue cars only, no parking, and so on. So, if players can't find an appropriate spot for a car, they have to park illegally and risk getting ticketed by other players. Giving out tickets is a money-earning proposition for the ticketer, and a money-losing event for the ticketed—receiving a ticket has the effect of creating a 2*ticket difference in score. As you earn more money from parking and ticketing, you level up and gain additional cars.

*Parking Wars* was originally developed as an advergame for A&E's *Parking Wars* reality TV show. Though play originally capped off at $1,000,000, people didn't stop playing. There were no rewards to be gained by going further, but that didn't deter people. Encouraged by their continued play and in response to their requests, in early 2008, *Parking Wars* developer area/code added badges for certain achievements and also let players buy new cars, including ice-cream trucks, which allowed cars to earn at a greater rate, and tow trucks, which could tow illegally parked cars, no matter whose street they were on.[3]

## WHAT WORKS BEST?

Games on social networks must have mechanics that take advantage of the social network. Ultimately, these mechanics give rise to dynamics that lead to propagation of the game's player base. In *Parking Wars'* case, when the player installs the game or tickets another player, it is reported in the player's newsfeed. The dynamics of the game, then, support its growth and reinforce its advertising message not just on the player's screen, but on all the player's friends screens, too.

In analyzing successful game design on social networks, some constants emerge:

■ **Turn-based:** Since players of games on social networks come and go as they please, the games that sustain play the best are turn-based games. All players may be present for play, as in online games of *Poker*, or not, as in games like *Go*. The key, however, is the freedom for people to come and go as they please.

■ **Multiplayer:** On a social network, allowing friends to interact with one another seems like a no-brainer. Surprisingly, many single-player games exist on social network sites. However, games that allow interaction within the social network are far and away the most successful.

■ **Friend affecting:** Games where players can do something nice or something mean to their friends tend to be particularly popular. *Vampires* allows you to feed on your friends, while *Parking Wars* allows you to ticket them and take virtual money directly out of their pockets. As with traditional games, beating your friends or helping your friends is more satisfying than beating a computer.

■ **Easy to propagate:** In order for games to be commercially effective and successful, they need to be played by a wide audience of individuals. Therefore, games that allow easy propagation from player to player or, better yet, provide tangible rewards for inviting friends, have the best chance of succeeding.

■ **Games with a status feature:** Players like to feel good about their performance in any kind of game. In fact, the pursuit of the high score earned many a quarter for owners of arcades. Games that make the display of a score (or the equivalent thereof) prominent in the main gameplay screen or in newsfeed updates are often attractive to players. One such game threatened (albeit unintentionally) to display the player's score in a financial quiz. More than one person publicly wondered why on earth anyone would want anyone else to know how little they knew about finances. For more information, see the section "High Score and the Social Network" later in this chapter.

■ **Games with a visual display feature:** Just as players like high scores or leader-boards in games, they also like games that allow them to customize their space and display that space to others. Games like Facebook's *Fluff Friends* offer players multiple opportunities to customize the play space on the player's page.

■ **Games that are easy to understand and play:** Casual games work the best on social networks, although the breed of social-network casual games is different from what one would expect of the traditionally popular single-player casual games like *Bejeweled* and *Diner Dash*. The most popular games are easy to understand, require interaction within the social network, and provide low-stress play.

■ **Games that require repeat visits:** Players are brought back to a game on a regular, predictable basis as a requirement of play. In *Parking Wars*, there are three specific mechanics that require players to return. These are the following:

■ Ticketing cars that are illegally parked on the player's street

■ Cashing in cars that have maxed out their earnings

■ Checking to make sure the restrictions on a spot haven't changed from, say, "Red Cars Only" to "Green Cars Only," rendering a player's car ticket worthy

This is different from games like *Scrabulous* that don't integrate time into the mechanics. People can go back to *Scrabulous* a week or more after the last move. There's no impetus to return to play like there is here in *Parking Wars*.

■ **Games that encourage community:** Increasingly, games on Facebook are encouraging players to work together in order to succeed. For instance, in order to discover how to get the badges offered by developers in their early 2008 update of the game, players worked together and announced their successes and raised questions in the *Parking Wars* forum.[4]

On the flip side, games that run contrary to these conventions tend not to do as well.

## SOCIAL-NETWORK PROPAGATION MECHANICS

In order to succeed on a social network, games need to move from user to user to user. How does that happen?

One of the authors of this book is currently studying the mechanics that developers use to propagate casual games throughout the Facebook community. Since the success of these games and the payout in terms of advertising dollars and impressions is related to the number of players and the amount those players actually play, a successful Facebook game must propagate within the social network in order to be successful.

In the absence of the traditional methods of advertising, AAA-level production values, or even a serious review structure for the games, what causes people to play Facebook games?

### THE PYRAMID SCHEME

The most successful Facebook games form pyramid schemes where you benefit from inviting people to play, and they, in turn, benefit by inviting still more people to play. This is exemplified in games like *Parking Wars* and *Fluff Friends*. Solo-player games, however, fail in this regard. Many of the non-game, popular apps on Facebook give people rewards for inviting people, too. So a player gets rewards for inviting people, and they get rewards for inviting people, and so on. Due to the structure of Facebook, few games are designed to take advantage of the full pyramid (for lack of a better term)—the player doesn't receive benefits for invitees of his or her invitees.

In the case of some popular Facebook apps, much of the work is automated, actually. The only "work" players need to do is selecting friends from their friends list. If they have a sizable list of friends, it's relatively easy to meet certain reward thresholds.

Modifications on this mechanic are bonuses for all invitees and additional bonuses for those who accept.

### NEWSFEED "TESTIMONIALS"

With the installation of a game, a report appears in the player's friends' newsfeed, and the newsfeed item then serves as a testimonial. The number of friends to appear in that newsfeed item (for example, "five of your friends have…") and the value of their opinion to the newsfeed reader affects whether or not that person installs the application, too. This suggests that faster propagation could lead to still faster propagation.

For instance, five game developers installed *Parking Wars.* When the item appeared in one of their friend's newsfeeds, they installed it immediately, based not only on the number, but on the value he placed upon his friends' opinions as game developers.

### NEWSFEED PLAY UPDATES

*Parking Wars* and most games continually provide newsfeed updates every time a certain milestone is achieved. For *Parking Wars,* the game posts an item in the newsfeed when the player tickets people or earns a badge. Other games post when the player reaches a higher score. *Fluff Friends* reports when people do something to the player's pet or there's an abstracted race. In each instance, these too serve as a form of testimonial.

### MULTIPLAYER MANDATE

Some games cannot be played alone. *Parking Wars* is one such game. When it was first released, however, some people were put into this situation: if the player had no friends playing the game, he was unable to play until he could get some of his friends to install the application, too. Eventually, however, *Parking Wars* added "neighbors" so that multiplayer playing was no longer a mandate. It changed the overall dynamics of the game, however. One can see this reflected in the later addition of "show only friends" or "show friends and neighbors." Evidently, it's not as satisfying to ticket an unknown person from *Parking Wars'* player list as it is to ticket one's friends.

### MULTIPLAYER OPTION

Some games provide an option that allows play either solo or with another player. *Scrabulous* is one such game. Its relative ease and familiarity make it one of the most popular Facebook games. Still, it's more pleasant to play the game with a friend than the AI of the game.

### REWARDS THROUGH INVITE

This ties into the pyramid scheme mentioned earlier. In this instance, the game prompts you to invite friends, and it unlocks content for you if you do so or provides a similar reward. For instance, *Fluff Friends* gives you 25 "munny" for each accepted invite. The player is generally enticed to invite other friends during the player's initial installation of the application.

### THE HOSTAGE SITUATION

"So and so has said [something] about you. Log in now to find out what!"

One of the more popular Facebook app-propagation mechanics is the "the hostage situation." You are notified by an application that your friend has evidently left some juicy information about you. In order to get the information, you need to add the application, too. This mechanic quite obviously relies on player curiosity to propagate itself.

### RETALIATION

Using the "retaliation" technique, a friend has done [action x] to you, and the app invites you to do it back to your friend, thereby forcing you to install the app. If you accept, it is likely to propagate still further, because if you go that far, you're more likely to do [x action] to others, too. For instance, one of the authors of this book got into *Superpoke* because a fellow game developer "slapped [her] with a trout." In order to do something equally odd to him, she needed to install the app, too. To its credit, *Superpoke* offers a wide range of options, from holiday greetings to the more inane things like… throwing a cow at someone. So, though someone may not have been likely to install the app to retaliate a trout attack, the diversity of options propagates it heavily among friends.[5]

## SLOWING THE SPREAD

As a gaming platform, Facebook is a relatively new medium, and the dynamics of play are different from many others with which we, as game developers and designers, are familiar. The whole paradigm's changed—the social nature of the game is, in many cases, more important than the actual game itself. In fact, a Facebook game can be threadbare in terms of actual game mechanics or not even fun at all, and still be wildly successful. On the other hand, a game can be deep and lasting and fail to propagate.

What slows down gameplay propagation?

### HITTING CRITICAL MASS

Over the summer of 2007, thousands of players received this message daily: "Dear victim, You have been bitten by [friend name]! Start biting chumps!" After deleting them, another wave of messages would arrive. It led one prominent game developer to use his status line to tell any potential werewolves, vampires, or other propagators precisely what they could do with themselves. The game had hit critical mass, and instead of becoming fun, it was becoming downright annoying to many, especially if they weren't playing the game.

After "chumps," some noticed a decided reservedness among the Facebook community to bite, kick, Sith, Jedi, or otherwise propagate anything that resembled these applications. Much like the early days of the Internet, at some point, it became bad etiquette to spam your friends with your personal amusements or interests.

Oddly enough, games can become victims of their own success.

### APPEARANCE/EMBARRASSMENT

People care about how others perceive them and value the contacts they have on their friends list. If people are annoyed by invites to use a particular application, they are much less likely to propagate that application on to other people. Propagating the application becomes the equivalent of a digital mullet.

### EMBARRASSMENT, AGAIN

When installing an application, the newsfeed reporting on said installation can affect whether or not the installation is installed in the first place. For instance, consider the thought process involved in adding the flirty *Are You Interested?* or the *Hotness* application. First of all, do players really want all their friends knowing they have installed this app? You don't always have the option to deny the report in your newsfeed. Furthermore, such apps are likely to be less appealing to women who, stereotypically speaking, are less likely than men to say, "Hey? Want to tell me how hot I am?" for fear that the answer may come back, "Not so hot." (See Sheri Graner Ray's book *Gender Inclusive Game Design* for more info on how women react to games and people playing games.)

## ME VERSUS YOU

In general, people care about themselves more than they care about others. Facebook applications that take advantage of this are more likely to propagate than those that don't. For instance, consider the *My Room* application. This application allows players to see all the things someone else has done to their virtual room. What is the *selfish* attraction? Apart from voyeuristic tendencies, why would one player want to see another's stuff, particularly if there were nothing in it for them? While players can create their own *My Room*, the message's appeal is to look at another player's stuff, not create their own. It fails to motivate.

Likewise, applications that immediately put the person in a subservient position aren't high on players' lists either. For instance some applications allow you to become a virtual knight and join another person's court. Again, the appeal here is to do something for someone else as opposed to doing it for themselves.

Compare this with other apps like *How will you die?* and *Which Rockstar are you?*, which target the player and not an assumption that they care enough about the person sending the app to want to be in their court or view their room. The nutshell here is this: In the propagation message on the target side, the game should target their interest in themselves and not the person who sent it.[5]

## HIGH SCORE AND THE SOCIAL NETWORK

People like to be noticed in real life and in games, too. Having a high-score list present on the page automatically ups the competitiveness of the game. Because of the transparency of social networks, high scores tend to have a more far-reaching effect than they do in traditional console or PC games where, at best, gamer tags are the norm.

When time is added into the mix (for example, you have to do something every x hours as you do in *Parking Wars*), the high-score list becomes an ever-moving target that the willing will continue to shoot at.

### HIGH-SCORE ALTERATIONS

If a game allows players to affect each other's scores through game mechanics, the high-score listing becomes that much more meaningful as a representation not just of the player's effectiveness in his or her own game, but also against his or her friends as well. It adds to the competitiveness and the enjoyment of the game if the player can affect not just his or her score but other players' scores as well.

### HIGH-SCORE LOSS

There is a down side to high scores, though. If the score starts at a particular point and keeps climbing from there, those new to the game may be turned off by that same score. It is a constant reminder to other players of a train they will never catch.

So they may decide not to play anymore. Players are reluctant to keep up the good fight when they feel that there's no real fight to be had.

Some games have addressed this problem in several ways:

- **Rolling score:** Rolling scores are calculated using a particular time period, frequently 30 days. The player's current score equals the individual scores from the last 30 days. This way, new players can still be competitive.[5]
- **Periodic resets:** Each game lasts for x days before the game resets. Sometimes, games preserve the highest score during that period for posterity.
- **Player-directed resets:** Instead of every x days, the game lasts until some game event happens that causes a player or a set of players to win. The end game can be tense with the entire community working together to stop a few players from winning.

## THE FUTURE OF SOCIAL NETWORKS AND GAMES

Predicting the future of social networks seems impossible, and it may very well be. However, just as Costikyan suspected that games would return to their multiplayer norm, likewise, social networks allow them the opportunity to return to their truly social, if virtual, nature.

Technologies are available and in development that allow people to build and propagate games within social networks. Some networks have even welcomed game developers by allowing them to host games on their network free.

Whether this will extend itself into a 3D virtual social network is hard to say. So far, 3D social games like *Second Life* have yet to attract the same volume of users, due to both technological constraints and player familiarity with the medium.

## CHALLENGES

Social networks are phenomenally familiar to many, but also an intriguingly new platform for game developers. Creating a game, let alone a good game, is a challenge for many. There are so many factors to consider that are not common to traditional games as we know them. Before exploring the challenges below, spend some time exploring social networks, and play a game or two for a sustained period of time to understand the experience and how the dynamics of these games work.

### CHALLENGE 1—GET YOUR FEET WET

Many businesses are eager to capitalize on the young professional market that lives by the millions on social networking sites like Facebook and MySpace. You've just been hired by one of them to lure in new job recruits. The company? Google. They want you to make a game for Facebook that will simultaneously provide the company with contacts to possible recruits and meet player expectation of a Google game.

### Components Required

■ Internet access for research

### Deliverable

■ One-page concept document describing the basic gameplay, networking component, and propagation techniques
■ Interface mockup

### Suggested Process

1. **Brainstorm the possibilities.**
   If you heard there were a Google game on Facebook, what would you expect? If you haven't played Facebook games (or used Google), take a moment to do so to familiarize yourself with their typical design.
2. **Sketch out a design.**
   With your basic list of expectations, determine a possible design for your game. What does the player do? What is the core of gameplay? Make a list of the game's features.
3. **Determine how the game is propagated.**
   How does the game travel from player to player?
4. **Consider the user interface.**
   What is your game going to look like? Casual games need to be understandable quickly by a huge range of people. Create mockup interfaces for your game.
5. **Create deliverable.**

### Challenge 2—The Social-Net Board Game

Somewhere out there, there are more than a few individuals wondering what all this "social-networking stuff" is about. After all, people have been social and networking since the caveman days. It's with that in mind that you'll apply the unique nature of social networks in a non-digital space: with the aid of digital networks, all of those wanting to be social and to network don't need to be present at the same time. Using the same series as described previously, create a board or tile-based game that up to 20 players can play. Players should be able to come and go as they please, solve missions, and function independently of other players or with them, provided they are playing the game simultaneously. As a designer, your biggest challenge will be to determine how the game ends or if it ends at all. How will you provide your players with continuing entertainment? What's to stop them from racing through in a single play?

### Components Required

- Board-game components

### Deliverable

- Complete set of written rules
- Interface mockup

### Suggested Process

Use the same process as in the previous challenge.

## CHALLENGE 3—WOW! THAT'S BAD

As with any platform, there are no shortages of bad games on social networks. Find one, analyze it, and design a fix for it. Remember, making good games for social networks isn't as easy as it looks.

### Components Required

- Access to the Internet
- An account on a social-networking site

### Deliverable

- Analysis of bad social-networking game, including coverage of what it did right, what it did wrong, and its performance to date within the social network (number of players, percentage of daily users, and so on) if available.
- Redesign of game

### Suggested Process

1. **Identify bad game.**
   As is the case with most bad games, this isn't too hard to do.
2. **Analyze the bad game.**
   Think about the aspects of a social game covered in this chapter. Does the gameplay involve a player's social network, and if so, how? How does the game propagate? Aside from the social aspects, is the gameplay itself compelling? Make a list of weak points in the game. Lastly, is there anything the game did right that you don't want to change?
3. **Brainstorm fixes.**
   For each issue that you've identified, think of ways that you could fix it. Consider changes to the mechanics, the user interface, and propagation methods.
4. **Create deliverable.**

### Challenge 4—LinkedIn Wants In

Throughout a lot of this chapter, we've focused on games within social networks. Games can also harness the information publicly available on these social networks while remaining external to them.

For this challenge, your goal is to create a game that is external to the popular professional networking site LinkedIn (www.linkedin.com). Study the site, the people who are on it, and its purpose, and using the publicly available information, create a game concept that fits with the overall aesthetic of the site itself.

#### Components Required

■ Internet connection, for research

#### Deliverable

■ One-page game concept or
■ Playable paper prototype demonstrating your game concept

#### Suggested Process

1. **Research LinkedIn.**
   Research LinkedIn and determine what information is publicly available to visitors to the site. Make a list of this information. In effect, this information will become the stats, resources, and attributes of your new game.
2. **Consider genres.**
   What types of games could you build with this information? A tycoon game comes to mind, as do games in the simulation genre. At the same time, a casual game, social net game, or an ARG are possible, too. Run through the list of possibilities and brainstorm within your group.
3. **Create deliverable.**
   Develop a concept pitch for a possible game.

### Iron Designer Challenge 5—Social Networking, the LARP

*Assassin* is a popular game played on college campuses. The game takes place in real time, in between classes, in the real world. There are many rules variations, but in general each player in the game must "assassinate" another player (in play form, perhaps using a Nerf gun or water pistol). In this way, every player is hunting someone else, and also being hunted *by* someone else. When a player "kills" his prey, he receives that person's target as his or her new object of assassination. As time goes on and players are eliminated, the circle narrows, until eventually two players are hunting each other. When only one player is left alive, he is declared the winner.

For this challenge, your goal is to take this game and adapt it to be playable on a social network such as Facebook.

**Components Required**

■  None

**Deliverable**

■  Game concept, including a description of core mechanics

**Suggested Process**

1.  **Find the mechanics that must change.**
    Some aspects of *Assassin* do not translate at all from the real world to a virtual social network. For example, part of the fun of *Assassin* is never knowing when some random person is going to attack you during your normal daily routine, but Facebook has no offline component. You will have to do something about that. (If your game requires action to be taken outside of Facebook, then you will need a way to notify the online game of what happens.)
2.  **Propagation.**
    In *Assassin*, a game usually involves people signing up in advance of the event. Most Facebook games propagate *after* people have already started playing. How does your game propagate through social networks?
3.  **Notification.**
    How are players notified when they assassinate someone? When they are themselves assassinated? Is this notification used to propagate the game? What happens to players who are eliminated?
4.  **Put the pieces together.**
    Assemble your list of mechanics and reflect on them. Is this a game you would like to play? If not, what changes could you make? Are your rules simple enough that anyone could start playing this game without feeling lost?
5.  **Create deliverable.**

## NON-DIGITAL SHORTS

Since the caveman days, games have inherently been a social experience. The new forms of social networking allow us to consider new forms (and reconsider old forms) of games. These shorts encourage this type of exploration.

1. Create a tile-based game that emphasizes the expanding territory based on an expanding network.
2. Create a card game that encourages players to work in teams to achieve their goal.
3. In the world of business, it's all about who you know. Create a board game that emphasizes this dynamic.
4. Birds move in flocks, and fish move in schools. Consider how this relates to social networking and make a game about it of any type.
5. Create a game that will help grow a non-profit organization that uses at least three successful social-networking mechanics noted above. The game will begin at their next yearly conference.
6. Create a game designed to help build a sense of community in a city with a high-transient worker population. The game will be launched at the building of a new community center in a large apartment complex.
7. Design a Facebook board game.
8. There is a game, simply called *The Game*, that is played in real life. The object of *The Game* is to not think about *The Game*. If you find yourself thinking about *The Game* when other people are nearby, you must publicly declare that you just lost, and you must explain the rules to anyone who asks. *The Game* spreads virally in a way that many Facebook games would like to, but it's not really much of a game. Design a better one—a game where the *mechanics* involve recruiting new players, which can grow infinitely.
9. Design a game to help people overcome shyness at parties or other social events.
10. Design a board or card game that gives players in-game rewards for every new player they introduce to the game. The mechanisms for doing so must be administered by the players themselves, not the game developer or some other third party.

## RESOURCES

[1] "I Have No Words and I Must Design," http://www.costik.com/nowords.html

[2] "Game design for Facebook is a very different beast," available online at http://numberless.net/blog/ 2008/01/12/game-design-for-facebook-is-a-very-different-beast/

[3] "Parking Wars: The Crack that is the 'Possible Prize'," available online at http://bbrathwaite.wordpress.com/2008/03/29/parking-wars-the-crack-that-is-the-possible-prize/

[4] "Facebook Game Player Propagation," available online at http://bbrathwaite.wordpress.com/2008/01/06/facebook-casual-game-player-propagation/

[5] "Facebook App Propagation: The Hostage Situation & Retaliation," available online at http://bbrathwaite.wordpress.com/2008/01/07/facebook-app-propagation-the-hostage-situation-retaliation/

# Index

# You're a teen with a great imagination...

Written specifically for teens in a language you understand, on topics you're interested in! Each book in the *For Teens* series features step-by-step instructions to help you conquer the tools and techniques presented. Hands-on projects help you put your new skills into action. And the accompanying CD-ROM or web downloads provide tutorials, instructional videos, software programs, and more!

...unleash your creativity with the  series!!

**Computer Programming for Teens**
ISBN: 1-59863-446-1 • $29.99

**Web Comics for Teens**
ISBN: 1-59863-467-4 • $29.99

**3D Game Programming for Teens**
ISBN: 1-59200-900-X • $29.99

**Game Creation for Teens**
1-59863-500-X • $29.99

**Torque for Teens**
ISBN: 1-59863-409-7 • $29.99

**Web Design for Teens**
ISBN: 1-59200-607-8 • $19.99

**Microsoft Visual Basic
Game Programming for Teens**
Second Edition
ISBN: 1-59863-390-2 • $29.99

**Game Art for Teens**
Second Edition
ISBN: 1-59200-959-X • $34.99

**COURSE TECHNOLOGY**
CENGAGE Learning
Professional • Technical • Reference

Check out all of the *For Teens* books
and order online at **www.courseptr.com** or call **1.800.354.9706**

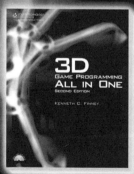